PUTIN'S LABYRINTH

RANDOM HOUSE TRADE PAPERBACKS
NEW YORK

PUTIN'S LABYRINTH

*Spies, Murder, and the Dark Heart
of the New Russia*

Steve LeVine

2009 Random House Trade Paperback Edition

Copyright © 2008, 2009 by Steve LeVine

Published in the United States by Random House Trade Paperbacks,
an imprint of The Random House Publishing Group,
a division of Random House, Inc., New York.

RANDOM HOUSE TRADE PAPERBACKS and colophon are
trademarks of Random House, Inc.

Originally published in hardcover and in slightly different form
in the United States by Random House,
an imprint of The Random House Publishing Group,
a division of Random House, Inc., in 2008.

LIBRARY OF CONGRESS CATALOGING-IN-PUBLICATION DATA
LeVine, Steve.
Putin's labyrinth : spies, murder, and the dark heart of
the new Russia / Steve LeVine.
p.   cm.
Includes bibliographical references and index.
ISBN 978-0-8129-7841-4
1. Political violence—Russia (Federation).   2. State sponsored
terrorism—Russia (Federation).   3. Putin, Vladimir Vladimirovich, 1952–.
4. Litvinenko, Alexander, 1962–2006.   I. Title.
HN530.2.Z9V55 2008
947.086—dc22   2008016581

Printed in the United States of America

www.atrandom.com

4689753

For Dolores LeVine
and for
Avery LeVine

PREFACE

Just before midnight on November 1, 2006, Alexander Litvinenko, a former Russian intelligence agent living in political exile in London, awoke terribly sick. Within days, a ghastly photograph of his wasted body in a hospital bed shocked the world. Three weeks later, he was dead. He had been poisoned by polonium-210, a radioactive isotope that investigators believed had been slipped into a beverage.

The forty-three-year-old Litvinenko had fled his native country with his wife and six-year-old son six years earlier. He was an unrelenting and harsh critic of President Vladimir Putin and the methods of Russia's intelligence apparatus, which he labeled immoral.

In life, Litvinenko had been only a foot soldier in the opposition to Putin, and his outbursts were often dismissed by journalists, politicians, and researchers. But his death became an international sensation, and many suspected the president's involvement. The poisoning of Litvinenko riveted attention on Russia's visible slide toward autocratic rule and its increasingly bellicose attitude toward the West, even as Russia's economy was booming, thanks to the surging value of its energy exports, and Putin was seeking to restore his nation's lost stature after the Soviet collapse.

I could find no precedent for an assassination of this type. Who was responsible? I traveled to Moscow to sort through the circumstances of his death. My investigation gradually widened to encompass what seemed to be an epidemic of assassinations and bloodletting, both inside and outside the country.

I came to view Litvinenko's assassination—and the spectacular use of polonium to kill him—as emblematic of the dark turn that Russia had taken under Putin's rule.

CONTENTS

INTRODUCTION

This is a book about death in Russia.

The world is familiar with Russia's long history of murderous rulers and ruthless assassins. But even now, a decade into the twenty-first century, brutality and violent death is so ordinary that it is usually ignored by all but the victims themselves, their families, and their friends.

After sixteen years of living in or visiting the former Soviet Union, I have come to believe that Russia's acquiescence to this bloody state of affairs sets it apart from other nations that call themselves civilized. I realize this is a harsh judgment, and can only say that it was not hastily reached.

When I first arrived in the country after three years of reporting in Pakistan and Afghanistan, I mainly felt awe. Russia's enormous size, remarkable history, and rich language wholly engaged me. I was assigned to cover territories on the fringe of the old Russian empire—Georgia, Armenia, Central Asia, the northern Caucasus mountain regions of Chechnya and Ingushetia. I maintained a Moscow apartment as a base of operations.

There were discordant notes from the outset. Resident foreigners and a disgruntled minority of Russians said the country was meddling beyond its borders—provoking wars in the Caucasus, blocking oil deals and energy pipelines in Central Asia, and generally working to preserve

Moscow's influence in the neighboring republics that comprised the former Soviet Union. At first, these complaints seemed unfounded; yes, Russia was seeking to reinvent and perhaps enrich itself, but it was not attempting to reestablish an empire. I would soon be disabused of this somewhat benign view.

In December 1994, a number of foreign journalists, including myself, gathered in Grozny, the capital of Chechnya. We were Americans, Britons, French, Russians, Azeris, and Georgians, including our translators and drivers. I was accompanied by my Georgian driver, Yura Bekauri, and assistant, Nana Kiknadze.

We headquartered in an inn that became known as the French Hotel and waited for the Russian military to attack the city. Russia's president, Boris Yeltsin, and his defense minister, Pavel Grachev, had threatened just such an assault—a show of force to quell the region's pretenses of independence.

Russia and the region of Chechnya had been antagonists for hundreds of years. They fought a long guerrilla war in the nineteenth century before Chechnya was subjugated. In the next century, the Chechens chafed under Soviet rule, and in 1944 Stalin, who thought they were siding with the Nazis, deported them en masse to Kazakhstan. Nikita Khrushchev allowed them to return, and when the Soviet Union broke up in 1991, the Chechens saw an opportunity at last for independence. They behaved as though they were governing an autonomous land. That led to Yeltsin's threat three years later to compel the Chechens to return to Russia's fold.

Yeltsin had set a deadline of December 12 for all foreigners to be out of Grozny. Journalists were separately warned that Russia could no longer assure our safety, but there was nothing about the notification that I construed as threatening. Western correspondents had heard similar cautions in other war zones, and we were unworried. But there was a palpable rumble among the Georgians in our group. Two or three Georgian drivers, Yura among them, began packing their cars. They intended to leave, and quickly. "You don't know what the Russians can do," Yura replied when I protested.

Why was Yura, an ordinarily unflappable man, so agitated? His behavior seemed unreasonable, but it forced me to reassess the situation. For one thing, his panic was clearly genuine. For another, he intended to take the car with him, which would leave us without personal transport in a war zone.

We left with him—Nana, my colleague Carlotta Gall, then of *The Moscow Times,* and I. As we drove away, I wondered how to explain to my editor that I had left the scene of a story. We traveled east, and a half-hour later Yura drove into a gas station and employed his usual magic. He struck up a friendship with another motorist, who invited all of us to eat and stay the night at his home in the city of Gudermes.

So began a several-months-long discovery of what was behind Yura's terror.

I returned to Grozny in January, in time to witness the main Russian assault for *The Washington Post* and its sister publication *Newsweek.* In my absence, the dispatches of my colleagues Anatol Lieven and Bill Gasperini, who had stayed behind, had kept me abreast of events there. Now Gasperini told me how he had been pursued by a Russian helicopter, first while on foot and then in a car, being shot at all the way. He was certain that the pilot had known he was a foreigner. It was my first realization that Western correspondents weren't necessarily regarded as neutral noncombatants by the Russian military.

The Russian term *bespredel* translates roughly as "anything goes." That describes how the Russians pursued their campaign in Chechnya. Grozny was a city under siege. More than half of its four hundred thousand inhabitants had fled. The Russian military subjected the remaining population to around-the-clock artillery bombardments, block by block, street by street, and building by building. It regarded no one as an ally, no one as a civilian.

Outdoor markets were a favorite target. After such attacks, people usually emerged from cover to retrieve the dead and wounded, only to be fired upon by Russian choppers returning for a second run. They typically dropped cluster bombs that fired shrapnel in an upward trajectory, seemingly designed to decapitate their victims. That was how a young Boston photographer named Cynthia Elbaum was killed in late December—decapitated when she left the safety of a bombed-out building to photograph the slaughter in a bazaar outside.

The assault reduced the city to rubble, leaving behind only the carcasses of buildings. Grozny resembled scenes in photographs from World War II depicting the carnage of Europe.

At the end of January, Nana and I returned without Yura, and we began to visit outlying villages. The war had shifted there as the Russians widened their assault. Now there was a new wrinkle in the stories we heard. Oleg Orlov, a distinguished investigator with the Russian human rights group Memorial, provided cassette recordings and written depositions from people claiming to be victims of torture and witnesses to murder by Russian officers and soldiers. The statements were said to come from both Chechens and ethnic Russian citizens of Chechnya.

We set out to find some of these victims and, in the cattle-breeding town of Goity, met Isan Matayev, a forty-year-old truck driver. His family went back three generations there, but he was born in Kazakhstan, his family among those exiled to that land by Stalin in 1944.

Matayev described eighteen days of imprisonment by the Russian army. He and about thirty other Chechens and ethnic Russian civilians had taken cover inside a Grozny bomb shelter, then heard troops outside. "The Russians gave us a two-minute ultimatum either to open the shelter door or they would smoke us out," Matayev said. "We opened the door, they checked us for weapons—none of us had any—and then they locked us back inside." The next day, the entire group was loaded into an enclosed truck, hands cuffed behind their backs. Guards whom he described as towering men wearing masks ordered everyone to lie facedown on the truck floor in rows. Then more prisoners were ordered to lie on top of others until there were five layers in all, "like lumber," Matayev said.

The truck hauled its human cargo seven hours north to Russian military headquarters in the city of Mozdok. En route, guards beat some prisoners with rifle butts and fired occasional gunshots. Matayev said one Russian man shouted that the troops "had no right" to shoot. The man was not heard from again. "I think he was shot, because he wasn't among us at the end" of the journey, Matayev said.

At Mozdok, the captives were ordered out of the truck two at a time and made to step over the bodies of seven or eight men who had perished along the way, having suffocated or been shot. They were marched to a makeshift prison that, in the Chechen wars, became known as a "filtration camp." It was ostensibly a way station for the Russians to separate Chechen fighters from mere civilians. The camp was that, but it also became a place where the Russians decided who would live and who would die. And that decision often was reduced to which captives' relatives could pay the soldiers enough to win their freedom. Some who had no one to pay the requisite bribe disappeared without a trace.

Matayev was imprisoned in a compound consisting of two sets of railway cars fitted with blackened windows and grates, and surrounded by barbed wire. About a dozen soldiers guarded the yard, along with incessantly barking German shepherds. The guards regularly clubbed the men; when Matayev went to the bathroom, two soldiers beat him along the way.

During interrogation, a masked man randomly struck his feet, his back, and handcuffs that had been positioned over his knuckles—"wherever was convenient." He was threatened with death: "Today is your death; we're definitely going to do away with you tonight; enjoy your last few hours." Matayev was released after relatives came up with enough money to free him and five others.

We left Matayev before dusk to make the long drive west to Nazran, in neighboring Ingushetia, where most correspondents were staying because Grozny had become too dangerous. Nobody wanted to be on the roads after nightfall, when nervous Russian solders seemed to shoot anything that moved.

The next couple of days, we visited villages where residents had signed pledges of neutrality in hopes that the Russians would not fire on them. At Achkhoi-Martan, a city dotted with large red-brick houses, local men armed with rockets, grenades, and assault rifles were lounging outside an office building. A local woman named Mariam Madiyeva, worried that they could attract hostile fire, shouted at them: "Go outside the village; don't do this here. I am asking you on behalf of the mothers and children to leave."

The neutrality pledges seemed to have dubious value. Mayor Abu Oshayev told us he was blindfolded and put in a flooded basement with other Chechen prisoners even after he had safely transported a wounded Russian officer to a Russian detachment. It was the very unit with which the mayor had negotiated the pledges.

"They were pushing us with the guns. They pushed us to our knees. Someone said, 'Shoot the bandits. All of them are bandits,' " Oshayev recalled. "Then they hit a person kneeling next to me. He fell down and shouted, 'Help me. Don't kill me!' "

Oshayev's ordeal finally ended when a Russian officer heard his account of assisting the wounded officer and ordered him released. "I told him, 'If you treat us like this, those helping you, how are you treating the civilians who you don't know?' " Oshayev said.

For the next few months, such stories were commonplace. It was tempting to dismiss them as the wages of war—there are excesses in all conflicts, everywhere. Yet this was something else—the Russians were not just trying to put down a rebellion. They were killing, attacking, and brutalizing anyone found on Chechen soil, including not only fighters for the resistance but also civilians and the elderly.

What crystallized events for me, however, was the arrival of the mothers. From across Russia, the mothers of young men conscripted by the Russian military to fight in Chechnya came to fetch their sons. I had seen similar scenes in Afghanistan during the late 1980s—Russian mothers, fathers, and wives arriving in search of husbands and sons captured by the mujahedin in the Soviet–Afghan war. But this was on Russian soil, not in a foreign land. This was their land. And the officers commanding their sons and husbands were on their side. Only, it didn't always seem that they were. The angry mothers were responding to the scandal of green, ill-trained Russian soldiers being used as cannon fodder or otherwise abused and neglected by their own commanders. It wasn't just the citizens of Chechnya who had been dehumanized by Russian indifference.

As with Chechen men who had gone missing, there was no telling where many of the Russian soldiers were. Many had been captured by the enemy. Some were prisoners at the Mozdok filtration camp—Matayev had observed a row of Russian deserters standing in a railcar, faces against a wall, being taunted by their Russian countrymen. "Do you want to be imprisoned with this group of Chechens, or that group of Chechens?" the guards shouted at the unhappy Russian conscripts.

There was one place to look for sure: The bodies of dozens of dead troops were kept in a freezer compartment in a morgue outside the war zone. But there was no systematic effort to identify the remains, and when we returned a year later, there were unclaimed corpses still stored there.

Carlotta Gall would go on to document the fighting, the brutality, and the blood thirst in her classic *Chechnya: A Small Victorious War*, which she wrote with our mutual friend Thomas de Waal. In the Second

Chechen War, launched by Vladimir Putin as prime minister in 1999, the tough-minded Russian journalist Anna Politkovskaya wrote similar accounts in articles and books. She herself would be seized in Chechnya by Russian troops and threatened with rape and execution before finally being released.

At first, Muscovites seemed to react with genuine anguish to the ugliness in Chechnya. This was attributable to the Russian media, which provided saturation coverage, including much dispassionate reportage. But even the shocking stories of Russian soldiers mistreated by their own military didn't seem to move many people; the main thing was to pay the necessary bribes so that your son was not conscripted or sent to fight there. Only the poorest, dullest, or most rural Russian youths seemed to end up in Chechnya.

Time softens memories. The images that had caused me to view Russians as callous toward the lives of most others gradually slipped from my mind. But then came a series of reminders of the anguishing events I had seen in Chechnya.

In 2000, a Russian nuclear submarine called the *Kursk* sank in the icy waters of the Barents Sea. All 118 aboard perished while rescue efforts proceeded at a snail's pace and Moscow spent most of its energy trying to blame the West for the slow response.

In 2002, Chechen militants stormed a Moscow theater, taking several hundred spectators hostage. Russian special forces pumped an opiate gas into the building, rushed it, and shot the terrorists dead. Only, they forgot to make preparations for rescuing the hostages, and 129 of them succumbed—untreated—in their seats, on the sidewalk outside, in buses on the way to hospitals, and elsewhere.

In 2004, Chechen terrorists took some 1,200 children, parents, and teachers hostage in an elementary school in Beslan, a town in the southern Russian region of North Ossetia. Bedlam erupted on the third day of the standoff; shooting and explosions killed some 330 children and adults as hostages and terrorists fled the building.

In the fall of 2006, two outspoken critics of Vladimir Putin, by then Russia's president, were murdered. Anna Politkovskaya was shot execution style and Russian defector Alexander Litvinenko, a former KGB officer, died of poisoning by a nuclear toxin.

I had been under no illusions about Putin. His bare-knuckle approach to governing Russia had been apparent for some time. But now it was hard to avoid the conclusion that something more ominous was happening. What I was seeing in Russia went beyond the question of leadership style. Putin had set about restoring the legacy of brute Russia.

It was not that his fingerprints were on every untoward event. They didn't have to be. Rather, it was the complicity of his inaction. A high-profile murder can go unsolved anywhere. A hostage situation can go awry even when police are highly skilled. But after the third, fourth, or fifth such outrage, it becomes clear that something fundamental is amiss. At the very least, in Putin's Russia the state cannot be counted on to protect the lives of its citizens. At worst, hired killers and those who employ them have reason to believe that they can carry out executions without fear of the law.

There has always been a certain amount of disorder in Russia. That is why many Russians are willing—even eager—to support a ruler with Putin's instincts. But I find it troubling that he has been unusually selective in exercising his power on behalf of the law. He seems disinterested in stopping or bringing to justice those who settle accounts with violence or worse. For example, the world has yet to hear him declare, "I will not tolerate, and indeed I will prosecute ruthlessly, anyone who orders or carries out a murder. Neither will I tolerate the death of hostages." If he had exerted such authority and issued such dictums, Russia might not have experienced the botched aftermath of the theater seizure or the retaliatory killings of Anna Politkovskaya and others.

Without question, he is willing and able to crush those who offend him. Consider this hallmark of the Putin era: his unyielding pursuit and prosecution of a select group of Russian oligarchs. The most notable target was oil kingpin Mikhail Khodorkovsky, Russia's richest man, who was arrested in 2003 by masked federal agents aboard his private plane on the tarmac of Siberia's Novosibirsk Airport. He was sentenced to eight years in prison, and his oil company, Yukos, was systematically dismantled and taken over by two state-controlled companies, Gazprom and Rosneft. (In 2008, when under ordinary circumstances Khodorkovsky might have been released on parole, Putin's prosecutors pursued a slew of fresh charges and his imprisonment for two dozen more years.) Khodorkovsky's crime? He had ventured into politics, financing Putin's opponents and presuming to form an influential—

perhaps dominant—bloc within parliament. That stepped over the line; politics is the state's purview, specifically the Kremlin's. The importance Putin placed on the case was evident. Dozens of prosecutors, auditors, and tax inspectors collectively spent thousands of hours making Russia safe from Khodorkovsky. There is no leniency for perceived political transgressors; Putin is hypersensitive in this regard.

Kukly, a weekly Russian TV show that employed puppets to represent the country's leaders, is another example. The Putin doll was a wickedly funny dwarf. Putin objected to the skits performed by his likeness, and the producers were warned that the president was off limits, I was told by Grigory Lubomirov, one of the show's creators. That didn't disturb the *Kukly* team, which was accustomed to such reactions. In Yeltsin's time, for instance, Prime Minister Viktor Chernomyrdin at first strenuously objected to his portrayal. But he relented under the pressure of friends and critics who advised him to acquire a sense of humor, and ended up appearing in a photograph grinning next to his puppet character. Putin was not so gracious. Two years after he became president, the show was canceled.

Khodorkovsky and *Kukly* were hounded out of the public sphere.

I don't mean to suggest that other countries occupy a higher moral plane than Russia. The post-9/11 world has upset many people's presumptions—including my own—that the West in general and the United States in particular can lay claim to generally noble status. We've discovered that an American president can treat foreign allies with swaggering bluster while conducting a war of opportunity and employing torture as a policy—with the support of a majority of Americans. In fact, a comparison of contemporary events in Russia, the West, and elsewhere in the world suggests that distinctions between countries and cultures have become barely discernible.

Except that they haven't. Notwithstanding America's slippage during the Bush years, the United States, Europe, and large swaths of Asia are not places where journalists are freely assassinated, defecting spies poisoned, or theatergoers gassed to death by their own police.

I deliberately use Japan, Canada, Germany, Britain, France, Italy, and the United States as a comparison group. These are the industrialized countries that were known as the G-7 until Yeltsin successfully argued that Russia was entitled to be a member of the club, and the G-7 became the G-8. In 2007, Putin threw an extravaganza in St. Petersburg as host of the organization's annual gathering.

But if you are a citizen of Russia, you are more likely than a person in any other G-8 nation to die a premature death, and to do so in a bizarre or cruel way. When I say premature death, I'm not thinking disease, stillbirth, or an automobile accident—although Russians die at a far higher rate in all these categories than citizens of the other seven countries. I mean the kind of death experienced by Anna Politkovskaya or Alexander Litvinenko or the theater hostages—all deaths that were countenanced or at least tolerated by the Russian state.

This book is a chronicle of violence in modern-day Russia, a place that seems unwilling or unable to escape its horrific past. My goal was to tell the story of some of the most prominent victims, people who are remembered largely for what they endured, and how they died. I sought—through the eyes of their friends, family, and colleagues, in addition to the victims' own writings and private and public utterances—to write a more complete portrait of their lives. Many survivors recounted their own ordeals. The shared testimony paints a disturbing picture of assassination and other brutality, and leaves the unmistakable impression that the Russian state under Putin is at least partly responsible.

CAST OF CHARACTERS

Elena Baranovskaya, Irina Fadeeva, and Ilya Lysak
Hostages in the 2002 terrorist takeover of a Moscow theater staging the musical *Nord-Ost*. From events before and after, the three were indelibly linked to Anna Politkovskaya.

Boris Berezovsky
Former Kremlin kingmaker largely responsible for Boris Yeltsin's 1996 reelection, and for Vladimir Putin's surprise elevation to power. He thought he would continue to manipulate events, but Putin rebelled and the two became blood enemies. Berezovsky is the financier of the London-based Putin opposition. His team included Alexander Litvinenko, the defector and former KGB officer.

Nikolai Khokhlov
The first-known victim of deliberate poisoning by a nuclear isotope. A KGB officer, Nikolai defected in 1954 while on an assassination mission; three years later, he survived the KGB's attempt to assassinate him. He regarded the Litvinenko assassination as a replay of his own experience.

Paul Klebnikov
Editor of *Forbes Russia* and American-born scion of Russian aristocracy. Klebnikov's best-known work was his highly critical biography of Berezovsky, whom he called "Godfather of the Kremlin."

ALEXANDER LITVINENKO

Former KGB officer, defector, critic of Putin, and member of Bere-zovsky's London-based opposition political team.

DMITRI MEDVEDEV

Law professor, chairman of Gazprom, and Putin's hand-picked succes-sor as Russian president.

ANNA POLITKOVSKAYA

Having grown up as a member of the Soviet Union's privileged *nomen-klatura,* Anna eventually became perhaps Putin's fiercest critic, and a lit-erary celebrity abroad.

VLADIMIR PUTIN

Anointed as president by an ailing Boris Yeltsin, who sought a succes-sor who would protect his family from charges of corruption. Soaring oil prices under his rule transformed Russia from a broken country into an increasingly prosperous land with renewed global ambitions. But Putin also created an atmosphere of impunity for killers.

PUTIN'S LABYRINTH

CHAPTER 1

Russia's Dark Side

A Land in the Grip of
a Brutal History

THE BOULEVARDS OF MOSCOW ARE VERY MUCH TWENTY-FIRST-century Russia, a kaleidoscope of flashing neon, ostentatious wealth, and the hectic traffic of a city too busy to stop. But walk down Maliy Karetniy Pereulok, a backstreet in the city's prestigious central Petrovski district, and step through the wooden door of the simple red-brick building at number 12. Here, time reverses itself. Visitors find themselves inside a musty archive of repression. Photographs of Russians executed during Stalin's purges in the 1930s are displayed in open shoe boxes. Storage boxes and cardboard file folders, their contents a history of state-sanctioned savagery, are stacked floor to ceiling along narrow corridors and crammed into seemingly every niche. Personal items that belonged to prisoners of the gulag invite inspection.

A human rights organization called Memorial, which documents the crimes of Stalinism past and present, maintains this museum and has its office here. The quarters have the feel of a relic, and the museum visitor traffic is low. But during the golden era of Mikhail Gorbachev's perestroika—roughly from 1988 through the first half of 1991—the building buzzed with researchers, journalists, visitors, and foreign dignitaries. Curiosity about the Stalinist period was intense then. (Remarkably, the reform-minded FSB, which had replaced the KGB in a convoluted bureaucratic change in 1995, assembled the photographs of purge victims that ended up in the museum's collection. "The current

FSB wouldn't do something like this, but then they did," said Nikita Petrov, Memorial's KGB expert. Petrov himself is a throwback to an earlier time, with long gray hair parted on the side, green T-shirt, denim jacket and pants, and trimmed gray beard.)

Perestroika was a flash in time when many Russians dared to hope for a break with the past. Tens of thousands marched in the streets for an evolving list of causes, scanned newspapers for the latest exposés of the Communist Party, and forced genuine change in the country. But when the economy crashed and the government of Boris Yeltsin wiped out their savings—not once, but twice—by summarily devaluing the ruble, Russians felt tricked.

Now Russia is again Russia, its dark side emergent and, for the most part, tolerated by the populace. Petrov, a chemist by training and a historian by profession, tried to explain why.

"Russian history taught its people to be indifferent toward the suffering of others at their death," he said. "It's hard to say whether history produced the culture or culture produced the history. Whichever, it's the consequence. People are used to death. It's a psychological defense toward death."

To underline his point, Petrov turned to Europe. "In 2004, there was a terrorist act in Spain," he said, referring to the Madrid train bombing by al-Qaeda that killed 191. "Lots of people went into the street in protest. That would never happen here. Why? Here it's 'Why should we go into the street? It would have no impact.'

"That's actually quite a logical response. [But] it has resulted in people not being brave. They take no responsibility toward events—they can't affect anything."

Some have interpreted this detachment as an inevitable outcome of Putin-era prosperity—many Russians had never lived better and so were not motivated to challenge the system. But my own observation was that Petrov had it right—Russians had reverted to what they had always been, which was generally passive.

It was not hard to find evidence that the state had turned back to its old self, too. In 2004, Qatar convicted two Russian intelligence officers of murdering Chechnya's former president, Zelimkhan Yandarbiyev, by blowing up his car in the tiny Gulf country. Moscow asked that the men be permitted to serve their sentence in Russia, and Qatar agreed. But once the officers were home, Russia set them free. That seemed to demonstrate that if one carried out a killing on behalf of the state—even if it was arguably terrorism—one would be protected. It reinforced an atmosphere of impunity for such crimes; there were few examples of anyone convicted for a major Russian murder. The Qatar episode and others like it mainly suggested that people should keep their heads down.

One of those who surprisingly did so was Olga Kryshtanovskaya, who for two decades was Russia's premier expert on the nation's elites and their wealth and position in government. Her most recent study, she told me over coffee, was a measure of the wealth accumulated by military officers and the FSB leadership under President Vladimir Putin, including their shares of ownership in Russia's biggest companies. Almost offhandedly, I asked where the study would be published so that I could pick up a copy. I didn't want to burden her with a request to send me one. She is an enormously busy woman, frequently published in Russia and the West and widely quoted on the Russian power structure. Even the Kremlin has sought her advice.

Her expression turned dark and awkward. She said she wasn't sure where—or if—she would publish her findings. After so many years of demystifying the elite, she suddenly felt at risk. "This type of information is dangerous to life," said the sixtyish woman. "A lot of people had unpleasant things happen to them. There can be accidental car crashes. A lot of people died and that is why I can't stop thinking about it. I don't know what I'm going to do."

I learned later that Kryshtanovskaya turned over her study to friends in a think tank abroad, who paid her and used it under their own byline.

One of the things that foreigners least understand about Russia is why ordinary Russians seem largely unperturbed by the violence and death around them.

Yuri Sinelshchikov, a former deputy Moscow city prosecutor who had dealt with murder his entire professional life, thought it was a matter of practicality or personal priorities. People simply lacked the inclination to care, he said. There was nothing in it for them.

"If people go in the street, they won't gain materially," he said. "Any murder can be compared to a show where an actor comes to entertain them. It doesn't really affect someone unless it happens to them directly. People get angry if they lose a meter of land, or their children are hurt, or someone installs a door that is heavy and could hurt someone."

The keenest observers on almost any matter in nearly any country are often the bankers, who have much to lose if their judgment is wrong. So I asked a few in Moscow to analyze the Russian mind-set. They were Americans and Europeans who admired Putin's government and were earning eight- and nine-figure payouts as lawyers, investment bankers, and investors thanks to the Russian juggernaut.

"The local attitude is, 'Shit happens,'" said Rory MacFarquar, Moscow research director for venerable Goldman Sachs. Slender, baby-faced, and bookish, MacFarquar was persuasive partly because of his long years and deep study of Russia, and also because of his clear and painstaking choice of words. He tended to see things in a historical context. "There is an enormous perception gap about life. It's not something trivial like 'life is cheap,'" he said. "Russia has gone through unimaginable tragedies in the twentieth century."

The United States reacts with great shock to events such as 9/11 and the 1999 Columbine High School massacre because they are so out of the ordinary, he said. But "enormous tragedies" occur with such relative frequency in Russia that its people become almost numb to them.

"One thing the West noticed [after 9/11] is how many people were put in danger. [But] that wasn't a big thing here," MacFarquar continued. "The level of routine ecological danger here is enormous. The systematic official lying has led to a universal assumption that the danger is pervasive, which leads to fatalism."

Al Breach, an executive at United Bank of Switzerland, put it this way: "Life isn't straightforward here. It's not significant enough."

It seemed to me that five or six hundred years of Russian history provided ample reason for its people to become inured to suffering. But two Russian historians told me that my thinking was too simplistic. "I would advise you not to make too much of a continuum of history," warned Alexei Miller, on a visit home from Budapest, where he was teaching at Central European University. Miller was especially contemptuous of anyone who would mention Putin and Russia's iconic sixteenth-century czar, Ivan IV—known as Ivan the Terrible—in the same sentence. Alexander Kamenskii, an oft-quoted professor at Russian State University for the Humanities, felt much the same way. "People say that Russians are used to being slaves, are used to dictatorship, and that's just the way it is. That's a myth," Kamenskii said. "Why should we think that people who lived under dictatorship liked it?"

Miller's and Kamenskii's admonitions made sense in the abstract—history is not science, and the past doesn't necessarily dictate the present. But it was hard to understand why in this instance they didn't see what seemed obvious: that Russians in a sense have chosen to live in the tradition of their medieval ancestors.

It isn't that Russians *favor* dictatorship. But they have gone along with autocratic rule even when offered an alternative, as in the parliamentary and presidential elections over eight years that cemented Putin's grip on power. And there does seem to be a straight line to the present from Ivan the Terrible and the Russian tradition of fear-based rule.

Russia's first crowned czar and grandson of the creator of the Russian state, Ivan, who took power in 1547, had thinning hair, deep wrinkles on his forehead, and was physically impressive, with a rippling beard and a barrel chest. His more sympathetic biographers thought that he was initially a conscientious and even empathetic leader. Emulating Spain, England, and Portugal in the pursuit of empire, he captured parts of Siberia, fought against Poland for control of the Baltic Sea, and against the Tatars in the east. Ivan opened Russia to the West, welcoming trade with Europe and forming a particularly warm relationship with Elizabeth of England; Elizabeth had a soft spot for Ivan and on at least two occasions offered him asylum should he require it.

Yet, though Westerners were accustomed to savagery against one's own kind, they were startled at what they witnessed in Ivan's Russia. An English merchant named Jerome Horsey wrote of a prince named Boris Telupa who, accused of treason, had a stake "thrust into his fundament through his body, which came out at his neck, upon which he languished in horrible pain for fifteen hours." Telupa's mother was gang-raped, Horsey wrote, and Ivan "commanded his huntsmen to bring their hungry hounds to eat and devour her flesh and bones, dragged everywhere." Anthony Jenkinson, England's envoy to Russia, described the punishment of an unfortunate aristocrat, as Ivan's men "cut off his nose, his tongue, his ears and his lips." Ivan had a particular fascination with potions. Convinced that one Prince Vladimir was out to destroy him, he handed a goblet of poisoned wine to the unfortunate man, who died in great agony. His wife and nine-year-old daughter similarly perished after being given the same concoction. When some of Vladimir's retinue refused to beg for mercy, they were stripped naked, shot, and left for birds and wild animals to eat.

That was how Russians grew up in the sixteenth century. Ivan was out to destroy Russia's power structure—shared by the Church, wealthy and politically powerful landowners called boyars, and individual princely rivals to the throne—and become its sole, almighty ruler. His enforcers were an ultra-loyalist six-thousand-man band of thugs whom he called the *oprichniki*. They roamed the countryside on horseback in black robes, a dog's head and broom etched into their saddles, massacring thousands, including much of the population of the ancient city of Novgorod. To retain their loyalty, Ivan granted them control of the richest part of the country, along with Russia's principal trade routes.

The consequence of Ivan's violence was a terrorized, terrified, and cowed population. In a letter to England's Queen Elizabeth, King Sigismund Augustus II of Poland asked in wonder why Russians, while no doubt fearful of their czar's savagery, also seemed to defend him as a mark of patriotism.

The most-admired historical figure in Russia is Peter the Great, who two centuries later presided over the torture and execution of hundreds of actual and alleged traitors, including his own son, Alexei. He doled out such punishment "to make an example, to terrify, to force submission," wrote biographer Robert Massie, but with the ultimate aim of gaining "the power to work his reforms and—for better or worse—to revolutionize Russian society." He fretted that the pain and death he inflicted might cause his Western friends to think less of him, and ordered that a lengthy letter be delivered to Europe's heads of state imploring them to ignore reports of his brutality against his son. At the end of the self-serving missive, composed the day after Alexei's death, Peter advised his European counterparts, "In case also that anyone wished to publish this event in an odious manner, you will have in hand what is necessary to destroy and solidly refute any unjust and unfounded tales."

The czars of the late nineteenth and early twentieth centuries were also to be feared, as exemplified by the organized attacks on Jews that they carried out. But some were victims of assassination themselves.

Among those suffering that fate were Czar Alexander II, who was killed by a bomb in 1881, and of course Nicholas II, who was shot dead along with the entire Romanov family in 1918.

Soviet rule brought a new wave of official violence. Josef Stalin executed nearly all of his senior-most comrades from revolutionary days, almost his entire upper echelon of military officers, and millions of others when one included deaths in labor camps and from forced collectivization. Stalin was Ivan's natural heir, and said as much himself. During the darkest days of Hitler's invasion, Stalin could be found scribbling the words "teacher, teacher" on the pages of a biography of Ivan. He "constantly compared his terror to Ivan's massacre of the boyars"—the landed aristocracy—according to a biographer of the twentieth-century dictator. Stalin thought that Ivan's only fault was that, in slaying the boyars, "he should have killed them all, to create a strong state."

One of the most credible and revealing accounts of Stalin's time is *Special Tasks,* the memoir of Pavel Sudoplatov, who directed overseas assassinations for the dictator. Contemplating his own and others' acts during the Soviet era, Sudoplatov wrote that "victorious Russian rulers always combined the qualities of criminals and statesmen." Indeed, his book is a dispassionate catalogue of official poisonings, stabbings, and other plots, including the killing of his first victim, Yevhen Konovalets, a Ukrainian nationalist whom he cultivated for five years before blowing him up in Germany with a booby-trapped box of chocolates. Sudoplatov played a leading role in one of the most infamous political assassinations of the twentieth century, that of Leon Trotsky. The revolutionary leader had fled to Mexico after earning the enmity of Stalin, who ordered Sudoplatov to make his slaying a priority. So in 1940, Ramon Mercader del Rio, a Spanish national working for a Sudoplatov deputy, dispatched him with a pickax to the head.

Musa Eitingon Malinovskaya is the daughter of Mercader's supervising agent, the legendary Soviet master spy Leonid Eitingon. Dressed in a silk scarf and a denim blouse for coffee at an upscale Moscow café, the sixty-year-old Malinovskaya told me how, as a teenager in the 1960s, she shared ice cream with Mercader and her father. She had no idea who he was, nor of her father's role in the Trotsky assassination, but the two men had an evidently warm relationship. "My father introduced him to me as 'my friend from the Spanish resistance,'" Malinovskaya said. ". . . I heard about him killing Trotsky only in 1989 when I read about it in *Literaturnaya Gazeta*." Malinovskaya was clearly proud of her mother, Musa, for whom she was named. She showed me a 2005 advertisement featuring a 1935 photo of her mother as a gorgeous twenty-two-year-old Army parachutist. But she was singularly devoted to her father and eager to talk about his association with Trotsky's slayer. One got the impression that it was the most important thing she could say about herself. The murder perhaps helped to break the ice at cocktail parties.

In 1954, a Sudoplatov protégé named Nikolai Khokhlov became the first Soviet defector to publicly divulge firsthand knowledge of the Kremlin's assassination program. He became a valuable source of intelligence for the CIA and survived an attempt by Russian agents to assassinate him using radioactive poisoning. The West usually prosecutes its traitors but, as Khokhlov was witness, the Soviets regarded them as fair game for murder.

Another defector, Bulgarian novelist and playwright Georgy Markov, died in a most exotic way. He was working as a London-based journalist for the BBC when Moscow and its Bulgarian allies joined forces to kill him. In 1978, an assassin jabbed a tiny ricin-laced pellet into Markov's thigh as he waited at a bus stop near Waterloo Bridge. Although the murder weapon wasn't found, an excited British press reported that the pellet was fired from an umbrella, and that idea stuck with historians.

Following the collapse of the Soviet Union, Russia became a fledgling democracy in 1991. It should have been an opportunity for the nation to demonstrate that murder and mayhem were not embedded in the Russian DNA, that the notion of a centuries-long continuum of violence was fatally flawed. The czars and the dictators were gone; tyranny no longer ruled the land. But its people quickly learned that democracy Russian style could be ruthlessly bloody. A historic tradition seemed to be reasserting itself. The chosen style of rule—tyranny or democracy or something in between—seemed to matter little.

There were, of course, differences between the old and the new. Ivan, Peter, and Stalin alike reserved the right to decide who would live and who would die. Ivan and Peter tortured their unlucky victims to death, and Stalin had them shot in the back of the head or sent to prison camps to be starved and worked to death. This was state murder. But none of these three strongmen permitted murder in the streets. On the contrary, they were very nearly pathological about order and concealing Russia's dark side from the rest of the world.

Under the rule of Boris Yeltsin in the 1990s, the old order was turned upside down. There was little if any state-sponsored murder. But contract killers brazenly murdered prominent bankers, metal traders, oilmen, and hundreds of others for violating unspoken "rules of the game." Kidnappers chopped off the fingers and heads of their victims, sometimes before even requesting a ransom. Russia's richest billionaires, known collectively as the oligarchs, left a trail of dead bodies—by coincidence or otherwise—as they accumulated unimagined wealth; these victims were often business rivals. The state solved few cases, and in that way seemed an accomplice to some of them.

But if Yeltsin, the nation's first popularly elected president, appeared to tolerate the bloodbath, it wasn't his creation. Rather, it filled the vacuum created when the once-feared KGB and other law enforcement agencies seemed to vanish in the unraveling of the Soviet Union. Grievances that previously would have been forgotten or settled through legal or other peaceable means suddenly poured into the streets. Bitter scores were settled in shootings carried out directly by, or ordered by, swindled business partners, gangs denied a piece of the action, and so on. The murders and murderers were cold-blooded and had unmistakable attitude. Bankers were among the most frequent victims because of their access to money; scores of them were killed in shootings, bombings, and at least one poisoning during the 1990s.

Lesser citizens also could be caught in the cross fire. In summer 1993, three gunmen murdered a café manager and then, at a kiosk where they found service unsatisfactory, shot a saleswoman and a customer dead. In April 1995, two gunmen killed a Russian stockbroker's six-year-old daughter, who was on the way to kindergarten. And in November 1996, a bomb buried in a Moscow cemetery killed some dozen mourners. Organized crime became Big Business. Experts said that more than four-fifths of Russia's banks were controlled by gangs, whose tentacles spread west to Israel, Europe, and the United States. These Russian gangs poured into Germany, for example, bringing with them the most grisly crimes the country had experienced in decades. In a 1994 case, German police came upon the bodies of a bordello owner, his wife, and four prostitutes, all of them apparently killed by a Russian gang. Police agencies such as the U.S. Federal Bureau of Investigation said they had never faced a challenge so difficult, a shadowy underworld that had come to be known as the "Russian mafia."

As the 1990s drew to a close, Yeltsin retired from the presidency. He was succeeded by a former KGB spy catapulted into office by powerful men confident that they could manipulate him—but who would turn out to be wilier than any of them. Once again, Russia would be ruled by a strongman.

CHAPTER 2

How Putin Got Elected

Boris Yeltsin Finds a Guarantor in a Man from Nowhere

BORIS YELTSIN WAS AN OBSCURE COMMUNIST PARTY FUNC-
tionary in the tough, mafia-ridden industrial region of Sverdlovsk
when Soviet leader Mikhail Gorbachev in 1985 summoned him to
Moscow. There, Yeltsin became Gorbachev's political protégé and
demonstrated an energy seldom seen among Soviet leaders. His mentor rewarded him with promotions, enabling Yeltsin to rise rapidly
through the ranks of party leadership. But the two began to butt heads
when Yeltsin pushed the president to enact political reform faster than
Gorbachev was willing. Yeltsin quit the Communist Party and soon became a political force in his own right. He captured the imagination of
many Soviets with such populist gestures as rushing into a Moscow
shop and demanding that their goods be stocked on open shelves, not
pilfered by the proprietors. Everything about him seemed larger than
life, including his distinctive shock of white hair.

Yeltsin showed he was willing even to put his life on the line, famously standing atop a tank in August 1991 to rebuff an attempted coup
against Gorbachev by Communist hard-liners. Although he was no
longer a supporter of the president, he would not allow a return to the
worst traditions of Soviet rule, Yeltsin declared. Four months later, Gorbachev resigned from the presidency and the Soviet Union collapsed.

Now Yeltsin was president of independent Russia. He set out to
improve the lives of Russian people by appointing a team of economic

specialists led by a brilliant mathematician named Yegor Gaidar. The team's assignment was simple: to provide Russians the economic lift from democracy that had been promised but not delivered during the last five years of Gorbachev's rule. Gaidar's strategy, dubbed "shock therapy," was driven not only by economics but also politics. It was designed to wrest control of the nation's means of production from Soviet-era bosses in order to create a middle class of stakeholders that would become the foundation of a new, freer Russia. And so the Yeltsin government ended state ownership of Russia's biggest moneymaking enterprises, including nickel, oil, aluminum, and media companies. These giant industries were sold off, at a relative pittance, to a half-dozen well-connected Russian businessmen—"the oligarchs." But the Russian economy ended up being the loser. Like the Communist bosses before them, the oligarchs mainly used their freshly won enterprises as a means to generate cash for themselves. Workers often went without pay, and the promised modernization of old and inefficient Soviet-era factories never happened.

In 1998, conditions worsened. The world price of oil, a critical source of revenue for Russia, plummeted below $10 a barrel. Already, an economic contagion had spread from Asia to Russia; for the second time in five years, the Kremlin impoverished ordinary Russians by devaluing the ruble and making their hard-earned savings nearly worthless.

Yeltsin took a pummeling. His popularity rating wallowed in the single digits. Despite his well-known personal frailties, such as alcohol-binging and depression, he had always been perceived as a giant of a man. Now he seemed physically and politically weak. John Lloyd of the *Financial Times,* perhaps the most able foreign correspondent in Russia at the time, wrote that Yeltsin had become a virtual tool of the oligarchs, "a mixture between an invalid and a puppet, his strings jerked by masters behind his throne."

The story of Vladimir Putin's ascent in the ruling circles of Russian government begins with the five heart attacks that Yeltsin suffered during his presidency. Yeltsin was routinely incapacitated for months. His staff ran the country, and it became plain to them in 1999 that the succession process—selecting who would follow Yeltsin, whose term was ending the next year—had to be accelerated. They had two aims: to preserve the political gains that their leader had achieved, and to ensure that the Yeltsin family would not be prosecuted once he vacated the ramparts of the Kremlin. In recent months, allegations had surfaced in Switzerland of Yeltsin and his daughters running up tens of thousands of dollars on credit cards provided by a Swiss man who had received millions of dollars in Russian government contracts. There was also the Russian tradition of political leaders persecuting their predecessors for retribution and political gain. The Yeltsins wished at all costs to avoid such an unfortunate retirement.

There is much conjecture about what happened next, chiefly that the FSB, the main successor to the KGB, decided to seize power. I looked to a longtime Kremlin insider for guidance, and he agreed to fill me in, but only anonymously so as to retain his access. I'll call him Viktor. As he recalled, at that time Yeltsin named yet another new prime minister, his fourth in fourteen months. The rapid turnover resulted from Yeltsin's opponents forcing on him candidates whom he did not favor, and Yeltsin in turn finding ways to install successors who were more to his liking. This time the lucky man was Sergei Stepashin, a former Interior Ministry officer from St. Petersburg. Although it was not made explicit, Yeltsin's camp intended only to give Stepashin a tryout for the presidency, Viktor said. Stepashin almost immediately proved not up to the task. He lacked backbone, Viktor said. He wouldn't take a stand. And that could only earn disrespect in a place where long knives were the norm. Yeltsin's handlers and family were dismayed and looked about for a replacement.

Meanwhile, Putin had made his unobtrusive way onto the Kremlin's radar screen as head of the FSB. By comparison with Yeltsin, he was wholly lacking in political charisma or presence, but he did have demonstrated decisiveness. In June 1999, Yeltsin announced to a visiting dignitary that in ten days he would appoint Putin as his new prime minister. Furthermore, he told his startled guest, he would soon name this up-to-now obscure functionary the next president of Russia.

Vladimir Putin was the archetypal man from nowhere—as in, how did this fellow get so far? He undoubtedly benefited from a convergence of probably unrepeatable circumstances. He had quietly gained recognition within the Kremlin, where the leadership was desperate for a competent successor to the erratic Yeltsin. The chief outside candidate seemed to be one of Yeltsin's former prime ministers, Yevgeny Primakov. But he was an ally of political forces whom Yeltsin and his allies had alienated and hoped to keep at bay.

The most telling factor appeared to be that Putin was slavishly loyal. In the early 1990s, he had attracted attention in Yeltsin's circles as the dutiful deputy to St. Petersburg's mayor, Anatoly Sobchak, for whom he served after returning from KGB duty in East Germany. When Sobchak slipped into political decline and suddenly faced corruption charges, Putin worked to exonerate him, while arranging his secret flight out of the country.

This act of devotion was impressive. But then he outdid himself in the eyes of Yeltsin and the president's advisers by helping to destroy the career of an official who had made a serious nuisance of himself with the Kremlin. Yuri Skuratov, a zealous prosecutor, had seemed bent on bringing criminal charges against the Yeltsin family. But at the height of Skuratov's high-profile investigation, a video of him carousing in the nude with prostitutes suddenly appeared on Russian television. To head off claims that the video was a fake, Putin took pains to publicly state that it was authentic. The Kremlin was nearly teary-eyed with gratitude.

Putin gained a reputation as a bureaucrat who would shield his bosses and their families from prosecution and possible prison terms. What made his record all the more meaningful to the powerful men who observed him was that he didn't appear to be self-serving; Putin had nothing to gain, for example, from aiding Sobchak, who was already out of power. Rather, Putin seemed to feel obligated by an almost quaint sense of honor and duty. As a former KGB boss, Oleg Kalugin, put it, he was "a man of Prussian-style obedience." That quality, so rare in Russia, combined with a willingness to work hard and avoid the spotlight, swept him into the most powerful post in the country.

I don't mean to discount his strong attachment to the state intelligence agencies. This outwardly emotionless man seemed to be moved almost solely by his feelings for the spy services and Mother Russia, both of which he believed had been scandalously maltreated by Gorbachev and Yeltsin. Yet Putin himself had a mediocre career in intelligence. To be a reasonably successful spy, one should land an assignment in the capital of an important enemy state, such as Washington or London, or in a zone of significant East–West conflict, such as the Middle

East. By comparison, the apex of Putin's career was a six-year posting to East Germany, a Soviet satellite with few secrets to learn and few foreigners worth converting to the Communist cause. Putin was not even assigned to Berlin, the capital, but instead to the singularly unremarkable outpost of Dresden. Upon returning home in 1990, he was not sent to the Soviet capital of Moscow—the center of intelligence work—but instead to St. Petersburg. In a collection of interviews conducted with him in 2000, called *First Person,* he claimed somewhat unconvincingly that St. Petersburg was his choice because he knew that the Soviet Union was teetering toward collapse. Whatever the case, his active intelligence career was over. He was thirty-eight.

Putin was elevated to the top job in the FSB eight years later—in summer 1998—but not because of his intelligence skills. The Yeltsin camp effectively installed him there. Putin was seen as someone who could be relied upon to defend the first family and those around the president. Any notion that the FSB on its own would choose an arguably failed spy to be the intelligence agency's champion seemed questionable to me. Indeed, Putin's first act upon assuming the presidency of Russia, on December 31, 1999, seemed to validate the thinking of Yeltsin's advisers. He signed a proclamation barring any prosecution of the outgoing president.

The state's intelligence operatives nevertheless are extremely influential. It is disturbing, for example, to witness Putin's benevolent attitude toward the remnants of the once all-powerful KGB. When the Soviet Union collapsed, thousands of *silovíki,* members of Russia's military and security agencies, had gone from being the cream of Soviet society to the dregs of the Yeltsin era. Their complaints about their fate and their mourning for Russia's past were largely ignored until Putin came along, tapped into their fury, and began methodically reappointing them to influential posts. By the end of 2006, they were in full control of both Russia's political and corporate worlds, according to Olga Kryshtanovskaya, the scholar and leading expert on Russian elites. She examined the top one thousand officials in the Kremlin, parliament, the ministries, and business, and found that 78 percent had some link to the *silovíki.* This is not surprising when one considers the extent to which Putin and the *silovíki*—and a significant portion of ordinary Russians, for that matter—were troubled by the same questions: What had happened to this nation that in the not-so-distant past had struck fear into the hearts of the West? How had its once-venerated army fallen into such shameful disrepair?

But the evidence shows that Putin summoned the *siloviki* to help him right the ship, to restore the Russia that he and they remembered. I could find no reason to believe that there was any more to it than that. The theory that Putin's ascendance was masterminded in FSB headquarters seemed vastly exaggerated.

As Putin assumed power over Russia, a kind of social contract was struck between the mafias and the state. The terms were unwritten but understood. The mafias did not disappear. But they were regularized and made to observe new rules of conduct—for starters, the wanton street shoot-outs that were a fixture of the Yeltsin era would no longer be tolerated. Among the chief beneficiaries of this contract were the hundreds of current and former agents of the FSB who had become part of Russia's dark underbelly in the Yeltsin years, acting as muscle and brains for the mafias and gangs throughout Europe. Now they became the visible superstructure of Putin's regime. Overnight, they were part of the new order, working in high-level security firms, assigned to jobs at every level in ministries, the Kremlin, and state-owned companies.

The Yeltsin period had been so rapacious that even some of the oligarchs recognized it as such. The most perceptive among them quickly understood that Putin would attempt to unwind their power. There is a belief that he offered the oligarchs a deal in the last half of 2000: Cease your political activity and most likely keep your fortunes. In fact, it appears that some of the oligarchs *themselves* sought this deal, to head off a Putin attack on all of them. One oligarch, Mikhail Fridman, told Lloyd, the *Financial Times* writer, that he and the other billionaires deserved Putin's wrath. In an interview at the time, Fridman said they asked only that past wrongs be forgotten. "I think the best plan would be if Putin were to declare an amnesty on everything that happened in the past," Fridman said.

Russia's increasingly hostile stance toward the West under Putin also has a more nuanced history. The prevailing wisdom is that he was emboldened to challenge the West when soaring oil revenues suddenly made Russia a wealthy nation to be reckoned with. It is true that Russia and the West enjoyed a relatively warm relationship from the Gorbachev years through the middle to late 1990s. But antagonism actually began to surface during Boris Yeltsin's latter years as president. It seemed to start as a pragmatic political response to a resurgence of Russian nationalism; Yeltsin's government decided that it could strengthen its domestic support by adopting a harder-edged foreign policy. That turned to seriously belligerent talk in the lead-up to NATO's 1999 decision to bomb Serbia in order to halt Belgrade's advance on Kosovo. Yeltsin warned that the NATO strike could lead to military action by Russia and a possible world war. When he first took power, Putin sought to moderate Russia's rhetoric, but that would soon change.

Domestic Russian politics and a series of terrorist attacks that shook the country in the latter half of 1999 were instrumental in creating the Putin we know today. Explosives shattered high-rise apartment buildings in the region of Dagestan, the city of Volgodonsk, and two districts of Moscow itself—a total of four bombings that killed more than three hundred and wounded scores more.

The Yeltsin presidency was in its waning months; Putin, who had just been appointed prime minister, went on the air to angrily declare that he would not negotiate with those responsible for the apartment blasts, who he said were undoubtedly Chechens. In fact, he would not negotiate with terrorists under any circumstance—a seeming swipe at concessions made by Yeltsin to end the First Chechen War of 1994–96. Whereupon Putin launched the Second Chechen War, in which tens of thousands of Chechens and Russians would be killed during the worst years of the fighting.

These events in latter 1999—the apartment blasts and Putin's retaliatory assault on breakaway Chechnya—"transformed the Russian political landscape," wrote Paul Klebnikov, a *Forbes* magazine reporter. "Prime Minister Putin declared the nation besieged. Paranoia swept Russia's cities. . . ." The fearful populace craved a strong leader and six months later elected Putin president with 52.6 percent of the vote. The results were a stunning turnaround from his popularity rating of a mere 2 percent when, as a stranger to the population at large, he was first appointed prime minister.

While most of the country was galvanizing around Putin, some were troubled by an explosion that *didn't* happen. On September 22, 1999, six days after the fourth blast, in Volgodonsk, nervous residents of an apartment building in the city of Ryazan became suspicious of strangers seen on the premises and called police, who found a bomb identical to the others and deactivated it.

Dogged local police work and reporting by Russian journalists turned up evidence that pointed away from Chechen involvement. One of the most tantalizing discoveries was a telephone call to FSB headquarters in Ryazan—tracked by a switchboard operator—that suggested contact between the security agency and someone involved in planting the bomb. Very quickly, the official story—that a terrorist attack had been thwarted—changed. Moscow now declared that the bomb was a dummy, placed in the apartment house as a civil defense exercise to test public vigilance. Local police, though, said it contained the working parts of a bomb, and tests indicated the presence of explosives.

In what became known as the Ryazan Incident, local and foreign reporters and opposition parliamentarians speculated that if the FSB itself wasn't responsible for planting the bomb, then rogue agents or officers might have been. It wasn't much of a leap to then suggest that similar elements in the FSB could have been behind the other apartment bombings.

It was a sensational scenario—that the deadly attacks had been staged by the FSB, acting on behalf of unidentified people with unknown motivations at senior levels of the government. Andrew Jack of the *Financial Times* bureau in Moscow took a skeptical view. He thought a likelier culprit was an affiliate of al-Qaeda in the neighboring region of Dagestan. But one of Jack's predecessors, David Satter, was a chief proponent of the FSB theory. In *Darkness at Dawn,* Satter delivered a riveting analysis of the event in Ryazan, bolstered by witness testimony. Satter was convinced that "Ryazan was planned by the same people who perpetrated the earlier bombings." He characterized the bombers as "those who needed another war capable of propelling Putin into the presidency in order to save their corruptly acquired wealth. These could only have been the leaders of the Yeltsin regime itself," meaning the FSB.

Some who continued to question whether the government had played a role in the bombings were killed or imprisoned over the next several years. Opposition lawmaker Vladimir Golovlyov was shot dead while walking his dog. Gunshots killed Sergei Yushenkov, a leading liberal parliamentarian, near his home. Yuri Shchekochikhin, a Duma deputy and reporter for the opposition Russian newspaper *Novaya Gazeta,* died after a sixteen-day illness resembling poisoning. Lawyer Mikhail Trepashkin was jailed on a weapons charge just before he was to testify at a court hearing into the explosions. He maintained that the firearm in question had been planted, and upon his release a year later he renewed his accusations of government complicity in the explosions.

The mystery of the four apartment house explosions that preceded the Ryazan Incident attracted the attention of Russian billionaire oligarch Boris Berezovsky. He had played a crucial role in getting Putin elected president by lining up cash, political support, and, more important, unabashedly positive coverage on his television station, ORT. But the two had a falling-out soon after and the tycoon now lived in self-exile in the West.

One of his key advisers, Yuri Felshtinsky, believed that the FSB had been involved in the apartment blasts. He also suspected that Putin, who was chief of the agency up until a month before they happened, had taken part in the planning. Felshtinsky, a bearish Russian émigré, had spent years prowling Russian archives, specializing in cataloguing the diaries of Bolshevik revolutionary Leon Trotsky. He became bored with his historical pursuits, longed to move into contemporary political analysis, and signed on with Berezovsky.

In a meeting at his suburban Boston home, Felshtinsky explained to me that one day while riding in a limousine with his employer he took the opportunity to advance his theory about the explosions. He told Berezovsky that the motives were obvious: power and wealth. As the Yeltsin era drew to a close, the future control of Russia was up for grabs. If the men of the FSB had to kill three hundred people to create a climate of fear that would enable them to claim the spoils, well, they would kill three hundred people. It followed that the leader of the intelligence agency would be rewarded with the presidency because he had taken the greatest risk. That's a mafia tradition—the person risking the most gets the most, Felshtinsky argued.

At first, Berezovsky was skeptical of Felshtinsky's suspicions. But later, he began to reflect on the run-up to Putin's election. As the struggle to succeed Yeltsin had begun to take shape, most observers viewed the taciturn prime minister as a relative unknown who stood little chance of political survival. Yet Putin had seemed highly confident, Berezovsky now recalled. In fact, the man had seemed to know something that he was keeping to himself.

"I am so stupid," Berezovsky finally blurted out, according to Felshtinsky. "I am so stupid."

Felshtinsky's scenario was entirely believable, Berezovsky decided. Putin's confidence that he would assume power could be explained by his knowledge of, or participation in, a plot that was unfolding within the FSB.

The oligarch now directed his attention to the particulars of the apartment house explosions. Who would know how such a terrorist plot might have been carried out and how to identify the likely culprits? Felshtinsky immediately thought of another Berezovsky adviser, a fellow named Alexander Litvinenko, who had served as an intelligence officer with some of the darkest units of the FSB. Litvinenko, already a pointed critic of the spy agency, was still living in Russia but would soon defect to the West.

At Berezovsky's request, Felshtinsky flew to Moscow to test his theory with Litvinenko. They drove out together to the latter's dacha outside Moscow, and strolled in the woods after leaving behind their cell phones—a standard precaution against possible electronic surveillance. Felshtinsky outlined his suspicions and posed the question: Was such a sequence of events possible?

Felshtinsky not only sounded reasonable, Litvinenko replied, but had hit upon a pattern.

"Find everything you can about Max Lazovsky," Litvinenko suggested.

"Who?"

Lazovsky was a former KGB officer and reputed criminal leader. As Litvinenko and Felshtinsky would later describe in *Blowing Up Russia,* a book they would write together, Lazovsky had helped bomb a Moscow bridge, an act coinciding with Yeltsin's 1996 reelection campaign, and was later arrested. In August 1999—a month before the apartment bombings—the Russian Supreme Court freed Lazovsky. Now he was dead—murdered eight months after the apartment explosions—and Litvinenko saw his fingerprints all over them. "If you understand Lazovsky, how he operated, how his organization was built, you will understand everything," Felshtinsky recalls Litvinenko saying.

It was hard to separate the Berezovsky team members from their inherent bias against Putin. These three intelligent people—Felshtinsky, Litvinenko, and Berezovsky—had looked at highly suspicious circumstances through a shared lens of anger, victimization, and vengefulness, and reached the most extreme possible conclusion: that Putin had conspired in the bombing of fellow citizens as part of a diabolical power grab by Russia's intelligence services. The circumstantial evidence was certainly prejudicial against the FSB. Yet as far as I could see, it would be very difficult to validate the three men's conclusions.

A contrarian attitude is healthy when it comes to conspiracies; though many are suggested, few turn out to be real. I myself learned that lesson on my first foreign posting, in the intrigue-filled Philippines, a place where there were no simple answers. The locals spun the most fantastic tales, into which it was easy to be drawn. The coup-prone counterintelligence officers of the Philippine Army were even more dangerous, skillfully persuading most of the foreign correspondents that President Corazon Aquino was destined to fall and that they—these handsome officers—would take her place. She didn't fall, and those who succumbed to the disinformation were embarrassed. David Briscoe, my Manila boss at The Associated Press, possessed one of the wisest approaches to seemingly sinister events. "Sometimes the answer is right there on the surface," Briscoe used to say of conspiracies, or the lack thereof.

So, what about the apartment blasts? Did the FSB and possibly Putin slaughter hundreds of Russians to achieve their aims? Putin himself called the Ryazan theory madness. "There are no people in the Russian secret services who would be capable of such a crime against their own people," he said. "The very allegation is immoral."

Yes, the possibility was intriguing, made so by the writings of Felshtinsky, ultra-smart Russian journalists such as Pavel Voloshin, who led the reporting on it at the time, and foreign correspondents such as David Satter. I was reluctant to dismiss them, even though my nonsense detector rejected their stated or implied judgments that a conspiracy was to blame. After all, the authorities had tried to sweep Ryazan under the carpet.

I reconsidered the competing theories—that it was al-Qaeda, Boris Berezovsky, Chechens, rogue FSB agents, or perhaps someone completely different. What if one group had blown up the first four buildings, but copycats had planted the Ryazan bomb? An FSB link of some sort seemed certain—former or current agents were basically caught in the act. But did that mean it was a plot approved at the top? Were they rogue operators hired to carry out a mission for al-Qaeda or the Chechens?. Were other forces at work?

There did seem to have been a plot afoot to bomb the Ryazan building. But it did not seem possible for a journalist to solve the mystery of who organized it. As far as the allegation of a conspiracy at the top levels of government, the most that anyone could say with absolute certainty was that the Kremlin had been guilty of its customary indifference to the welfare of Russian citizens.

In the years to follow, Putin would preside over a revival of Russian prosperity at home and influence abroad, fueled by a great flood of wealth from the country's tremendous store of oil and natural gas. Russia possessed 26 percent of the world's natural gas—the largest reserves of any country—and the seventh-largest oil reserves, at 6.6 percent. Putin would trumpet the return of a Great Russia and tell his people to be proud of themselves and their past. He would glorify leaders and events regarded as odious by much of the outside world; Josef Stalin's murderous 1930s purges, he would say, had been exaggerated by Russia's enemies. (As prime minister, Putin had toasted Stalin on the dictator's birthday. And he threw a lavish, nationally televised Kremlin party to honor Felix Dzerzhinsky, the brutal founder of Cheka, the early Bolshevik-era prototype of the KGB. It all smacked of a personal love affair. "This profession employs those who love our Motherland and who are selflessly devoted to their people," Putin told a room of intelligence agents. ". . . Those who are ready to execute the most difficult and dangerous tasks at the first order work in the security services.")

The Russian people would respond to Putin's steady withdrawal of their individual liberties with obedience combined with defiant nationalism, a standard set four centuries earlier under Ivan IV. In the West, Ivan's nickname, Grozny, was translated as "Terrible"—but to

Russians, Ivan was "Fearsome" or "Awesome," an image that Putin would successfully cultivate.

Putin maintained no torture or execution chambers. Yet his matter-of-fact responses to the domestic assassinations that occurred with some regularity invited the impression abroad that he was cold-blooded and at minimum a protector of murderers.

Consider the month of October 2006. A killer fired four shots into Anna Politkovskaya, killing the journalist in her apartment house. Three days later, gunmen killed banker Alexander Plokhin, the head of a Moscow branch of Vneshtorgbank. Days after that, the victim was Anatoly Voronin, business director of the ITAR-TASS news agency. Finally, a lone assailant used a Kalashnikov with a silencer to execute Dmitry Fotyanov, a mayoral candidate in the mining town of Dalnegorsk. None of the murders was solved.

Litvinenko was assassinated the following month in London. The United Kingdom concluded that a former Russian intelligence agent had done the killing, and sought his extradition from Russia. Putin could have acquitted himself and Russia as a whole by cooperating with Britain. Instead, he rejected the extradition request and looked on approvingly as the suspected assassin won election to the national parliament, thereby gaining immunity from prosecution within Russia while a wanted man in Europe. Opinion abroad hardened that Putin was, in one way or another, complicit in the murder. I could think of no similar behavior by the president of an industrialized country. Putin seemed to be deliberately putting himself in the same camp as the world's most disreputable leaders.

It was altogether possible, of course, that Putin and his circle intended to convey precisely the menacing impression that foreigners had of them, sending a message that said, Don't mess with Russia. But that seemed like overthinking. The greater likelihood was that Putin was simply being Putin.

CHAPTER 3

Getting to Know The Putin
Morning in Russia—
at a Price

EVEN THE MOST TOTALITARIAN GOVERNMENTS ARE PUBLIC RELATIONS conscious. Journalists can usually count on at least one reasonably informed—if not entirely believable—person to serve as the face of the country. Afghanistan's brutal ruler Najibullah himself met routinely with reporters during the late 1980s and early 1990s; Uzbekistan's Islam Karimov delegated the task to an economic lieutenant; and Sudan's Omar al-Bashir had Islamic radical Hassan al-Turabi speak to me, in the days before Bashir threw him in prison.

In Vladimir Putin's Kremlin there was no such person. Putin's usual spokesman was Dmitri Peskov, baby-faced and charming. But I did not want to hear from a mere spin doctor. I wanted access to an actual player, a *participant* in events, so that I could better understand the Kremlin's view of why certain things happened as they did. I got nowhere.

As one of Peskov's assistants explained, Putin's men saw no benefit at the moment in candid conversation with someone writing for an essentially Western audience. Whatever they said would be misperceived, and in any event why should they care what the West thought about them?

I raise my experience not out of pique at being rebuffed, but to note the larger truth it illustrated about Putin's Russia. Now on top of the world, it owed no one an explanation. It was up to the West to accept that Russia was back. Unlike in the 1990s, when the nation was, economically speaking, on its knees, it was now self-sustaining, on the move, and didn't need Western help nor the West's understanding.

A sharp rise in oil prices was behind the Kremlin's huge confidence. Crude oil sold for about $20 a barrel when Putin succeeded Yeltsin. It was pushing $100 a barrel when he announced in late 2007 that, since term limits barred him from reelection as president, he would assume the mantle of prime minister, thereby assuring his continued hold on power. Next to the country itself, Putin was the greatest beneficiary of Russia's new oil riches; its people credited him personally for the resulting improvement in their standard of living. Never in history did such a large percentage of the Russian population have so much money to spend.

The impact of this wealth was especially evident on my trips to the capital in 2007. Moscow had become one of Europe's most grand and fashionable cities. Each time I visited, the number of exclusive boutiques had multiplied along Tverskaya Street, all the way to Red Square and the Kremlin. This slice of Moscow now boasted one of the world's largest concentrations of billionaires. The swelling middle class spent its salaries with seeming abandon at new shops and malls that encircled the city. Wealthy Russians bought up lavish villas, mansions, and chateaux along Montenegro's Adriatic coast, in southern France, and in central London.

Russia's new muscular profile earned it global deference. It ran neck and neck with Saudi Arabia in the contest to be the world's largest oil producer, paid off its foreign debt, banked some $200 billion in a rainy-day fund, and began to invest in international stocks and bonds. For the first time, the country burst out of its borders not at the point of a gun, but through the strength of its purse.

Europe was an important energy customer; in 2008, Russia provided a third of the continent's oil and natural gas, and indications were that the percentage was not going to drop. Foreign oil companies assiduously courted Russia, one of the few petro-states willing to entertain their proposals. But the price of admission became steep, and giants such as Britain's BP could no longer negotiate the advantageous terms they had when Russia was far weaker. Oilmen from the West not only had to pay cash up front but also give Russian energy companies a share of their prized energy possessions elsewhere. Gazprom accumulated an impressive list of shareholdings in gas storage, marketing, and pipeline companies across Europe—in Germany, the United Kingdom, Italy, the Netherlands, and so on—and pressed hard for more. Investment banks, too, courted Moscow and earned tens of millions of dollars in fees by enabling a wave of Russian public offerings, mergers and acquisitions, and other financing deals.

Meanwhile, Putin's exercise of power was applauded by much of the country. After moving aggressively against Chechnya, he took on some of the best-known titans who had amassed their wealth during Boris Yeltsin's presidency. In 2000, Putin forced two of Russia's seemingly invincible oligarchs—Boris Berezovsky and Vladimir Gusinsky—into exile and turned their broadcast empires into pro-Kremlin propaganda vehicles. Putin's campaign against Mikhail Khodorkovsky began in 2003; by the time it was over, Russia's richest man had been sentenced to eight years in prison and his Yukos oil company had become the property of the state.

After eight years of paralysis under Yeltsin's rule, Putin's display of testosterone—dutifully reported on state-controlled television—sent his popularity rating over 70 percent. From the outside, Russia might have appeared to be under the thumb of a rogue regime. But at home, Putin was seen as demonstrating that Russia was governable. He had taken a perilous gamble, to be sure. His modus vivendi with criminal elements required that he tolerate their routine crimes and even murders in exchange for their fealty. To bind Russians together, he encouraged a campaign of sometimes frightening nationalism and xenophobia against non-Russians in Moscow, St. Petersburg, and elsewhere. Hate crimes soared. According to the SOVA Center, a Russian activist group, that kind of violence killed thirty-three people across Russia in the first three months of 2008, compared with seventy-two in all of the previous year. Racist attacks tripled in four years, SOVA reported. But that was the nation's Faustian bargain—acquiescence to a much-compromised, all-powerful state in exchange for the freedom to emerge from their homes, sweep away the rubble from their streets, and send their children to school.

The fresh pride that Putin instilled in his people bore resemblance to the feel-good mood that Ronald Reagan inspired in many Americans with a famously successful political slogan. Vladimir Putin created what a clever Moscow ad man might have marketed as "It's Morning Again in Russia."

The more confident Putin became about Russia's ascendancy, the more willing he seemed to rattle Europe occasionally and poke America in the eye with some frequency. He bluntly criticized the invasion of Iraq and complained about U.S. unilateralism. His assertiveness drew occasional scolding in America, which seemed to say, well, what can one expect of those impossible Russians?

But Putin's increasingly disagreeable manner was not simply a Russian being difficult. It was at least in part a result of the West's condescending attitude toward Russia when it was still deep in the throes of economic crisis. Russia's sense that it had been humiliated when it could least defend itself helped set the stage for worsening relations as the years wore on.

Putin had begun his presidency ready to find a way to reconcile Russia's profound differences with the West and develop friendly relations. As they did with Yeltsin, the policies of NATO would become an irritant for Putin. When the West, in the 1990s, began proceedings to absorb Eastern Europe and the former Soviet Baltic states into its military alliance, Russia objected. In nationalist circles, the NATO expansion was seen as a potential move to blackmail Moscow militarily should it mount any serious challenge to Western aims in the region. But Putin regarded the NATO dispute differently. He thought Washington simply didn't understand the basis for Moscow's opposition, according to Viktor, the Kremlin insider I consulted. If he was patient and made every effort to explain, Putin told his aides, "they'll see we're normal people, and we'll have a different relationship," Viktor recalled. So Putin sat for hours with major and minor Western visitors—a government minister, a vice minister, whoever was willing to hear his thoughts on Chechnya, NATO, and energy.

By the beginning of 2000, the NATO expansion was well under way. Putin met with President Bill Clinton, Secretary of State Madeleine Albright, and National Security Adviser Samuel Berger, and floated a question: What would be the West's attitude toward Russia applying to join NATO? Putin was serious, according to Viktor. He saw dual benefits to NATO membership: Russia could integrate more tightly with the West, and, more important from Moscow's point of view, have an opportunity to "reform" the Cold War–era organization from within. Like the other nineteen NATO members, Moscow would wield a veto. Among other things, it could stop the alliance from repeating acts Russia opposed, such as the bombing of Serbia.

As Viktor recalled the strained moment, Berger suddenly found a fly on the window to be extremely intriguing. Albright looked straight ahead. Clinton glanced at his advisers and finally responded with a diplomatically phrased brush-off. It was something on the order of, If it were up to me, I would welcome that.

Not dissuaded, Putin's entourage raised the idea again with visiting congressmen. But they reacted similarly, getting "this tricky expression on their faces and saying, 'Ah, you want to destroy NATO from within,' " Viktor recalled.

The congressmen had a point, of course. If Russia had been a NATO member in 1999, for example, Serbia would have simply overrun Kosovo as it and its surrogates had previously done with Bosnia and Herzegovina. It made sense to exclude Russia from NATO, notwithstanding the organization's absorption of other members of the former Soviet bloc, I thought. But Viktor had been offended at the American suggestion that Russia's motives were disingenuous. So too, apparently, had Putin. My mind wandered to Shakespeare's admonition about protesting too much. Only minutes earlier, Viktor had openly stated that Putin wanted to join NATO in part to "reform" it. But I presume there was something irritating about Russia not being given the benefit of the doubt and instead being accused of deception.

A truly serious outrage came after the September 11, 2001, terrorist attacks on the United States, Viktor said. Putin was among the first to reach President George W. Bush with condolences and an offer to provide any needed assistance. It wasn't long before Bush requested that Russia acquiesce to the establishment of a U.S. military presence in Uzbekistan and Kyrgyzstan, from which an offensive would be mounted against the Taliban-ruled government in Afghanistan. The American president promised that the bases were temporary and only for the Afghan attack, said Viktor. He recalled Putin giving a positive response, saying, "We've got to help our friends."

A year and a half later, the active phase of the Afghanistan campaign was concluded. The Kremlin asked when the United States intended to withdraw. Viktor paraphrased the American reply: "This is a zone of our strategic interests and we're not leaving."

Vyacheslav Nikonov, a dapper fifty-one-year-old historian and Kremlin insider, said America's assertion that it intended to stay in Afghanistan pushed Putin beyond his threshold of patience. "I heard it from the Kremlin, 'We're fed up,' " Nikonov told me. Putin increasingly felt that Russia had made too many unrequited concessions since the Gorbachev years. "It's, 'You guys do what we Americans want or the relationship is terrible.' This is what the relationship has been for the last fifteen years," Nikonov said. "We did what the U.S. wanted, and it got us zero."

And that was the end of Putin as sometimes-friendly interlocutor. If Washington and the rest of the West were going to treat Russia as a second-class country, well, Putin had his own message to deliver. He told off Washington, saying it had "overstepped its national borders in every way." When the United States said, in 2007, that it would install anti-missile devices in Poland and the Czech Republic, Putin's commander of missile forces threatened to re-aim Moscow's nuclear rockets at the installations. Then Putin struck the West's true soft underbelly: energy. He forced both Royal Dutch Shell and France's Total to sell controlling shares in their Russian oil properties to state-run companies at low prices, and warned that a similar fate might await Britain's BP and the biggest company of all, ExxonMobil.

The West called Putin belligerent. But his disparaging remark about the extent to which America had extended its presence seemed altogether reasonable to me—the United States clearly had over-reached around the world. America's reaction to Putin's complaint showed once again that it could be just as thin-skinned as the Russians, tending to vilify any outspoken critic abroad.

Viktor found it telling that Boris Yeltsin and Vladimir Putin—two wholly different people—started out and ended up at the same point in their attitudes toward the United States: hopeful at first, quite disenchanted and antagonistic in the end. What Viktor might have added was that their separate journeys reflected Russia's historic problem since Ivan the Terrible: Much of the world felt uncomfortable with Russian ways and kept the country at arm's length. Russia's modern ruling elite recognized the dissonance, yet thought that over time other nations might become more accepting. Putin in particular thought that Moscow's willingness to shelve its misgivings and bow to the West in certain situations would motivate the West to reciprocate in other instances. When the West largely failed to do so, he was hotly resentful.

The story line put forth by Viktor and Nikonov presupposed that Russia and Putin wouldn't have adopted their chin-out attitude if the West had behaved differently. While it must be recognized that the West does not have entirely clean hands in all of this, I am not as confident as my two Russian informants. There is no way to dial back, but my own experience in the former Soviet Union is that Russia is predisposed to some amount of bullying self-importance. Russia and the West quite likely would have ended up in the same spot no matter how much more accommodating the West had been. The West likely would never accept certain Russian demands, and vice versa. For instance, it is difficult to imagine Russia willingly acceding to the West's Balkan policy, specifically the independence of the region of Kosovo. Likewise, it's improbable that Washington will abandon its determination to see NATO expand all the way to Russia's borders. No matter how many diplomatic courtesies might have been exchanged during the post-Soviet years, these two issues would have remained incendiary in Russia and resulted in continuing antagonism.

Part of Putin's in-your-face defiance may be the lawyer in him. In a 2007 interview with *Time* magazine, for example, its correspondents questioned him about corruption within the Kremlin. Putin figuratively coiled into a fighter's stance—if *Time* was making such allegations, he assumed the magazine was certain that it had the facts right; if that was the case, his team was prepared to examine whatever *Time* published and take unspecified action should it find error. In other words, prove it.

The *Time* interview coincided with its selection of Putin as Person of the Year for 2007, an exceptional honor, although Putin seemed only grudgingly to recognize that. In a video excerpt of the interview, what I saw was the president of Russia in so many words putting up his middle finger. The writer, Adi Ignatius, in his account of how Putin behaved during their three and a half hours together, confirmed my impression. Putin was king of the world. Ignatius and his colleagues were supplicants. Here was one of the West's most prestigious publications declaring him a man of global importance. So what? He would act as he wished. Though the interview and a dinner were obviously strained, Putin was more or less indulgent through much of it. But each time he sensed that his interrogators were using events or Russian history to patronize or bludgeon his country, he would have none of it. When his tolerance had reached its limit—before the main dinner course arrived—Putin called it a night and summarily dismissed the journalists.

In a famous remark, Sergei Yastrzhembsky, Putin's senior envoy to Europe, said, "Gentlemen, Russia has returned. It should be reckoned with." That's certainly how Putin felt, and his toughness was probably necessary to move Russia along the path toward renewed greatness. In the same way that Gorbachev opened Soviet society and made peace with the West, and Yeltsin stood down the Communist Party and forced it to yield, Putin brought a sense of order to the country and prepared it for prosperity. With chaos all around, the country's economy in tatters, and the oligarchs dictating what they were going to make off with next, he said "Enough." He pushed back, creating space for the state and reclaiming much of the property that arguably should never have been relinquished—certainly not at such bargain-basement prices—to profiteers who enriched themselves at the country's expense. When oil prices went up, the system was poised to benefit and take off, and that's what happened.

For some, the lesson was clear: Anyone who aimed to rule effectively in a rowdy neighborhood like Russia had to demonstrate muscle. It was a limited vision, to be sure. Where Gorbachev and Yeltsin suggested that the Russian people could be more than they had perhaps imagined, controlling their own lives in a democracy, Putin told the people through his actions that the state had first claim to greatness, ahead of individuals for the most part.

But many Russians were tired of high-minded ideas anyway. They wanted to be paid their long-overdue salaries and pensions, and to have some stability in their lives. Putin by and large delivered both, and began 2008 with enviable popularity, leaving the presidency after two consecutive terms with his 70 percent approval rating intact. His chosen successor, a former law professor named Dmitri Medvedev, campaigned in a rigged election and received 70 percent of the vote. As part of the bargain, he named Putin his prime minister, with the stated intention of maintaining the policies of the previous eight years. It was no surprise: Putin had chosen Medvedev with the presumption that he, Putin, would continue to exercise his power over matters of state, then manipulated the election to make it happen.

Vyacheslav Nikonov, the Kremlin adviser who helped me understand some of Putin's disillusionment with the West, now explained the plan for the long-term future. Nikonov was a grandson of Vyacheslav Molotov—Stalin's foreign minister and the namesake of the Molotov cocktail—and a former assistant chief of staff to Gorbachev. He also was a chief adviser to Vladislav Surkov, Putin's domestic policy chief, and that interested me the most. The forty-three-year-old Surkov was the mastermind behind the making of what I call The Putin—the transformation of the president's visage into a savior-of-Russia icon, gargantuan and granite-faced, gazing from billboards, television screens, and newspapers throughout Moscow.

Although neither of us used the term during our conversation, Nikonov was a firm believer in The Putin, both the idea and the man, and seemed to expect him to rule for some time to come. He thought he would run again for president. "Putin may be back in 2012 and 2016, then 2024 and 2028," he said, naming the years of presidential elections, with a single break to satisfy Russia's term limits.

In other words, Putin's circle had settled in for a good two- or three-decade run. We journalists often joked about the creative ways that this or that dictator would devise to be president for life. I remember speculating that my five-year-old daughter, who has Kazakh grandparents, would be old enough to succeed the sixty-six-year-old president of Kazakhstan by the time he agreed to step down. Yet, faced with Nikonov's on-the-record declaration of pretty much the same ambition, I was momentarily speechless. "This is not extremely visionary," he assured me, "but pragmatic."

What did this exceedingly articulate Russian, dressed in a blue blazer with gold buttons and Scottish knit tie, mean by "pragmatic"? In Nikonov's own words, Putin had created a "rich, cynical, professional" group in their late thirties and early forties who "like their jobs. They are hand-managing the government. They'll be there another thirty years." Maybe that was pragmatism, Russian style. In any event, Nikonov was serious. And there was no reason to doubt that Putin felt the same way.

Putin has been unfairly criticized for playing a "double game," the multilevel chess cherished by spies everywhere. In fact, his governing strategy was transparent from the outset. He surrounded himself with people whose discipline and loyalty he trusted—other intelligence agents, military officers, and lawyers and colleagues from his old St. Petersburg days. Writers called it "Russia Inc." or "Kremlin Inc." A more apt label might be the "Gazprom State," since he rode Russia's oil and natural gas riches to global influence for himself and Russia. As the fall of the Berlin Wall marked the end of the age of the Soviet empire, Putin's style signaled the emergence of a coolly pragmatic state (as Nikonov would put it) overseen largely by ultra-patriotic spies and former spies.

But critics warned of a downside to Putin's approach. Boris Volodarsky, a former Russian military intelligence officer, told me of a messianic "KGB mentality" in which "everything is the state. . . . They will make a decision and carry it out, without limits." By its very nature, Putin's corps of intelligence agents will use whatever it deems necessary to achieve its goals, he said. Volodarsky was describing *bespredel*, anything goes.

In Soviet times, this single-mindedness among spies was suppressed by the Communist Party, according to Oleg Gordievsky, a KGB defector I met in the United Kingdom, where he lived in self-exile. He thought the dangerous thing about Putin was not that he was reverting to Soviet ways, but that he was failing to sufficiently reconstitute control over the spy services. As he put it, "The KGB without the Communist Party is a gang of gangsters." It was a rich assertion—as if the Communist Party didn't have its own gangster-like figures. Yet the central point remained valid—that the KGB's successor, the FSB, now answered to no one.

Coincidentally, my contacts included another man who possessed intimate knowledge of the spy services in Soviet times. And so I headed to California for a visit with Nikolai Khokhlov, a former captain of the KGB, a defector to the West, and an intended victim of murder by radioactive poison. He knew something about *bespredel*.

CHAPTER 4

Nikolai

The First Victim of Deliberate Nuclear Poisoning

DEATH IS ALWAYS A SAD EVENT, BUT ON THE DAY OF NIKOLAI Khokhlov's funeral the mourning was tempered by a sense of triumph. In his lifetime, the old Russian spy had not only outlived the KGB agents who relentlessly pursued him, but had reinvented himself in America as a man of accomplishment.

A half century earlier, on a garden terrace in West Germany, a Soviet operative had slipped a nuclear isotope into his coffee. The deadly substance—a derivative of the heavy metal thallium—was intended to kill Nikolai, a KGB officer who had unforgivably gone over to the West. It turned his face into a mask of dark spots and brown stripes that oozed blood and a sticky secretion, and caused his hair to fall out in tufts. Below his neck, his "copper-colored skin was tattooed with blood swellings." The attending physician said death was certain.

Instead, Nikolai survived. No one knew precisely why, except that perhaps his intended killers failed to dispense a sufficiently strong dose of the poison. Whatever the case, the KGB's failed attempt on his life only burnished his already considerable celebrity as a Cold War refugee in America. He settled in the small California community of San Bernardino, where he taught college psychology classes for two decades. In retirement, he tended his fruit trees and maintained his scholarly interests.

"He had the last laugh," observed his widow, Tatjana, as their four grandchildren scampered about and funeral guests mingled in a tree-filled backyard on the day of the September 2007 funeral.

Inside the house, photographs from a lifetime festooned walls, a piano, and a table—images of Nikolai's daughters, his son, who died from kidney failure, the German-born Tatjana. But there were no images from the long-ago years when he was trained as an assassin for Stalin's Kremlin, then defected to the West, and finally survived the first-known attempted murder by radioactive poison.

It would have been easy to dismiss Nikolai as a relic. But he seemed less a man past his time than a powerfully authoritative witness who could testify to the chilling practices of his native country's spymasters. He was certain, for example, that successor agencies to the KGB had carried out the notorious 2006 assassination of Alexander Litvinenko, in London. Litvinenko, the former Russian intelligence officer who had defected six years earlier, was poisoned by another radioactive toxin, polonium-210. Nikolai and Litvinenko thus shared an unusual distinction: They were the only known victims of radioactive poisoning in the entire history of assassinations worldwide.

After months of telephone and e-mail exchanges, in June 2007 I went to San Bernardino to meet Nikolai, a man who was once a decorated agent of state-sponsored assassinations, in the service of the Soviet Union. In his old age, Nikolai had a cane always at his right hand, the blond hair of his youth now a silky mane of white, his accented voice soft with no hint of menace. We kept in regular contact until failing health took his life nine months later, at age eighty-five.

Nikolai was still a teenager when he enrolled in a Moscow school for vaudeville, hoping it would lead to an acting career. After six months of learning to be an "artistic whistler," he was ready to join a traveling company. Then World War II intervened. Germany invaded the Soviet Union in the summer of 1941, and Nikolai was drafted for a role in a military film. Soon Hitler's troops were massed at Moscow's door, and an evacuation of the city was imminent. Soviet intelligence officers hit on a scheme to leave behind a vaudeville troupe that would become part of the resistance; Nikolai and three other young actors were recruited to make up the troupe.

In the end, the Germans were beaten back and the services of the would-be partisans were not needed. But Nikolai had impressed his superiors, especially Major General Pavel Sudoplatov of the NKVD, as the KGB was then known. The general, overseer of Leon Trotsky's slaying in Mexico, was one of the Soviet Union's most accomplished assassins. In short order, Nikolai signed on with Sudoplatov and joined a squad assigned to kill Franz von Papen, a Nazi appeaser who was Germany's ambassador to Turkey. But Nikolai contracted typhoid fever en route and was not there when the attempted assassination went awry.

His next mission sent him behind enemy lines. He was only twenty-one years old, but was about to become a Soviet hero.

Nikolai's target was Wilhelm Kube, the Nazi leader of German-held Belorussia. Secreted into the Belorussian capital, Minsk, by the Soviet underground in August 1943, Nikolai tracked down a housekeeper who serviced Kube's quarters. He showed the woman how she could place a bomb with a delayed fuse beneath the Nazi's bed, and argued that the killing would be an act of patriotism. The housekeeper finally agreed to do her part. Less than a week later, a courier awakened Nikolai with urgent news: "Kube is killed. . . . The bed and Kube blown to bits!" The housekeeper escaped with a partisan unit.

The Nazi's assassination was one of Nikolai's proudest moments, perhaps *the* proudest. In his memoirs, he wrote that it had been a chance to "kill a man whose name to millions symbolized fear and terror!" Stalin ordered medals for all who had participated in Kube's demise, and Sudoplatov himself pinned Nikolai's on the young spy's lapel.

As I researched the episode, a small detail seemed to reveal a side of Nikolai that surprised me. In his memoirs, published in 1959, he wrote that he had brought the bomb to the housekeeper, showed her how to attach it to a bed frame, and left it with her. But a retired CIA agent referred me to a book by the late British writer Gordon Brook-Shepherd that cast doubt on that account. When I put the question directly to Nikolai, he indeed backed away from the version in his memoirs. He said he had instructed the housekeeper how to use the bomb, but that the actual explosive was provided to her by Nadya Trayan, a partisan who later became one of the Soviet Union's most famous war heroes. Five decades had passed between the time he published his memoirs and I interviewed him. But I had trouble believing the discrepancy was the product of an old man's fading memory; Nikolai seemed to have excellent recall of past events. The more likely explanation was that his memoirs omitted Nadya Trayan's participation simply because it was a better story, at least from his perspective. The fact that he immediately owned up to the inaccuracy persuaded me that there was nothing malign about it.

The more time we spent together, the more Nikolai displayed those self-serving and self-absorbed aspects of his personality—but with an infectious charm. Probably his closest friend in San Bernardino was Nick Andonov, an émigré from Macedonia who practiced psychology. He said Nikolai could be quite demanding, calling at any hour to insist that Andonov come over for a long talk on some arcane subject the professor had been ruminating on. Nick would comply; he felt he had to—he wanted to—out of friendship.

To Andonov, Nikolai was an extremely sensitive, complex, and difficult figure who felt misunderstood by almost everyone. To that, I would add deeply emotional and sometimes self-pitying. When an effort to republish his memoirs failed, Nikolai retreated into an "it doesn't matter" mode, sullen and withdrawn—why would I want them published anyway; no one wants to read about such archaic matters.

Nikolai also didn't always own up to his embellishments. During our conversations, he would feign puzzlement if I asked a question that he found insulting, especially one that challenged the veracity of one of his stories. He would say, "I don't understand the question."

But in all these cases—when he withdrew at perceived slights by publishers or by me—he would get over the offense in a couple of days and return for more. He loved the attention.

His relationship with Tatjana was a bit of a mystery. The two of them had separated two decades before. (Nikolai blamed it on their age difference—she was nineteen years his junior. Also, she was too practical, while he was "metaphysical.")

They did not attempt to hide their disagreements. He was rude and condescending toward her, extremely chauvinistic. When she attempted to speak, he simply talked over her or said, "May I have the floor?" and then took it. He especially reacted that way when the talk turned to politics (his were decidedly right wing). She could be equally dismissive, responding to one of his tirades with, "Right, Nikolai, umm-hmmm," while rolling her eyes.

And yet they still had obvious affection for each other. After his physical condition worsened, they spoke almost every day. She screened calls for him, cooked for him, and let him entertain guests at her home. (His apartment was a disaster, he explained.) How many estranged wives would do all that for their husbands?

Most often, Nikolai was extremely polite and possessed of a self-effacing sense of humor. He had a coughing fit at one point and Tatjana asked if he needed anything. "Yes, a new throat," he replied.

He also was an articulate, intelligent, and erudite man who was utterly riveting when he discussed psychology and why he found parapsychology to be the discipline's ultimate form.

Did I find him heroic? I would say I respected and admired him. He was a man of conscience, and I didn't mind his affection for the spotlight.

In 1945, the war concluded, Sudoplatov dispatched Soviet operatives to Eastern European countries, as what were called "sleeper agents" in an earlier age. Nikolai ended up in Romania, where for four years he posed as a Polish immigrant and readied himself for undercover assignments. Then he was recalled to Moscow to engage in intelligence missions against Moscow's new enemies, the United States and its allies.

Acquaintances thought Nikolai a ladies' man, dapper and slim. Sudoplatov praised Nikolai's "blond, blue-eyed good looks" and "suave ways" as valuable assets, especially if "turning" a woman was part of the assignment. The general treated his protégé with sometimes astonishing indulgence and seemed to see Nikolai as "a young Sudoplatov." "I have big plans for you," the general had promised when Nikolai left for Romania.

But now Nikolai was losing his zest for the spy game. The romance and patriotism that had motivated him as a wartime intelligence officer had not carried over to peacetime. He wanted to try his hand at filmmaking or the theater, and lobbied Sudoplatov to release him from duty. The general refused, and Nikolai thought he knew why. Sudoplatov could not go to Stalin and admit that he had so wrongly judged an agent and vouched for him in the past; such a lapse was inexcusable, and "if he admitted it, he could be liquidated, and if I did, I could be," Nikolai said.

In 1952, Sudoplatov told Nikolai he had been chosen to assassinate Alexander Kerensky, who ruled the provisional government between the abdication of Czar Nicholas II and the 1917 Bolshevik revolution. Stalin wanted Kerensky killed because he seemed about to unite anti-Soviet émigrés in Europe. Nikolai tried to talk his way out of the assignment, but managed to avoid it only when Stalin decided that Kerensky was not a serious threat and called off the mission.

The following year, Stalin died, and a purge followed. Led by Nikita Khrushchev, Stalin's heirs executed Lavrenty Beria, chief of the NKVD, the secret police agency that was a forerunner of the KGB. He possessed incriminating dossiers on virtually all of them; the fear was that he would use the documents to intimidate any opposition and become ruler of the Soviet Union. Then they went after those with real or imagined links to Beria, and Sudoplatov and scores of others were swept into prison. Nikolai was suddenly without a protector. In his memoir, he wrote that Sudoplatov was "the finest and most intelligent man I had known in the service. And now his turn had come to be sacrificed to the machine." But when I questioned Nikolai in person about Sudoplatov, he said he "didn't care" when he heard of the general's arrest: "To him, I was his protégé. But to me he was my superior, not my mentor." At the time, I thought that was Nikolai's bravado speaking. And, indeed, a few months later, he revealed himself to be genuinely torn about the general. "I looked at him almost as my stepfather," he said, "until the moment he told me to go to Paris to kill [Kerensky]. That was a surprise that he would do that. That's when everything fell apart."

The new boss was a "short-witted" colonel named Lev Studnikov, who soon had an assignment for Nikolai: the assassination, in West Germany, of an anti-Soviet Russian nationalist named Giorgy Okolovich. But an inspection of Okolovich's file led Nikolai to conclude that the émigré leader, while clearly opposed to the Soviet leadership, was not "an enemy of the state" bent on destroying the Russian nation or people. Thus, he hardly seemed deserving of assassination.

According to Nikolai's account, his doubts about the mission multiplied. He told his then-wife, Yana, that he was being asked to murder "apparently a very good man." Yana, who had always been uncomfortable with her husband's chosen occupation, issued an ultimatum. If he carried out this killing, she warned, their lives together would be over and he would never see their son, Alik, again. Nikolai, already troubled by the grim task that awaited him, was finally persuaded: He would not carry out the assassination.

He concocted an elaborate ruse to make it appear that he would proceed with the mission, in which he was to supervise the poisoning of the émigré leader by two German secret agents. The three of them trained together for months. They rehearsed how to approach Okolovich at his five-story Frankfurt apartment building, and how to use their weapons—two tiny pistols secreted inside metal cigarette cases that Nikolai bought at a West Berlin gift shop. A special weapons shop in Moscow adapted the gear so that the cases, if opened, would reveal nothing but the tips of unfiltered Chesterfields, and the pistols, from their hiding space, would almost soundlessly fire pellets filled with poison.

In January 1954, preparations were complete. Nikolai said his good-byes to Yana and Alik in Moscow, and promised that an intermediary would warn them if anything went wrong. As they parted, he could not help but feel uneasy. He was thirty-two years old, about to throw aside his life as he had known it for the past decade.

"Is it possible that this is really the last?" he thought.

In his memoir, Nikolai describes how he confronted Giorgy Okolovich at his Frankfurt apartment weeks later and told his would-be quarry, "I've come to you from Moscow. The Central Committee of the Communist Party of the Soviet Union ordered your liquidation. I can't let this murder happen."

So began what must be one of the most curious friendships of the Cold War. Eventually, the episode would gain him worldwide fame as a traitor to his homeland (the Russian view) or a principled man who could no longer stomach the brutality expected of him (the opinion held in much of the anticommunist West). But it required a bit of convincing to get there. Okolovich quickly led Nikolai to the émigré's American "friends," agents from the CIA whose immediate reaction was to suspect that this supposed Russian assassin was a fraud, perhaps a double agent.

They subjected Nikolai to "rigorous questioning," before finally concluding that not only was he telling the truth, but he was a high-

value catch: the first serving officer ever to defect from the Soviet terror unit known loosely as Special Tasks. He could provide detailed descriptions of its personnel, its missions, and so on.

His interrogation then took an unexpected turn. The CIA agents
began pressuring Nikolai to go public with his story, intending it as
"blow for blow" retaliation for the NKVD abduction of another Soviet
émigré. Nikolai reacted with disbelief, fearful that exposing himself to
the world press would put his wife and son in grave danger.

Here is Nikolai's recollection of what happened next: Struggling to
preserve their relationship with their prized defector, CIA agents came
up with a compromise. He would tell his story to the press and make an
impassioned appeal for the safety of Yana and Alik in Russia. At the
moment he did so, either U.S. diplomats accompanied by Western reporters—or the reporters on their own—would go to Yana and the boy
and offer them sanctuary in the American embassy. The CIA even produced a State Department man calling himself "Mr. X," who offered assurances from President Eisenhower that the United States would
"keep Yana in the embassy until victory."

It was naïve to think that, in a police state, either diplomats from a
Western embassy or foreign reporters could simply drive to the apartment of a turncoat Soviet intelligence agent, pick up his wife and child,
and make it safely back to the embassy. It was a goofball plan, worse
than a Hail Mary pass. It was a Hail Mary with the almost certain
knowledge that there was no receiver in the end zone to catch the ball.
Nikolai—who was no innocent, after all—should have known better.
But events seemed to be spinning out of control. "I was desperate," he
told me.

On April 22, 1954, he unmasked himself before more than two
hundred reporters in Bonn. A reporter described him as "a slight,
scholarly-appearing blond young man . . . neatly dressed in a dark blue
suit" and wearing glasses. Nearby was a table displaying weapons to be
used in the assassination, conveniently placed there by the CIA. Nikolai posed for photographs with the émigré Okolovich and holding a
portrait of Yana. His plea on behalf of her and Alik went out over Voice
of America broadcasts, along with their Moscow address and telephone
number.

A week passed without word from the Soviet capital. Then Mr. X
called. "Nobody went to your family in Moscow," he said. ". . . I don't

know why. It looks like at the last moment they got cold feet." All Nikolai could think was that he had lost Yana and Alik.

Five decades later, in all of our conversations Nikolai never deviated from the above narrative. But I wondered, was it entirely credible?

Two retired CIA agents who were posted in Germany when Nikolai defected did their best to convince me that his story was fiction or at least greatly exaggerated.

Thomas Polgar, then intelligence adviser to the CIA station chief there, said that a CIA agent would have been willing to "say anything" to exploit the opportunity that Nikolai presented. But he said that he had never met Nikolai and knew of no ironclad promise that his wife and child would be rescued.

David E. Murphy, a principal agent on Soviet affairs at the time, was present during the interrogation of Nikolai. While the Russian might have thought he had a deal, "he was never told this would happen," Murphy said. "The State Department had no interest at all in such a risky activity in Moscow. How would you have done it? I don't think it would have worked."

Nikolai, Murphy suggested, was clinging to what he had wanted to believe would happen. Moreover, the Russian's version of events was convenient, considering that he had left his family behind in Moscow. "He has to justify having decided to defect. That's why he insists on this portrayal," Murphy said.

When I told Nikolai that I was in touch with Murphy and Polgar, he urged me to be skeptical since CIA people "are trained to lie." (Well, I thought, so are KGB people.) He said Polgar, despite asserting that he had never met Nikolai, had attended at least one interrogation session. Murphy, he said, conceived the idea of the press conference and spiriting Yana and Alik to the American embassy—and assured Nikolai that Washington had approved the scheme.

In the end, there was little overlap between the competing firsthand versions of events. But I heard enough from these two CIA agents and others posted to Germany at the time to understand that honoring promises was less important than outwitting the Soviets in the Cold War. American interrogators did and said what was necessary to turn possible KGB defectors and convince them to cooperate. And it seems clear that's what they did with Nikolai. He was deliberately misled into thinking he had a deal. The propaganda payoff for the United

States was obvious: the saga of an idealistic young Russian agent seeking refuge in America after suffering a crisis of conscience.

But why did the CIA allow his version of events to stand unchallenged all these years? Was this mere humanism, empathy for a guy in the same business who had lost his family? Not likely. The greater probability was that the agency didn't want to push Nikolai too far and risk losing his cooperation.

In an unpublished chapter of his memoir, Nikolai wrote that he was "often close to suicide" after his defection, enduring "endless hours of loneliness mixed with feelings of guilt and failure." Two months after his Bonn press conference, word arrived from Moscow that his wife and son were missing. Nikolai feared the worst. (Much later he would learn that Yana had been arrested the day after the press conference and sentenced to five years of internal exile, in the Russian republic of Komi. She was able to take Alik with her, work, and receive visitors. Her punishment seemed relatively benign; Yana once observed that her interrogators had become "nauseatingly friendly.")

But by late 1954, his spirits were lifting. Private committees were formed in the United States to support Yana's immigration. While none succeeded, the effort comforted Nikolai. He became a sensation in America, telling eager audiences across the country what it was like to be a Russian secret agent: bombs concealed in soap, salt, and tea; offices hidden behind bookcases; shadowing a subject.

The remarkable detail of Nikolai's revelations set him apart from other spies who were defecting from the Soviet bloc to the West (in such large numbers that the CIA had to establish a reception center in Frankfurt to process them). He was one of the first to publicly divulge the most intimate secrets of the Kremlin's assassination program. The Russians reacted to his and a series of other security breaches by curtailing political killings.

With the CIA looking on approvingly, Nikolai became a favorite of Cold War propagandists, testifying on Soviet wrongs before the House Un-American Activities Committee and otherwise lending his voice to the anticommunist crusade in America. He made the rounds of network television talk shows such as *Meet the Press* and wrote a series of articles entitled "I Would Not Murder for the Soviets" in *The Saturday*

Evening Post, then a dominant U.S. magazine. Nikolai told me the CIA arranged the articles.

In fall 1957, he attended a Frankfurt conference of the anti-Soviet organization of Russian émigrés led by Giorgy Okolovich, the man he was once ordered to assassinate. He remembered drinking a rancid cup of coffee and then dropping by an adjacent concert hall to hear a performance featuring opera singers. Suddenly his ears were ringing and his stomach was queasy. Around him "things began to whirl . . . [and] the electric bulbs were swaying," he wrote.

Nikolai retreated to his room and began vomiting violently. Okolovich was summoned, and took him to a hospital, where he was treated for acute gastritis. The reddish-copper hue that appeared on his ordinarily pale skin would soon fade, doctors assured him.

But the morning of his sixth day of hospitalization, brown stripes and spots emerged on his face. His pillow was drenched in blood and his hair came out in clumps. After a battery of tests, the German doctors suspected poisoning by thallium. They administered a compound called Prussian blue, the recognized—and generally effective—treatment for exposure to the heavy metal. Nikolai's body failed to respond, leaving his doctors baffled. The chief physician told Nikolai's friends, "To be honest, it's hopeless. . . . Wait with your questions until the autopsy."

Twelve days into the crisis, Nikolai was moved to an American military hospital in Frankfurt. Under tight security, doctors administered continuous blood transfusions and injections of vitamins, steroids such as cortisone, and so on—anything that might fortify his immune system. On the eighteenth day, the symptoms finally receded. Gaunt and bald under a beret, appearing two decades older than his thirty-five years, Nikolai walked out of the hospital. He later told crusading Russian journalist Anna Politkovskaya that it took a full year to recover; his legs in particular hurt.

What had nearly killed Nikolai? The commander of the U.S. hospital concluded that his suffering was "due to poisoning, probably by thallium and/or other chemical agents." In his memoir, Nikolai says that a New York specialist later analyzed the evidence and confirmed the presence of radioactive thallium. The near-fatal dose had in all likelihood been dropped into his coffee at the conference. When I asked Nikolai the doctor's name, he said he could no longer recall it, his typical reaction to a perceived challenge. I decided that, given the symptoms and the advice of chemists that thallium does have relatively stable nuclear isotopes, there was no reason to seriously question his assertion.

Nikolai had no doubts about what had happened. The poisoning was the handiwork of his former colleagues in Soviet intelligence, who had finally had enough of his public denunciations and wanted to "square accounts" with him. But why had this method been chosen? Was its aim not only to kill, but to kill cruelly? Nikolai thought Moscow's intention was more prosaic—to avoid detection. His assassins never expected that anyone would discover the presence of radioactive thallium.

In the years that followed, Nikolai became "disgusted" with what he regarded as an ineffectual anticommunist movement and decided to move on. Now a U.S. citizen, it took him just three years to earn both master's and doctoral degrees in psychology at Duke University. Then he began his teaching career, at California State University, San Bernardino. Two decades later, in Russia, Boris Yeltsin pardoned Nikolai for turning against the Soviet intelligence service. Nikolai attributed Yeltsin's act to blind luck—he had asked for permission to visit Moscow at a moment when, for one reason or another, the Russian president saw political advantage in welcoming such a visitor.

Nikolai and Yana spoke frequently by telephone in the time leading up to the Moscow visit, his first since defecting. In the Russian capital, they spent an emotional evening together. He would not share the details of their visit, other than to say that she told him he had "done everything right." They were divorced by now; he had since married Tatjana, who was a sister-in-law of Giorgy Okolovich's chief lieutenant. He remained in contact with son Alik, now a biologist at Moscow State University.

Nikolai's years as a spy never left his soul, and in a very real way he was still living them when I knew him. He thrived on the past. His voice turned childlike whenever our discussions turned to his World War II exploits, and the descriptions of those adventures are the best parts of his memoir. He remained bitter at the CIA's failure to rescue Yana and Alik; it was a betrayal, proof that the agency cared nothing about human beings. His friend Nick Andonov told me Nikolai was desperate to find someone who would portray him in film or print as a man who was not a traitor. When he failed, he was certain that the CIA simply didn't want his story to be told and had pressured media executives into shunning him. I chalked that up to paranoia.

Until the very end, Nikolai insisted he was never an assassin and spoke contemptuously of those who portrayed him as having been one. Everyone got him wrong. I thought it was an absurd position to take. Did he ever kill anyone with his bare hands? Not that I could find out. But he was obviously capable of directing murder plots when he so chose. He was making a distinction between assassinations that he thought were justified—during wartime as a Russian partisan—and those he found distasteful after the war. One type was patriotic, the other mechanical and ideological.

I came to believe that stagecraft was a large part of Nikolai's psyche. The Okolovich affair seemed to be a prime example. If Nikolai had simply wanted to stop the murder of the émigré leader, he only had to warn Okolovich to get out of town and no one would have been the wiser. He extended what should have been a temporary intersection with Okolovich's life into an elongated drama, quite possibly because of the very theater of it—he couldn't help himself.

Now I wanted to understand something about the nature of the current regime in Moscow. I decided to take a look at the events of October 2002 in a popular theater in the Russian capital.

CHAPTER 5

Nord-Ost

Once Again, Mother Russia
Fails Her People

ILYA LYSAK, A BOYISHLY CHARMING TWENTY-FOUR-YEAR-OLD bass player with a confident manner, seated himself in the orchestra pit and began tuning up. It was October 23, 2002, and he and thirty-one other musicians were about to perform in the hit musical *Nord-Ost,* or "Northeast," a World War II love story. He knew the score by heart, having already played it some three hundred times for theater audiences. But he was ever mindful of the need to stay sharp—it was a coup that he had landed this job in Moscow, one of the world's most musically talented cities, and he knew it.

Irina Fadeeva, a thirty-seven-year-old blond woman with striking blue eyes, took her seat in row 11 of the theater. She was accompanied by her equally lovely older sister, Victoria; her fifteen-year-old son, Yaroslav; and her eighteen-year-old niece, Anastasia. The foursome ended up here entirely by chance. Irina had bought tickets for another show at a different theater, only to discover at the last minute that the tickets were for the previous night's performance. But she was determined that the evening would not be wasted. She hurried everyone to another theater just down the street. *Nord-Ost* was playing, and she managed to buy four of the few remaining tickets.

Elena Baranovskaya, a well-spoken, elegantly turned-out woman, sat seven rows away with her husband, Sergei, a retired military officer, and her nineteen-year-old son, Andrei. They were marking a new life together—she and Sergei had been married just over a year, and only the day before had moved into a large new apartment. Elena had bought the *Nord-Ost* tickets to celebrate their good fortune; a bottle of wine and late dinner awaited them at home after the play was over.

Five years later, in separate conversations, the young bass player and the two women would guide me through the nightmare that soon unfolded inside the theater. Here are the stories of Ilya, Irina, and Elena, three who somehow survived while more than one hundred were dying.

It was during the second act that events on stage began to seem out of the ordinary. Ilya looked up from the orchestra pit to see armed strangers, dressed in masks and fatigues, suddenly appear. His initial reaction was bemusement: Two years into the musical's run, its eccentric director must be still fiddling with the cast, introducing new characters without warning. Ilya watched as one of the masked men ordered a principal actor to leave the stage, then a second and a third.

Some in the audience, including Irina and Elena, laughed at the seemingly impromptu staging. But not Elena's husband, a war-hardened former colonel in military intelligence. His intuition told him that these new "actors" were about to take hostages. "Everyone relax. We will be here awhile," Sergei cautioned those around him. Images flashed through his mind of the 118-man crew that had perished in the submarine *Kursk* two years earlier, absent any Russian rescue attempt. Putin "will not save us," he said.

Now something was going wrong in the orchestra pit. The conductor continued to wave his baton, but the music began to trail off. One by one, the confused members of the orchestra were putting down their instruments, in such perfect order that it appeared the surreal scene had been choreographed. Finally, there was only silence in the pit.

Videos captured some of the drama. A sequence from the theater's in-house recording system opens with four men walking on stage in camouflage jackets. One barks orders to a comrade. Another is identifying himself and the other invaders as Chechens from the republic in southern Russia where President Vladimir Putin is conducting a savage war of conquest. Their leader, twenty-two-year-old Movsar Barayev, appears in a separate video shot during the siege with British newsman Mark Franchetti. The only one not wearing a mask, he is a nephew of a famously fierce Chechen commander. "We want an end to the war," he tells the intrepid reporter.

From his vantage point in the pit, Ilya estimated that there were four dozen Chechens scattered about the theater. He wasn't far off. There were forty-one. Many of them were women; they were known as "black widows" because they were the wives or sisters of slain Chechen men and had volunteered to be suicide bombers in this assault. Each one kept a hand at all times on a belt around her waist; each belt was said to be loaded with explosives and shrapnel. Ilya could see what appeared to be detonators—small buttons atop some belts; two wires extending from others, as if waiting to be touched together.

As the hours ticked by, tensions heightened. Some of the intruders wired bombs to pillars that supported the theater's structure. Others fired weapons over the heads of audience members. "Just look straight ahead," said one masked man. "Anyone who ducks will be dealt with." It was ultimate terror, Ilya thought—was he more likely to die from a bullet as he sat in his seat, or if he ducked down next to his bass? He looked directly ahead, as did everyone else.

Later, when the attention of the Chechens seemed to be directed away from the orchestra, Ilya sensed that the time might be right for escape. His seat was close to a door leading to the musicians' dressing rooms. He reached over and opened the door, and the players quietly filed out of the pit, locking the door behind them. But the Chechens quickly noticed their absence. A few militants climbed into the pit and demanded that the musicians come out. If they did not comply, the door would be forced open and a grenade tossed in. What could Ilya do? He opened the door, and the musicians returned to the pit, with their hands behind their heads. Now they were made to sit with the audience, directly in front of Movsar Barayev so that the Chechen leader could keep an eye on them.

Only a few rows away, Irina expressed confidence that the standoff would soon end. Even if these were genuine Chechen terrorists, they would be satisfied to have made their point; the show would then go on and she and her son would be home by eleven o'clock. "No, this will be two or three days," came the voice of one of the black widows, known to audience members only as Asya. She had been standing nearby and overheard the conversation. Her prediction would prove to be eerily accurate.

Russians were not unused to mass hostage-taking by Chechen insurgents. In 1995, after an assault on the town of Budyonnovsk, invaders from Chechnya retreated to a hospital and held some 1,500 patients hostage. About 30 died in fighting with Russian forces before a truce was finally negotiated. The following year, two villages were raided in Dagestan, a territory adjoining Chechnya; more than 2,000 were taken hostage and about 340 died before the standoffs ended. In all three of these episodes, many Chechen fighters were able to escape.

I was more accustomed to the criminality that erupted after the First Chechen War ended in 1996. It sorely tested the sympathy that many Western reporters felt for the quarrelsome republic that had been nearly obliterated by the Russian military. The main crime was kidnapping-for-ransom. It wasn't only the abductions themselves that disillusioned me, but the way victims were treated. They were typically held for months without word, sometimes in pits dug under homes, even if family members were ready to pay up. Most victims were Chechens, many never to be seen again. Some were foreigners, including a Russian journalist named Yelena Masyuk, who was held for 101 days before being ransomed for $2 million.

In August 1997, I visited the northern Caucasus city of Nalchik, a two-hour drive west of Chechnya, where sixteen residents had already been kidnapped that year. Thirteen had been released for an average ransom of $300,000. Among the lucky ones was Alim Tlupov, a muscular twenty-three-year-old with a butch haircut. He and two friends had driven into Chechnya to barter belongings for diesel fuel. But two Chechen acquaintances led them into a trap. Alim and his friends ended up with pillowcases over their heads and their hands tied, while the captors telephoned Alim's father, Zauddin, with a demand for the equivalent of $300,000. The sum was absurd, since Zauddin was only a factory driver.

So began an ordeal in which the three young men were moved from one basement to another, beaten, and prevented from bathing. Alim described it as a family enterprise. The kidnappers' wives and sisters wandered about, sometimes delivering bread and unsweetened tea to the captors—their main diet. Neighbors strolled by, clearly aware that kidnapping victims were being held a few steps away, Alim said.

After two months, the captives managed to escape. Before they could reach home, the infuriated Chechens telephoned Alim's father. "Your son has been killed in a skirmish," one of the captors said. "Come right away." Now the father would become the victim. When Zauddin arrived at the rendezvous point, the Chechens abducted him. Another two months passed. Finally, the kidnappers accepted a reduced ransom of about $22,000, which the Tlupovs managed to raise from relatives. What seemed to most anger the family was the tepid response they received from authorities in Russia and Chechnya when they asked for help. Everyone pleaded impotence against the kidnappers.

Some victims who managed to escape—especially Europeans—tried to explain away the kidnappings as a natural outgrowth of the abuse the people of Chechnya had experienced. But that was absurd. The truth was that kidnapping became a way of life for many Chechens. Obviously nowhere near the whole population was involved, but sometimes it seemed so.

At the same time, Chechen militants fighting for a cause became interwoven with unholy characters such as Arbi Barayev, a sadistic Chechen insurgent who, among other outrages, had decapitated four Western telecom workers—three Britons and a New Zealander—in 1998 and left their heads in a sack by a road.

Now Barayev's nephew was standing on a theater stage in Moscow, glaring down at hundreds of terrified hostages whose lives were in his hands.

Anna Politkovskaya was in Santa Monica, California, to receive an award for courage from UCLA. Swooping into the sun-drenched lobby of her hotel, the celebrated Russian journalist was handed a message: Call Moscow.

"The terrorists want to see you," a colleague told her.

What terrorists?

Anna turned on the television and saw news of the siege for the first time. She rang her hosts to express regrets and booked the next available flight from Los Angeles to Moscow, via New York, a grueling trip. On the way, she telephoned her twenty-two-year-old daughter, Vera, in Russia.

Here is where coincidence proved difficult to believe.

Ilya, the young bassist now sitting quietly under the watchful eyes of his Chechen captors, had been a favorite of Anna's family since childhood. She had been like a mother, someone he could turn to for advice. More than once he had slept over on their couch after a study session with Anna's son, who was Ilya's best friend. For a time, Anna's daughter had been Ilya's girlfriend.

Mother, Ilya just telephoned me from *Nord-Ost*, the daughter told Anna.

Ilya is in *Nord-Ost*? Quite apart from concern over his fate, Anna had an idea. If he calls back, she instructed her daughter, please make two requests. Could he ask the Chechens if it was all right for her—Anna—to enter the theater when she reached Moscow? And would he also relay her request that they not do anything rash before she arrived?

Ilya did call back. That was one of the oddities of the hostage-taking—the Chechens' leader, Movsar Barayev, allowed his captives to make as many cell phone calls as they wished. He saw it as a way to increase public pressure on the Kremlin to negotiate. The only limit was how much power remained in one's cell battery.

But Barayev was not one to trifle with. He was the proud heir of his uncle Arbi, whose reputation for brutality was well known. The nephew apparently had not carried out any major operations before *Nord-Ost*—and, unlike his uncle, had not decapitated anyone. He commanded respect nonetheless, specifically because of his family link.

From where he was sitting, Ilya had almost line-of-sight eye contact with Barayev. "Can I talk to you?" he called out. The Chechen looked over and then motioned for Ilya to approach.

"I have a message from Anna Politkovskaya," Ilya said when he reached the stage.

"How do you know her?" the suspicious Barayev inquired.

Ilya recounted his long-standing friendship with the journalist's family.

Barayev asked for the phone number of Anna's daughter, then sent Ilya back to his seat.

At three a.m. in Moscow, the daughter was awakened by the ringing phone.

"This is Barayev. From *Nord-Ost*."

Anna had his permission to enter the theater.

For Ilya, conditions improved at once. He was allowed to roam the theater aisles, no longer forced like the rest to stay seated. He took it to mean that Anna enjoyed "undisputed authority" among the Chechens.

Ilya noticed a curious thing during his wanderings. At night, when the hostages were mostly asleep, the black widows were much less menacing. They appeared rather relaxed, unlike during daytime, when they were ultra-serious and seemingly ready to set off their belt bombs at any moment.

And there was something puzzling about the belts themselves. Ilya saw one woman reflexively pushing her thumb detonator without causing her belt to explode. Screws dropped regularly to the floor from other belts. Such observations made Ilya and some fellow musicians wonder if the belts were fake.

Anna Politkovskaya arrived in Moscow the second day of the hostage-taking. She went directly to the theater, on Melnikov Street, in the Dubrovka district. She was used to danger, having reported stories in the most remote and treacherous parts of Chechnya. But walking into a hostage situation with terrorists ready to explode bombs was quite another matter. She was admittedly frightened.

The theater was not what one might call cavernous; it was more like a large cinema house, with two decks of red-covered seats set on a slight incline down to a moderate-size stage. Anna entered the lobby area, accompanied by an elderly doctor who had volunteered to check on the condition of the hostages. There was no one in sight. "Hello, is anyone here?" she called out. "This is Politkovskaya." There was no reply. Again she called out.

At last they heard a voice. "Are you the one who was at Khotuny?" A masked man made himself visible. He was referring to a Chechen mountain village that Anna had visited some twenty months earlier to investigate the reported presence of a brutal Russian prison camp. Yes, I was there, Anna told him.

That made her welcome, but not the elderly doctor, who was ushered out after being accused of various misdeeds. Anna went on alone until she came face-to-face with a man calling himself Abu Bakar. He was nominally Barayev's deputy. But it was clear from his authoritative manner that the relatively inexperienced Barayev relied on him heavily for most of the crucial decisions.

Here was an opportunity to try for a negotiated settlement. Anna spoke first. She assured him she wanted to hear everything the Chechens had to say, but first the children in the audience must be released. She was instantly rebuffed. Russian soldiers made a practice of arresting Chechen males as young as twelve, Abu Bakar replied, so why should we show mercy?

At least allow the hostages to have something to drink and eat. Abu Bakar gave a little ground. He would permit juice and water to be brought into the theater, but no food. The hostages could eat the same as the beleaguered Chechen people, meaning little or nothing.

Anna could understand Abu Bakar's bitterness. She felt that Putin had victimized not only the Chechens, but also Russian civilians, by inuring them to a vicious war, and his own military, too, by turning professional soldiers into callous killers.

What were the Chechen demands? Anna wanted to know.

There were two, Abu Bakar replied. Putin had to declare the war over. And, as a confidence-building measure, he had to actually withdraw troops from one part of Chechnya. Once those demands were fulfilled, the hostages could go home.

And what about Abu Bakar's masked comrades and the black widows?

"We will stay here, take the fight, and die," he said.

Anna knew there was no chance that Putin would agree. Perhaps there was some other way out. But for now, the hostages needed attention.

She returned to the street and went looking for drinks. But the Russian commandos surrounding the theater had come ill prepared to satisfy such a request—there were no food supplies of any kind for the hostages. So Anna solicited cash donations from fellow journalists and some firemen—enough to buy water, juice, and candy at a nearby kiosk. The candy was not explicitly permitted, but Anna figured that it was worth the risk. In several relays, the drinks and the sweets were carried inside.

Anna felt better after having brought some relief to the hostages. But she was newly distressed by a message whispered to her furtively by one of Ilya's orchestra mates. Word was circulating that the Chechens intended to begin shooting captives soon.

Anna telephoned a trusted friend, Dima Muratov, her editor at *Novaya Gazeta*. He told her to stand by while he called someone. *Novaya Gazeta*—"The New Newspaper"—was the only national opposition paper that had survived Putin's purge of rival voices in the media. It did not have a lot of friends in the Kremlin, but Muratov did possess the phone number of one important person—a suave survivor from the Yeltsin era named Alexander Voloshin, who was Putin's chief of staff. Perhaps Voloshin could make a difference. The editor put in the call.

"Can Anna leave the theater area? Is she free to leave?" the Putin aide asked. Muratov didn't know. He had to call his reporter back.

"Yes, I can go," Anna told him.

"Tell her to leave," Putin's man said when the editor called back. The meaning of his words was ominously clear. The Russian security forces had their own timetable—they were about to storm the theater. If Anna were there, she risked being swept up in the violence. The trouble was, if her editor told her the truth, she was sure to refuse to leave. She was just that way.

Muratov called Anna. "I need you to come back to the newsroom— now," he said. "I need you to write your story."

Apparently not suspecting her editor's subterfuge, Anna returned to the office and wrote up the events of the previous hours.

The clock ticked past midnight, and Irina's fifteen-year-old son began saying his good-byes to those sitting around him. "I will not survive," he said.

A few rows away, Elena's son, a third-year chemistry student at Moscow State University, wondered aloud why authorities didn't pump in a gas that would simply put everyone to sleep. "Such gases exist," he said. But his stepfather, the retired colonel in military intelligence, said it wouldn't work.

"If they spray gas, it is not physically possible for everyone to be put to sleep," the older man said. So "they will just start shooting."

Elena thought that if anyone was about to die, it would be her. She turned to her new husband. He had to promise that if anything happened to her, he would not abandon her son. "You'll help him," she said.

She was thinking of her former husband, who had walked out two years earlier to live with another woman. The colonel looked at her with tense eyes but spoke in a calm voice. "Don't doubt about this," he said. "I would never abandon him." A reassured Elena relaxed. She was certain he would not.

Suddenly, there was hope. "You can rest. Someone is coming from the government," the Chechens' leader, Barayev, called out. General Viktor Kazantsev, Putin's special envoy for Chechnya, had called to say he was flying in to Moscow and would come to the theater for face-to-face talks. The standoff, now in its third day, might actually be near an end.

Everyone—the hostages, the Chechens—was buoyed. The masked men tossed candies and juice into the audience.

About five a.m., Elena's son told his mother that he smelled something sweet. Irina saw one of the Chechens on stage pull his mask up over his face and look about the theater in seeming puzzlement. Was there a fire? she wondered. Ilya glanced up and saw a faint, cloud-like mist floating down from ventilators in the ceiling.

Barayev shouted a sudden warning. "Now they are storming us!" he cried out. "Lay down!"

Ilya didn't know what to think—did the Chechens intend to be their killers, or their rescuers?

"I'm afraid," said Irina's son. "Don't be afraid," she replied. "Whatever happens, we'll be together. I'll hold your hand." She was startled to see the black widows begin to slump against walls where they had been standing at attention, then slide to the floor unconscious.

Something perilous was in the air. Irina wrapped her scarf around her son's face and told her sister to cover her daughter's face, too. Elena dampened three handkerchiefs with water she had saved. She handed one to her son, one to her husband, and placed the third over her face.

Ilya heard shouting, glass breaking, and shooting. The Chechen gunmen scattered in panic. But the gas had made him woozy and indifferent—who cared about the Chechens? He and a fellow musician lay side by side on the floor and covered their faces with a jacket they shared. Then Ilya blacked out.

Russian commandos waited at a command post about two hundred yards away as the gas was released into the theater's air-conditioning system. It was a derivative of fentanyl, an opiate anesthetic many times more powerful than morphine. The Kremlin's expectations were that everyone inside would fall safely asleep. Then security forces could storm the building and kill the Chechen invaders before any bombs were detonated.

The assault had been organized with the care of a watchmaker, according to Mark Franchetti, the British journalist. Commandos placed ultrasensitive sound devices beneath the floor of the auditorium, enabling them to track the movement of the Chechens inside. They also drilled a peephole and ran a tiny camera through it, allowing some limited viewing of the theater's interior. After hours of such monitoring, the security forces were able to establish the approximate position of each terrorist. Commandos were then assigned specific Chechens to shoot when the assault began. They conducted practice raids in another theater a few miles away.

Still, after the fentanyl was released, signs of movement continued inside the auditorium. The gas apparently had not circulated as well as expected. Fentanyl was usually dispensed via an injection or pill; the aerosol had been tested and judged safe by scientists, but never in a space this large. Some parts of the theater seemed to be getting quite a bit of gas, other parts very little.

More fentanyl was pumped in, and then yet more. At last, all seemed quiet inside the theater and troops from the elite Alpha Unit poured into the building. Fifty-seven hours after the hostage crisis had begun, it was all over. The Russian commandos shot the black widows point blank where the women had collapsed. They pursued the Chechen men through the theater and executed them on the spot, including Barayev. (There were rumors later that one or more of the terrorists had escaped, but they were unsubstantiated.)

Ilya felt someone shaking him. A masked commando was shouting in his face, "Get up! Get up!" Although he could barely move his arms and legs, he managed to stumble out of the building to an ambulance, which whisked him to a hospital. When he was released four days later, four thousand rubles, the equivalent of $160, was missing from his trousers. Other hostages admitted to the hospital had the same story—all their cash, jewelry, and furs were stolen. Later, Ilya learned that ten of his fellow musicians were dead.

Elena awoke in a hospital bed about four hours after the gassing. "Where is my husband?" she pleaded. A few hours later, her mother and sister arrived with the answer. Her husband, Sergei, and her son, Andrei, had both perished.

Irina awoke in the crowded emergency room of another hospital. Her clothes, blood soaked, had been removed, and she was naked except for a blanket that someone had wrapped around her. She realized that her son was not with her and began to scream.

"Why are you shouting?" a doctor demanded. "Everyone is fine. No hostages died." That, at least, was the official word—all the hostages were safe.

A friend retrieved clothes from Irina's apartment while she used a borrowed cell phone to call other hospitals in search of her son. There was no trace of him, and she decided to go look for him herself. The first obstacle was getting out of the emergency room and off the hospital grounds, which were surrounded by soldiers with orders not to allow anyone to leave. Irina was stopped on her first attempt. But when in desperation she began to climb over a fence, she felt a hand under her—a kindly soldier provided the final boost.

Irina's first stop was her apartment, to retrieve a photograph of her son in case it would be needed for identification purposes. The building's lobby was already crowded with friends ready to join in the search. A television was turned to the news.

Suddenly, a friend brandishing a cell phone burst into tears. They killed him, she cried. On television, the bad news was confirmed. Some hostages in fact had died, and their names began scrolling across the screen. The first on the list was Yaroslav Fadeev—Irina's son.

A stillness came over Irina. She felt nothing and showed no emotion.

"Where is he?" she asked simply. She found his body at a morgue, where she sat alone, gazing at his face and caressing his head. She felt a wound and realized he must have been hit in the fusillade directed at the Chechens. That explained why her clothes had been so bloodied—it was her son's blood.

All she could think of were her final words to him—whatever happens, we'll be together. She felt she had deceived her son. And she couldn't live with that.

Irina ran out a back door, flagged a taxi, and directed the driver to a bridge over the Moscow River. She had no money so she paid the fare with her gold wedding band, and stepped out. She stood on the bridge where she and Yaroslav had often strolled, and gazed down at the icy water. The words kept going through her mind—whatever happens, we'll be together.

Then she jumped.

Irina opened her eyes. She had briefly gone underwater, but then floated right back to the surface. There was too much ice in the river. It was impossible to drown.

"Are you crazy? Why are you swimming there?" a man shouted from the riverbank. He and a friend pulled Irina out. "Where are you from?" the man's friend asked.

"I'm from the morgue," she replied. The men looked at her as if she was crazy.

"Listen," she said. "I'm from *Nord-Ost.*"

The two men instantly understood. Anyone in Moscow would have. "Where do you want to go?"

Home, she said.

Irina did not even catch a cold.

The official death toll was 129. In a statement, Vladimir Putin congratulated the commandos for rescuing more than seven hundred hostages. "We could not save everyone," he said. "Forgive us."

A chorus of criticism arose among survivors and their relatives. Why had the Kremlin not given negotiations more of a chance? What happened to Viktor Kazantsev, the Russian general who supposedly was on his way to attempt a negotiated settlement? Had that been a ploy to gain time for the commandos to prepare their assault? And what about the reckless use of the aerosol?

Those killed by the gas had gone into hypoventilation, slow and shallow breathing that leads to a dangerous buildup of carbon dioxide in the blood. It is the way that heroin addicts often die. The appropriate treatment is an injection of naloxone, a medication that counters the effects of opiate overdose, especially from heroin or morphine. But it must be administered immediately.

In fact, some rescuers carried syringes of naloxone. Judging by the welt on his upper arm, Ilya reckoned that he received a shot from the commando who shook him awake. But there were not enough doses, or not enough people delivering them, to make much of a difference. Ilya said that no other musician appeared to have gotten a shot; he had simply been lucky.

Outside the theater, medical personnel were either absent or disorganized. The commandos themselves, rather than a waiting crew of paramedics, carried the liberated hostages from the building. Witnesses said there were no waiting stretchers and virtually no medical supervision; the commandos simply laid the hostages on the sidewalk, sometimes in the snow. Proper medical procedure called for the victims to be laid on the side, arms down at their sides, and heads back and aligned with their bodies, so as to keep their air passages open and tongues safely away from their throats. But that care was not taken.

Even those who made it to hospitals alive could not expect to receive appropriate treatment. Government secretiveness left doctors and nurses uncertain for hours as to how to proceed. In the emergency room where Irina was treated, it was apparent that few medical workers had been told anything about the nature of the gas that had been used, not even what it was.

And so the doctors tried improvising. Irina recalled that one prescribed milk for all the survivors. Another doctor ordered the milk exchanged for mineral water. Then a third ordered the mineral water withdrawn. "It's no good in this case," he said.

Some doctors did receive word to inject naloxone, which they reasonably interpreted to mean that the gas was an opiate. But no one could be sure what sort of opiate, a crucial bit of information. Under pressure, the Kremlin finally began to characterize the gas as a fentanyl derivative, but even that was too inexact. Was it an analogue of fentanyl called carfentanil, ten thousand times more powerful than morphine and used to sedate large animals? Was it sufentanil, an anesthetic for heart surgery that is a mere ten times more powerful than fentanyl? Or simple fentanyl? Doctors were left wondering how much naloxone to administer.

Five years later, authorities whom I interviewed responded to their critics in pretty much the same way. The government had certainly not intended that the hostages should die. Therefore it was blameless.

A former Kremlin official who had been involved in the planning, and who asked for anonymity, said no one was sure how much gas to pump in. Nor, he added, did anyone anticipate that a large supply of antidote would be needed. It was assumed that everyone would simply wake up. "In my opinion, the operation was successful," he said.

As for the bitter complaints of survivors, he turned philosophical. "When there are victims, they will always seek answers," he said. "They say we could have continued negotiations. They will do so until the end of their lives. People live in a certain myth in which some things were done well, and some things bad. But I'm absolutely certain that there was no evil plot to kill people."

The Kremlin political adviser Vyacheslav Nikonov replied similarly. "The gas was rather harmless. The only thing they needed was a breath of fresh air—oxygen. A mask on their mouths," he said. "Most of them died because of their tongues going down their throats. When they started bringing people out, there was a long line of medical cars. They concentrated on bringing people to the cars rather than on giving them oxygen."

The government's review of what precisely happened was lackadaisical at best. Yuri Sinelshchikov, a former deputy prosecutor of the city of Moscow who supervised part of the investigation, believed it was not a serious effort. Written findings by his own investigator were altered to be in agreement with the conclusions of the FSB and the federal prosecutor, he said.

Sinelshchikov did not elaborate, but in other remarks he indicated there could be no conclusive investigation because the crime scene was politicized and corrupted. "I would leave the scene sick because of the mistakes, criminal mistakes," he said. "Important witnesses were not immediately interviewed, not until two or three weeks later. There was missing evidence. In the beginning someone didn't think something was important, and when he went back it was gone. People were not detained for interrogation. If someone was under suspicion and needed to be followed secretly, they were not doing it well at all, and it was obvious. For the first ten days there was chaos, and there were too many people from the top involved."

Anna Politkovskaya had her suspicions about the events—she believed there had to be complicity of some kind within Russia's intelligence agencies. How else did so many fully armed terrorists reach the center of Moscow? she asked. Six months afterward, she backed up her case by publishing an interview with a man who identified himself as a surviving member of the Nord-Ost terrorist band. The man, named

Khanpasha Terkibayev, was working for Russian intelligence, Politkovskaya alleged. After the interview, Terkibayev denied telling Politkovskaya that he was at Nord-Ost. He was killed in a car crash a few months later.

Like the allegations regarding the 1999 apartment blasts, the suggestion of FSB involvement at Nord-Ost seemed fantastic. Even though I trusted Anna's work, I had trouble taking such notions seriously. What I could say was that something worse than simple incompetence had led to the outcome at Nord-Ost. From the moment the hostage crisis began, the Kremlin and its security forces were focused only on killing the Chechens, on demonstrating the resolve of the state not to be pushed around. It never occurred to any of them to make the survival of the captives a priority.

An outsider could only wonder: If terrorists seized a theater in a major Western city, would the New York police or the FBI or the London, Paris, or Tokyo police use gas to subdue the hostage takers? Possibly. But would they neglect the need to have massive and well-organized medical care waiting outside the theater? The Hurricane Katrina debacle in 2005 notwithstanding, it is hard to imagine that fully equipped rescue trucks and ambulances would not have been lined up on Broadway by the dozens. I think it would be the same in the United Kingdom, in France, in Germany, and so on.

The most dangerous place in the industrialized world to be a rescued hostage is Russia.

The Nord-Ost survivors tried to get on with their lives, some more successfully than others. Two months after the hostage episode, Anna Politkovskaya's phone rang. It was the police.

"We've got Ilya Lysak down here. He is asking for you," a voice said. Ilya had been disorderly again; since his brush with terrorism, the young musician had gotten into a bar fight, inexplicably erupted at passersby on the street, and thrown a chair at someone.

"What's wrong with me?" he asked Anna, after she signed him out of jail. That night, he dozed off on the Politkovskaya couch next to the family's pet Doberman.

A few months later, a car jumped a curb near Ilya's apartment and ran him down. He suffered multiple broken bones and spent eleven months in the hospital. Anna arranged for his treatment, cashing in a favor owed her by a wealthy acquaintance, who paid the bills.

When I met him five years later, he spoke as though the hours he spent as a hostage weren't entirely frightening for him. Indeed, I had the sense that he was feeling fairly full of himself some of the time. At one point, he said, he decided that the Chechen leader, Barayev, was not *that* imposing, and that he, Ilya, could "take him one-on-one" if the two had ever been alone together. But there also was something affecting about Ilya. He described himself as a big, muscular man prior to the auto accident; now, at age twenty-nine, he was skinny, almost wiry, and, while a captivating speaker, he was more boy than man. When I saw him, Ilya was working two jobs—sound director at the country's main television station and, on the side, composing music for a film.

Elena noticed that people acted strangely once they learned of her connection to *Nord-Ost,* and so she stopped mentioning it. For the previous eighteen years, she had taught chemistry. But she could not see herself returning to the classroom. Instead, she began attending classes on the tourism industry, and there she met an elderly woman named Diana who was already a success in the business. As their relationship warmed, Elena revealed that she had been a hostage.

Diana responded instantly. "I'm going to give you my firm," she said. Elena was floored by her classmate's extreme kindness. "She was seventy-five and decided to do something else. She could see my circumstances," said Elena. "She asked an absolutely symbolic amount" of money in exchange.

When Elena spoke to me over tea in spring 2007, she was about to fly to Paris to personally select a hotel for clients. This courageous woman was on her way.

Irina, anxious that her son not be forgotten, presented herself at Anna Politkovskaya's newspaper office with a sheaf of photographs. Until then, the two had never met. But the sympathetic journalist made Irina and her dead son part of a feature article entitled "Nord-Ost. 11th Row," and churned out other pieces on the survivors and the government's plodding investigation. Irina read them all; Anna, she said, had "taken me by a finger and pulled me out from drowning. . . ."

But the *Novaya Gazeta* story offended the city prosecutor's office. An investigator summoned Irina for an interview and demanded that she retract the claim that her son had been shot by commandos. The official version was that firearms had been used only against the Chechens. Irina refused to back down; the prosecutor's office kept phoning, then began calling her parents.

Finally, Anna called the prosecutor's office: "Leave this family alone," she said, according to Irina. The calls stopped.

In America, the HBO network commissioned a documentary entitled *Terror in Moscow,* based on the work of Mark Franchetti, the British reporter who had interviewed the terrorist leader Barayev. Ilya, Elena, and Irina were brought together for the HBO program, and it in turn gave rise to the formation of Nord-Ostsi, or the "People of *Nord-Ost*"— survivors and families of the dead, bound together by the shared tragedy. They met at Elena's new apartment, and their common vow was to keep the memory of the theater massacre alive. Some joined in a suit against the Russian government, filed in international court in Strasbourg, France.

On the first anniversary of the gassing, a bronze plaque bearing the names of all 129 victims was installed outside the theater during a memorial service. Irina placed a photograph of her son amid the bouquets of flowers. Elena slipped in a photo of her husband and son at the seashore. No one from the Kremlin attended. President Putin sent a statement from abroad, calling the deaths "a severe wound in our heart that will take a long time to heal. But you and I know well that once you let terrorists raise their heads in one place they will immediately appear in another place using territories they are comfortable in as bases of rear support."

I last saw Irina at a Nord-Ostsi dinner in September 2007, where she sat before the camera of Russian documentary filmmaker Marina Goldovskaya. She was in despair that her life had become, like the setting for the theater massacre, a sort of play. "Just turn on the camera, and we can perform," she said of herself and the other survivors.

Her story fascinated the media—how she had found her son's body in a morgue, how she had jumped from the bridge. She was entirely genuine each time her tears welled up, which is why journalists and filmmakers kept returning. She had dedicated herself to crusading on behalf of the victims of *Nord-Ost,* which guaranteed that she would be a constant object of attention.

And yet she was troubled by the freeze-frame in which she found herself. It seemed frightening at times. In the years after the massacre, she had married and given birth to two children. She was a mother again, and she did not want her children to pay a price for the life she had chosen to lead. But how could they not be affected?

Would it have helped if Irina had sensed that there was some understanding of her pain amid the highest levels of government? An understanding among the Kremlin leadership that defense of the state had to be tempered with compassion for the Russian people?

Probably.

CHAPTER 6

The Exiles

Boris Berezovsky and the Sanctuary of London

THANKS TO ITS LIBERAL ATTITUDE TOWARD POLITICAL ASYLUM, the United Kingdom is a haven for the outcasts of autocratic countries around the world. Expatriates from former Soviet nations once ruled by Moscow make up a significant portion of this community of political refugees. My introduction to their universe was provided by a genteel Kazakh man named Akezhan Kazhegeldin, a KGB-trained former prime minister who presumed to lead his homeland's political opposition from London. Ten years earlier, he had stepped over the bounds of permitted ambition by aspiring to be president of his onetime Soviet country. Now he passed the time by dreaming of political plots against Kazakhstan's president, Nursultan Nazarbayev. Some dismissed him as a self-promoter, but this ungenerous characterization never gained traction with me.

I had known the fifty-seven-year-old Kazhegeldin for a decade. He was an enduring survivor, an admirable but sad figure. Admirable for standing up as an often lone voice against the autocratic politics practiced back home. Sad because, even if he were able to return to his country some day, there was little chance he could ever make a political comeback. And he likely wouldn't return, not with the discouraging example of Boris Shikhmuradov to consider. This somewhat vain political exile from former Soviet Turkmenistan sneaked back into his native country in 2002, thinking he would force the country's dictator into retirement. Instead, he was rapidly captured, drugged, forced to give a televised "confession," and imprisoned for life. Something similar certainly awaited Kazhegeldin were he to return to Kazakhstan. So that meant stewing abroad, forever planning unlikely conspiracies and hoping for a miracle.

Kazhegeldin supplied the number of a friend who could introduce me to the Mayfair district, a London haunt for the kind of people I was seeking: the political exiles, the denizens of the city's underworld of spies and former spies, and the often shady businessmen who moved comfortably among all factions.

Mayfair enjoyed a certain James Bond mystique, a hangover from the time that MI6, the British spy agency, was based there. But it was also august London writ large, housing Savile Row, Christie's and Sotheby's, and the Ritz. When I visited in 2007, its office space was the most expensive in the world at $212 a square foot, far higher than midtown Manhattan, Hong Kong, or Tokyo. You couldn't know by merely walking Mayfair's streets, but hedge funds had moved into the district alongside the luxury boutiques and exotic restaurants. The most intriguing businesses of all were the myriad detective agencies. These were run by clubby characters whose success seemed to hinge in part on how well they could create the impression that they knew the darkest secrets and kept company with the most dangerous characters.

Kazhegeldin had availed himself of such services, and sometimes reciprocated with information that enabled the agencies to plumb the vicious Russian business and political rivalries that their clients were keen to understand. With his help, I was able to contact agency detectives who were happy to talk, but not for attribution. While their openness might seem surprising, such professionals often trade information with journalists, particularly foreign correspondents with experience in opaque parts of the world.

One of these operatives, call him Andrew, said his usual clients were lawyers for British companies anxious to vet potential partners before signing a contract. But he also was profiting from a stream of new clients with business interests that involved the former Soviet Union. Some were tycoons in Russia and other newly independent republics who had built thriving enterprises from the wreckage of the Soviet states. They were willing to pay tens of thousands of dollars for compromising material on their enemies, a defense against rivals doing the same. Others were businessmen in the West, mainly Americans and Europeans, who were wondering if they should deal with such people. They routinely ordered $20,000 to $40,000 background checks on Russian, Kazakh, Uzbek, Georgian, or Chechen entrepreneurs who were offering what seemed like attractive deals.

The Mayfair detectives reckoned that most of the Western businessmen were just going through the motions; they fully intended to get in bed with these possibly nefarious fellows, if only to demonstrate their executive boldness. But, while they wanted to play near the edge, they hired the detective agencies to show shareholders that they were not doing so recklessly.

The agencies cared little about what motivated their clients. Their main concern was how to check out businessmen with murky pasts in Moscow, St. Petersburg, and elsewhere. Their staffs were thin on Russian expertise, and so their first reports were based on simple data searches on LexisNexis. Clients figured out that racket soon, however, and demanded more. So it was that the Mayfair agencies began to employ active-duty FSB men, reminiscent of the way that 1930s gangsters and Chicago policemen entered into mutually beneficial relationships. The agencies also hired former Russian intelligence agents, based on the assumption that, as with the mafia, no Russian spy ever truly left the service. It seemed that any Russian with an intelligence background who passed through London could pick up work.

The stock-in-trade for these gentlemen became known as the "KGB report." Once given an assignment, an agent would visit the FSB's file cabinets, pull records on whoever was of interest to the client, and pass them on. The level of detail delivered—property ownership, salary, marriage status, arrests—was astonishing compared with what was available publicly in the West.

There was no telling how much was accurate, but that didn't seem to matter. The KGB reports, at $2,000 or so each, would be gussied up and delivered to clients who mainly accepted them at face value and didn't question their provenance.

Andrew and the other detectives depicted their Western clients as strange combinations of voyeurs and cowboys, wanting to peek inside the strip show and boast to their friends about what they saw, but terrified to enter. Company lawyers ordered up the KGB reports, one detective said, but forbade his agency to conduct live interviews or hunt down revealing documents outside the KGB files. Such investigative methods could "violate little-understood laws," the lawyers said. I could not fathom what laws they were talking about. Most likely, they themselves didn't know and were simply trying to insulate themselves from whatever legal troubles might arise later.

William was the operations director of an agency that specialized in particularly gritty investigations. When he examined a Russian company, his aim was to provide a reality-based judgment on whether or not a client should do a deal, and if the answer was the former, how to do so prudently. He offered this theoretical example: If a client came to him with a Moscow property deal, it was not necessary to collect the voluminous detail that would appear in a KGB report. The sole relevant question was whether the deal included Yelena Baturina. She was Russia's only woman billionaire, the wife of Mayor Yuri Luzhkov, and the queen of Moscow property development. If she was a participant, well, that would be fantastic, full steam ahead. But if not, it might be best to pass; a reasonably successful deal was probably unlikely. While such a calculation might seem rather crude, in fact it reflected some sophisticated sleuthing—it reflected how deals really got done in Russia.

The detective industry had its turbocharged side as well. I learned this from Dmitri, once an officer of GRU, an intelligence arm of the Russian military that deploys more spies abroad than any of the nation's other espionage agencies. Dmitri worked now on contract for the Mayfair detective agencies, and a British friend recently retired from MI6 provided me the necessary introduction. Dmitri described his specialty as public relations—pee-yar' in its Russian adaptation of the English acronym, except that in Russia it was more often than not essentially a black art. Its objective was the destruction of a client's opponent through defamation. "We gather information for businesses that have problems," Dmitri explained. "We can find out what are your rivals' strong points, and can suggest how to damage the rival's strategy. Everyone has skeletons."

Unsolicited, Dmitri offered up Putin critic Anna Politkovskaya, the investigative reporter, as an example. He argued that her fundamental honesty could be challenged because she was in violation of Russian law by holding dual citizenships (she was born in New York when her father was a diplomat at the United Nations). Thus, he said, she should be regarded not as a crusading truth teller, but a questionable reporter who framed innocent Chechens and Russian soldiers.

It is best in such company to hold one's breath and focus on blinking normally so as not to betray any particular opinion. Dmitri occupied a ruthless world.

Yet I was sure that Dmitri himself had skeletons, so I ventured a question: Given his inclinations, why was he living in London and not in Russia? His reply: That's where he had found employment once he decided in the mid-1990s to leave the GRU, whose central tenet—discreet penetration of foreign militaries and businesses—had been watered down to a naïve belief that "Russians have nothing to be afraid of. Everybody is our friend."

"It was like a kindergarten" during the 1990s, Dmitri said, echoing Putin's realpolitik disdain for that period in Russia. In fact, in dealings with other states, "interests are eternal and friendships transitory."

Dmitri was a bag of hot air—a spinmaster with a huge mouth, an annoying attitude, and a bucket of money from his employment by the U.K. detective agencies.

I liked him. He was wholly transparent.

One reason such individuals sound like mafiosi is that the two camps regularly associate, said Mark Galeotti, a bearded professor at Keele University. He is an expert on the intersection of Russian organized crime and intelligence services, and was introduced to Russian gangs while working on a doctoral degree in the 1980s. Russian-based detective agencies are often partners with criminal gangs, said Galeotti. The gangs, in turn, are tolerated by Putin as long as they respect the Kremlin's domination of politics and business. Putin "doesn't go out to cleanse the stables," Galeotti said. "He just wants [the regions] to run efficiently."

Alexander Litvinenko's road to political exile in London began with a similar observation—that Putin was inexplicably tolerating criminality within the Russian state. His accusations would become more incendiary over the years, sometimes crossing into the fantastic. Galeotti, who once attended a speech by Litvinenko, found him to be earnest and committed, a decent person who was simply out of his depth. That was a perceptive observation. For all of Litvinenko's precautions as a KGB-

trained officer accustomed to attack and betrayal, he was ultimately un-
prepared for the precarious course his life took.

Litvinenko was raised by his paternal grandfather in the northern
Caucasus city of Nalchik, left there by parents who divorced when he
was a young boy. His first wife thought his upbringing in this relatively
wild region of southern Russia contributed to his being a bit of an odd
character. Natalia Litvinenko, who had met the blond, blue-eyed
Alexander in the suburbs of Moscow when he was fourteen and she a
year younger, told me that he glorified his boyhood. As they fell in love,
wed, and had two children, Litvinenko would abruptly turn cold and
intimidating, and defend himself by saying that Caucasus people "have
hotter blood so are capable of more cruelty," Natalia said. But ultimately Litvinenko was a self-pitying sort, "like an abandoned puppy,"
she said, troubled by an indifferent mother who refused to cook for
him, an abusive stepfather who once forced him to jump on and off a
couch one hundred times as punishment, and the general feeling that
no one at all loved him.

In later years, Litvinenko would regard the period spanning his
boyhood and first marriage as something of a lost time before he found
his bearings. But he seemed to appreciate Natalia's main point, according to *Death of a Dissident,* a memoir cowritten by his second wife, Marina,
and his colleague and spokesman Alex Goldfarb. Rather than loved, he
"felt sidelined" while growing up, the authors write. Absent an autobi-
ography, I treated *Death of a Dissident* as a primary source for Litvinenko's
mind-set. Unsurprisingly, it differs from Natalia's description of some
events, especially Litvinenko's abandonment of his family after eleven
years of marriage. Natalia said that his departure was sudden, coming
on a tempestuous 1993 night when he returned home smelling of per-
fume. She accused Marina of stealing him from her. *Death of a Dissident,*
however, describes the first marriage as an unhappy one that collapsed
of its own accord.

I found both wives attractive. Marina, a ballroom dance teacher, has
more city sophistication and flair, and is less prone to paranoid and eye-
brow-raising remarks. (For example, Natalia told my assistant that Litvinenko is still alive, and that his funeral was faked.) Yet I also felt sympathy
for Natalia and the two children she had with Litvinenko; twenty-two-
year-old Alexander and sixteen-year-old Sonya were both bitter and
clearly hurt over growing up without their father for long periods.

Meeting Marina clearly was an important personal turn for Litvinenko. *Death of a Dissident* says that their relationship enabled him to finally shed his feelings of alienation. But far more dramatic in terms of Litvinenko's ultimate fate was his crossing paths the next year with Boris Berezovsky, the wealthy Russian oligarch.

Moscow was bursting with swaggering billionaires in the 1990s, but few matched the outsized figure of Berezovsky. Made rich by his media empire, he presumed to influence all matters within the Kremlin, where he was part of President Boris Yeltsin's inner circle. Litvinenko at the time was a major in an anti-terrorism and organized crime unit of the former KGB.

The two met when Litvinenko was investigating a reported assassination threat against Berezovsky, and they spoke again a few times after that. Then, eight months later, Litvinenko received an urgent message on his pager. Berezovsky said he was in trouble—Moscow police had shown up at the club he owned with the intention of taking him in for questioning in the investigation of a sensational murder. Vlad Listyev, general director of the Berezovsky-controlled television station ORT, had been shot dead. Litvinenko rushed to the club and held off the police until more members of his own unit arrived, and the altercation was defused. Berezovsky underwent police questioning, but at the club rather than some remote location.

The event quickly cemented the relationship between Berezovsky and Litvinenko. Both felt that, short of the latter's intercession, the oligarch might have been taken away, only to disappear and later be reported as accidentally killed. Such things happened in Moscow with disturbing regularity. "[T]hey developed a bond shared only by people who have faced mortal danger together—not friendship or attachment, but a special kind of loyalty that no other can surpass," Marina Litvinenko and Goldfarb wrote in *Death of a Dissident*.

In other words, Berezovsky more or less owed Litvinenko a blood debt.

In 1997, Litvinenko took command of a four-member team that was part of a shadowy anti–organized crime unit. A superior officer summoned the team and told the men that Berezovsky had to be killed. Speaking directly to Litvinenko, he said, "You will be the one to take him out." The officer did not say who was ordering the assassination, but implied that the decision had been reached within the leadership of the anti-crime unit itself.

The events that followed reminded me of the old KGB agent Nikolai Khokhlov and his life-changing knock on the door of an anti-Soviet émigré—"I can't let this murder happen." Like Nikolai forty-four years earlier, Litvinenko did not perceive his assigned target as a "grave threat to our country"—the words of the superior officer that day. Extreme measures were warranted in wartime Chechnya, but not in peacetime Moscow. The order to kill the oligarch made Litvinenko and his men uneasy; he balked at it inwardly, but was careful to guard his feelings.

During the following three months, Litvinenko's squad did nothing to carry out the order, and the superior officer never brought it up again. It was a curious situation, to say the least. Litvinenko and his men were dismayed that, whatever criminality had crept into their profession, someone was trying to reinvent them as a moneymaking political hit squad. That was not what they had signed up to be. At the same time, they suspected the threat wasn't necessarily serious, and they might be able to outwait the officer who had issued the assassination order. So they dragged their feet, and heard nothing more from the officer.

Litvinenko did not immediately make Berezovsky aware of the order to assassinate him. When he later briefed the oligarch on the odd situation, Berezovsky thought the whole business sounded outlandish, but went straight to the director of the FSB. Was it true, what Litvinenko and his men said?

The FSB boss, Nikolai Kovalev, seemed to know nothing about the assassination order. But the accusations were explosive, and he assured the oligarch and Litvinenko that he would investigate. Soon they received word that whatever order had been issued—serious or not—was no longer in effect. Berezovsky would not be killed. However, the officer whose directive had set off the entire brouhaha went unpunished.

Litvinenko would not be soothed, and for good reason. Other troubling propositions were put before him: One superior asked if he was willing to help kill a former FSB man named Mikhail Trepashkin, who had accused the agency of corruption. Another sought his assistance in kidnapping a Chechen hotel owner. It seemed to Litvinenko that he and his men were still being pressured to act as an outlaw force.

Over subsequent months, Berezovsky arranged for Litvinenko's men to air their complaints outside the FSB—to a Kremlin security official, who passed them on to the federal prosecutor's office, which took formal depositions. It seemed they were being taken seriously, particularly when Kovalev was fired as FSB chief and replaced by someone whom Berezovsky recommended—Vladimir Putin.

Litvinenko and the other whistle-blowers were now on temporary suspension pending an investigation, but they thought the momentum was going their way. Their testimony could well lead to the reform of the FSB and promotions for all. Litvinenko in particular thought he might be in line for a senior position in the agency, given Berezovsky's influence. The powerful oligarch had become a Putin zealot and was championing the new FSB boss as a presidential candidate to succeed Yeltsin. Within a relatively short time, he would emerge as one of Putin's most important political strategists.

But the whistle-blowers had underestimated Putin's fealty to the intelligence community. When Litvinenko provided a briefing on questionable events at the FSB, Putin listened silently without committing to any action. Whatever had been said about killing Berezovsky reflected "thoughtless statements," but "did not constitute an intent to commit murder." Putin reassigned all members of the anti-crime unit—except the Litvinenko group. Litvinenko and his men seemed not to grasp it, but they had become outcasts within the FSB.

It was clear that Putin cared most about being solidly loyal to the intelligence agency he held dear, and less about changing the FSB's practices.

One day in November—almost a year after the original threat to Berezovsky—Russian émigré Yuri Felshtinsky flew in to Moscow to assume his new duties as a political adviser to the oligarch. Felshtinsky, now a scholar living in Boston, was no fan of the FSB. When, some two years hence, Russia would be shocked by a string of apartment house bombings, he would become a proponent of the theory that the FSB had been involved and that Vladimir Putin had been in on the planning.

But for now, his main interest was "a strange-looking man who was talking and talking and talking" while Felshtinsky and Berezovsky looked on. The talkative man was Litvinenko, who was preparing his men for a press conference the next day at which they would air their grievances against the FSB in public for the first time. There was much cursing and raising of voices as they debated whether to wear masks, weighed the risk of arrest, and wondered if their wardrobes were suitable for such an event. Litvinenko set about writing an opening statement to be handed to reporters.

"Do you mind if I look over the text?" Felshtinsky asked. Berezovsky agreed, and the new man concluded that Litvinenko could write pretty well.

The next day, Litvinenko and five FSB colleagues faced the press. Litvinenko was one of two who did not wear masks. He told reporters that he was deeply troubled by his unit's activities, and he recounted kidnapping and murder plans to which he had been witness. The FSB had become a criminal organization, "used for settling scores and carrying out private and criminal orders for payments. Sometimes the FSB is being used solely for the purpose of earning money." Senior officials within the agency were complicit, he said.

There simply was no precedent for such a public confession, at least not in Moscow itself. (Nikolai Khokhlov's dramatic 1954 news conference had been at a safe distance, in Frankfurt.) The Litvinenko event was televised and widely reported around Russia and in the West as well. The London *Independent* called it "extraordinary" and a *New York Times* report said later that "Moscow has talked of little else since."

What had brought matters to such a remarkable turn? Berezovsky, Litvinenko, and his men had lost faith that the FSB would reform itself and decided their only hope was a dramatic gesture that would marshal public opinion. But still they were not blaming Putin, and indeed shielded him by only citing events that had occurred before he took over the agency. They blamed the system, not the man.

Before the end of the year, they had their answer. FSB chief Vladimir Putin fired Litvinenko and the others for making "internal scandals public."

Berezovsky stuck by Litvinenko and his men. The whistle-blowers continued to nurse the hope that they would prevail, and the relationship between Felshtinsky and Litvinenko warmed. The latter, prone to nonstop banter, "was glad to have me as a listener," Felshtinsky recalled.

They were opposites in physical appearance, as was apparent in the jacket photo of *Blowing Up Russia,* the book that they would later coauthor. Standing beside each other, the hulking Felshtinsky and the comparatively small, boyish Litvinenko reminded me of the broad-chested John Steinbeck and his diminutive Hungarian photographer, Robert Capa, in a snapshot taken during research for their classic *Russian Journal.* In the case of the two Russians, it was the smaller man who had the spellbinding stories to tell.

As Felshtinsky listened, Litvinenko described torture he witnessed during his months of service in Chechnya, including once when soldiers burned a Chechen captive alive over an open fire and another occasion when they flayed a Chechen man. A startled Felshtinsky wondered why he didn't halt the outrages. Litvinenko replied that he couldn't have even if he wanted to, and that if he had tried, his companions would surely have killed him.

Then and later, Felshtinsky heard Litvinenko defend himself against implied and direct accusations that he had blood on his hands. Litvinenko said he never broke any law, Russian or international. Felshtinsky interpreted this to mean that while he killed men in battle, as dutiful soldiers must do, he never tortured anyone, nor violated any other standard of civility such as the Geneva Conventions.

But Felshtinsky decided there was something over the edge about these whistle-blowers. Hearing them bicker, he thought they sounded much like the gangsters they were trained to round up.

Berezovsky was providing them with monthly stipends of $500 to $1,000, good pay for Moscow. But that wasn't how the whistle-blowers—indeed, almost anyone around the oligarch—saw things. His retainers clung to the largely unsupported belief that anyone working for him inevitably would become rich, even super-rich. "When you are dealing with Boris, you are not thinking of tens of thousands of dollars, but hundreds of thousands or millions of dollars," Felshtinsky said. "Even if you are getting enough or a lot, you are disappointed or getting angry at him."

When one of the whistle-blowers angrily demanded a lump sum payment of $100,000, Litvinenko replied that "We didn't do it for money." After a few more rounds of similar sniping, everyone calmed down and the men recovered much of their optimism. Berezovsky was the key to promotions for all; the big money would come eventually. All they needed to do was push the oligarch harder.

Litvinenko himself thought so, too, until the moment, around three p.m. on March 25, 1999, when he was imprisoned.

The FSB charged him with beating up a suspect about two years earlier and planting bomb-making evidence to force the man to confess he was a terrorist. Litvinenko spent seven months in prison before being acquitted, then was jailed again, this time for three weeks. According to *Death of a Dissident,* Berezovsky obtained his release the second time by intervening with Putin.

One had to question Litvinenko's judgment in pursuing the FSB corruption matter so assertively. For instance, if the threat against Berezovsky was so serious, why didn't he call the oligarch at once and tell him the details? After all, he and the oligarch had developed "a special kind of loyalty" to each other, according to *Death of a Dissident.* And if the order to kill the oligarch was genuine, didn't the whistle-blowers think it odd that no superior officer demanded to know whether it was being carried out? Perhaps one answer is that, like Nikolai Khokhlov, Litvinenko wasn't satisfied with quietly saving a life. Rather than remaining behind the scenes, he had indulged a flair for the dramatic and an appetite for the public spotlight.

Almost everyone involved seemed to be looking out mainly for his own interests—the whistle-blowers hoping for enhanced status and more money, and Berezovsky seeking to tame the FSB and extend his political influence. When FSB boss Kovalev was fired and replaced by Putin, the dissidents saw it as evidence that "Berezovsky was winning," Felshtinsky recalled. Instead, "Litvinenko was fired and imprisoned. . . . Putin was not Berezovsky's friend, and Berezovsky was the last person who knew this."

That Litvinenko was no longer safe seemed obvious. He began planning his escape from Russia. Felshtinsky's recollection is that the two of them met at Litvinenko's dacha after his release from prison. Felshtinsky and Berezovsky had recently discussed Litvinenko's safety in Russia, and both figured it was time for him to leave the country. Now at Litvinenko's dacha, Felshtinsky related the conversation to him.

"What will I do? Where will I go?" Litvinenko asked. Felshtinsky said he could help. During the early 1980s, difficult years when the border was closed after the Soviet invasion of Afghanistan, he had run an illicit emigration scheme in which he charged Soviets $6,000 each to get out by marrying a Swede or a Finn. Given that he managed to settle people fairly easily during those years, he didn't see much of a problem once Litvinenko got over the Russian border.

In the meantime, Felshtinsky said, give Marina some money, and tell her to depart separately and meet him—Felshtinsky—somewhere abroad. Berezovsky would help. Litvinenko agreed.

According to *Death of a Dissident,* Litvinenko had already decided to flee before his émigré friend suggested it. He had been doing his best to evade FSB surveillance, which he was certain was under way. But how would he get out of the country, since he had been refused a passport the last time he applied? He began studying a lengthy land route south.

Not too long after, Natalia Litvinenko—his first wife—had a rare visit from her former husband. He had some plans, he said. It had become too dangerous for him, and he was going to go live on an island somewhere, write a book, and live off the royalties. Did she think that was all right? If he no longer felt safe, she replied, he indeed should go.

A month after the meeting at Litvinenko's dacha, Felshtinsky was back in Boston. His telephone rang. It was Berezovsky calling from London. "You know we have a common friend in Moscow?" the oligarch said in the vague way that former Soviets speak when they fear their phone is tapped. "Well, he's no longer in Moscow."

Felshtinsky understood instantly. Litvinenko had not taken long to act.

His first stop was the Russian Black Sea resort of Sochi, from which he took a steamer south to the neighboring republic of Georgia, a trip that didn't require a passport. He traversed seaside towns before finally turning inland and reaching the Georgian capital, Tbilisi. He knew people there and could purchase a false passport.

Litvinenko needed to obtain asylum in a Western country if he was to be out of Russia's reach. But where? One possibility was London. Another was Germany. Litvinenko had a sister there, and his father had other connections. The Berezovsky machine went into motion.

Berezovsky himself was in trouble with Putin at the moment. The strain had begun a half year earlier, soon after Putin won election as president. In Berezovsky's estimation, Putin's rise meant business as usual for him, meaning that he would maintain his profit-making enterprises and continue to exercise influence in the Kremlin.

And that's how their relationship was initially. But quickly, Putin became offended by Berezovsky's attitude, which smacked of entitlement. The billionaire argued forcefully against Putin's plan to rein in much of the country's power and transfer it to the Kremlin. Berezovsky's television station, ORT, strongly criticized Putin's performance during the 2000 *Kursk* submarine disaster. And, in an interview, Berezovsky had seemed to compare Putin to Chilean dictator Augusto Pinochet.

Berezovsky had stepped out of line. The punishment would be Kremlin seizure of ORT, Putin decided.

In their final Kremlin meeting, recorded in *Death of a Dissident* and confirmed by Berezovsky, each seemed to regard the other's behavior as betrayal.

"Tell me Boris, I don't understand," Putin asked. ". . . Why are you attacking me? Have I done anything to hurt you? . . . You are supposed to be my friend."

". . . You forgot our conversation after the election, Volodya," Berezovsky replied, using Putin's nickname. "I told you that I never swore allegiance to you personally. You promised to continue the Yeltsin way. He would never even think of shutting up a journalist who attacked him. You are destroying Russia."

That was about it.

"Good-bye, Boris Abramovich," Putin said.

"Good-bye, Volodya," said the oligarch.

The two never spoke again. By the time Litvinenko decided to flee, Berezovsky was already an exile living in Europe.

It was vindication for Felshtinsky. Berezovsky's relationship with his political consultant had gone through a rocky period, mainly because the oligarch felt that Felshtinsky didn't understand the changes that had transformed Russia in the last two decades. But now, Berezovsky wanted Felshtinsky to serve as his man on the ground, and get Litvinenko to safety. The oligarch instructed Felshtinsky to come meet him in London. Working as a team, they would spirit Litvinenko into Munich via commercial flights and even private planes if needed. Berezovsky provided $10,000 in cash to be funneled to Litvinenko.

At this point, Marina and her six-year-old son, Anatoly, learned for the first time what was going on. Her husband had left Moscow saying he was going to visit his father in the Caucasus. Later, he had called to suggest that she take a vacation in Spain. It was left to Felshtinsky to go to Marina and explain the escape plan.

He began to shuttle between the husband in Georgia and the wife in Spain. Arriving in Tbilisi, Felshtinsky found Litvinenko in a petulant state. He now had Berezovsky's cash, along with an authentic-looking Georgian passport, and wanted to go straight to the U.S. embassy. He threw a tantrum when Felshtinsky refused to take him there. Berezovsky had ordered that they stay away from the Americans—the oligarch wanted no one to know of the pair's presence in Georgia, worried in particular that the episode would be associated with one of his longtime business partners who had a reputation for criminal connections.

Litvinenko would have none of it. "If we don't go to the American embassy, I'm going back to Moscow," he said defiantly.

Finally, Felshtinsky relented. Okay, we will go, he said, but on one condition—that you never tell Berezovsky. Litvinenko agreed.

Felshtinsky held several meetings at the embassy. The American diplomats were mainly interested in gauging Litvinenko's usefulness as an intelligence source. Did he know any Russian agents operating in the United States? Or Americans operating for the Russians? Beyond that, the diplomats seemed in no hurry to move things along.

Felshtinsky and Litvinenko became increasingly nervous. For security purposes, they carried several cell phones, including one with Felshtinsky's Boston number. But only his Russian phone worked in Georgia—and it began to ring. Acquaintances in Moscow were calling, having noted the absence of the entire Litvinenko family and concerned that something was amiss. Felshtinsky worried that it had become too dangerous to remain in Georgia.

He and Litvinenko rushed to the airport and boarded a fourteen-seat luxury Fokker jet rented by Berezovsky in Paris. On the tarmac as the pilot prepared for takeoff, Felshtinsky heard his cell phone ring. It was the American embassy in Tbilisi.

"Call me in an hour," Felshtinsky said, notwithstanding that they would be in the air at that moment. Then Berezovsky called. Felshtinsky briefed him. In line with the original plan, he said, they were headed for Munich.

"I think you should go to Turkey, not Munich," Berezovsky replied.

That did not go over well with Litvinenko. Turkey was a nether-world that swallowed up all manner of people. It sounded like Bere-zovsky intended to abandon him, and he insisted that they head for a Western country—Germany, he said.

Felshtinsky handed the phone to Litvinenko.

Berezovsky went to work on him: I'm not going to abandon you. We just need more time to figure this out.

Berezovsky had a commanding manner. It also mattered that he was financing the escape. Even Litvinenko, prone to argue with anyone, didn't challenge him too vigorously. Finally he told the billionaire that he trusted him, and switched off the phone.

But then he resumed bargaining with Felshtinsky. Litvinenko would go to Antalya—the Turkish resort region that Berezovsky had in mind—only if Felshtinsky dropped him off, then flew at once to Spain to retrieve Marina and Anatoly.

By now Litvinenko was under tremendous stress, and the arrival of his family the next day with Felshtinsky didn't ease him that much. He was suspicious of certain men he saw in the hotel lobby. "I know these people," he insisted. "They are FSB. I know them from Chechnya." He was sure they were preparing to kill them. Felshtinsky ignored him. He thought that was Litvinenko's game—using staged nervousness to get what he wanted, which could range from checking into a new hotel, to going to a new city, or simply attracting attention.

Whichever was the case, Felshtinsky was losing confidence. A month earlier, he had thought it would be easy to arrange asylum for Litvinenko. The obvious route was the Americans, but so far that wasn't working. In Tbilisi, the U.S. embassy had seemed more inter-ested in bargaining for information than rescuing an FSB defector. Berezovsky's camp had made Felshtinsky even more anxious by sug-gesting they rent a yacht and sail into international waters—they could wait at sea while asylum was arranged. But Felshtinsky thought that could leave them exposed to an attack, with no escape route should Putin learn their location.

Now Berezovsky dispatched an additional adviser, Alex Goldfarb, to the mission. Goldfarb had an unusual talent for public relations. While still a Soviet citizen in the 1970s, this microbiologist came to be known by Western journalists as a conduit to Moscow dissidents. After the Soviet breakup, he ran the Moscow office of the Open Society Institute, an organization established by hedge fund billionaire George Soros to promote democracy in formerly communist states. Berezovsky eventually hired him to run a foundation that financed anti-Putin political activities. With Goldfarb, it was often difficult to determine where the truth ended and the propaganda began. But if you wanted something to happen, he was your man.

Felshtinsky and Goldfarb began instantly to quarrel. Goldfarb's first suggestion was that Litvinenko be brought to American diplomats in Turkey, accompanied by a lawyer to protect his interests. Felshtinsky thought this was a terrible idea after their Tbilisi experience, but couldn't let slip that they had defied Berezovsky's instructions and already gone to the Americans.

"It's an idiotic idea," Felshtinsky said.

Goldfarb said he would dispatch a lawyer.

"If you are going to send in a lawyer, you might as well go yourself, because I'm not going to go with a lawyer," Felshtinsky replied. He announced that he was leaving, causing Litvinenko to become even more alarmed and his wife to sense betrayal. Felshtinsky had deliberately escalated the argument out of dread that this mission was going very wrong. But his departure would turn out to be a welcome development. While a nice guy, he was not an operator of Goldfarb's caliber.

Within hours after Felshtinsky left, Goldfarb and the Litvinenko family were on the road to the capital, Ankara. There, they met with diplomats at the U.S. embassy—but again, no one seemed prepared to make a deal.

That night, Litvinenko went into his familiar routine. He called Goldfarb's attention to a fellow in the hotel lobby. "They're here already. . . . We have to get out of here," he declared, identifying the man as an FSB agent. Goldfarb took Litvinenko seriously and hustled the family out of the hotel. They drove all night to presumed safety in Istanbul. Along the way, Litvinenko stepped up the drama. He directed Goldfarb to stop the car and wait ten minutes to see whether anyone was following them. "I won't go alive," Litvinenko said. "If the Turks turn me in, I'll kill myself."

Was there a genuine danger? One couldn't tell, Felshtinsky had said of Litvinenko. And even if you knew he was bluffing, and kept saying to yourself, "He is bluffing, he is bluffing," Litvinenko was a very good actor, and it was hard to be absolutely sure.

Felshtinsky, back in Boston, received a call from local CIA agents. Could they come meet with him? Before long, a man and a woman showed up at his door. "You left Tbilisi without talking to our friend who was expecting to meet with you," one said.

"I was trying to check how quick you are," Felshtinsky replied, remembering the snippet of phone conversation moments before taking off from the Tbilisi airport. He explained what was going on in Turkey. "We left Tbilisi because it's dangerous, and it's more dangerous in Turkey." Could these agents help rescue his Russian friend? "It's difficult," the U.S. agents said simply. "It's difficult."

Goldfarb telephoned from Istanbul. If the Americans didn't act quickly, he told Felshtinsky, he would hold a press conference and say that an American's life was being put in danger, meaning his own. Felshtinsky should pass that message on to his CIA contacts. Felshtinsky advised against such an approach.

"It's my life, not yours," Goldfarb replied. "The FSB is already here. It's our lives, and I ask you to do this on my behalf."

So Felshtinsky called his contact at the CIA.

"We can't be subject to blackmail and pressure," the CIA contact replied. "You're on your own."

Goldfarb, left to his wilier instincts, improvised. He bought Turkey-to-Moscow tickets for everyone—with a transit stop in London. At Heathrow Airport, Goldfarb introduced Litvinenko to an immigration officer and requested asylum on behalf of him and his family.

Within hours, the Litvinenkos were under the protection of the British government. As for Goldfarb, the United Kingdom declared him persona non grata and sent him on his way.

Berezovsky put up Litvinenko and his family in an apartment in London's upscale Kensington district and arranged a £5,000 monthly allowance, a handsome sum, considering that their housing expenses were already covered.

Litvinenko and Felshtinsky saw much of each other, laboring over *Blowing Up Russia,* their book about the 1999 apartment blasts. Berezovsky published the resulting work in Russian, but the Kremlin security services foiled his attempt to smuggle five thousand copies into Russia. The opposition newspaper *Novaya Gazeta* came to the rescue by printing several chapters in one hundred thousand copies of a special edition.

But the transition to life in London was hard for Litvinenko. Unlike Berezovsky, now in self-exile there, he did not speak English and was not very diligent about learning it. That left him isolated, glued to satellite television shows beamed in from Moscow, and unable to wander much beyond the Russian-speaking community.

He sought a meeting with Oleg Gordievsky, the ex–KGB station chief who was the hub and glue of all the U.K.-based spies and former spies. Gordievsky had become a cause célèbre in 1985 when he defected and was spirited out of the Soviet Union by British spies in the trunk of a car. He had traveled to the United States a dozen times, visited Ronald Reagan and George H.W. Bush in the White House, and by his own count had written some ten thousand intelligence reports for the West.

Newly arrived Russian exiles regularly made pilgrimages to Gordievsky's home in Godalming, a village outside London. But the old spy at first refused to see Litvinenko. This new defector from the FSB was not the type of exile he was inclined to meet. This fellow was a mere operative for Boris Berezovsky, and not a genuine dissident.

Berezovsky, on the other hand, was always an interesting guest, especially with all the billionaire's supplication. Gordievsky recalled their first meeting, at which Berezovsky presented himself as "quite a positive figure" who spent his money on good causes.

"He came here in a limousine, and sat at this table, and told me the story of his life. It was like he felt he had to explain himself to me," Gordievsky recalled. The two shared a mutual contempt for Vladimir Putin. Gordievsky dismissed the Russian president as one of the "blanket lifters" who spied on Russians abroad when he was a KGB officer based in Dresden, Germany, during the 1980s. Not a professional he could respect.

Litvinenko was finally able to see Gordievsky after another exile vouched for the newcomer. The two quickly hit it off, and Litvinenko visited regularly for lunch, sometimes bringing his wife and son. "Like Berezovsky, he carried two mobile phones," Gordievsky recalled. "He was always on them."

Once, Litvinenko brought along Anna Politkovskaya, the crusading Russian journalist with whom he had been exchanging stories of

Putin's war in the restive region of Chechnya, and her glamorous elder sister, Elena Kudimova, a London-based derivatives trader. They dined at the village hotel, called Inn on the Lake, with a view of the surrounding forest.

I took the train down to Godalming, where Gordievsky met me in a blue blazer, with a peach shirt and a violet silk hanky sprouting from his jacket pocket. There was no visible security at his home, but I knew this man—the West's biggest Cold War catch ever—was well protected by surveillance. Gordievsky was cordial, inclined toward coarse humor punctuated with hearty laughs. At dinner with his English girlfriend along, he whispered conspiratorially, alerting me that she shouldn't hear.

"Russians want to hear rough language. They think it brings life to the conversation," he said, giving both sides of his face a light slap for emphasis. This is why Russian men can speak impolitely to their wives, he said.

Like Nikolai Khokhlov, Gordievsky fled Russia without his family. There was much explaining to do when he and his wife, Leila, reunited a few years later. She flew into London with their two daughters— eleven-year-old Mariya and ten-year-old Anna—but reconciliation proved elusive. After a few days, the wife and daughters returned to Moscow, and divorce followed. By the time I met Gordievsky, no one in the family was speaking to him.

I asked why his wife had bothered to make the trip. "She wanted the money," he replied. He was clearly bitter. "There was £200,000 to her, plus £170,000 of private education for the two girls. Plus she receives £1,250 a month as compensation for being an 'abandoned wife.' She brainwashed the girls that I am a traitor."

CHAPTER 7

The Crusading American
Paul Klebnikov and
Glorious Russia

IN MOSCOW, I STARTED ASKING AROUND ABOUT AN AMERICAN named Paul Klebnikov. The *Forbes* reporter's investigative stories, especially on billionaire Boris Berezovsky, had attracted wide attention there. I had run across his work while writing a book on oil and been struck by his obvious confidence when describing Russia's elites. Much of the nation's super-rich—guys I couldn't get to—granted him access, and the insights that he gained led to a number of exclusive reports on corruption. The detail that filled his stories made them especially enjoyable to read.

I was surprised to discover that Klebnikov seemed a kindred spirit of Vladimir Putin. That set him apart from his more skeptical—in some cases, downright hostile—journalistic colleagues. But then Klebnikov wasn't an orthodox reporter. He was an unabashed crusader on a shared mission with the Russian president. Both saw themselves duty bound to assist in the restoration of a great Russia—prosperous, powerful, and respected by the world. Both attacked anyone who appeared to be impeding that goal. Neither seemed to pause to consider that his vision of historic Russia might have been more romantic than real.

Klebnikov's leanings were more understandable when one considered his origins. Unlike Putin, who was most strongly influenced by his sentimental loyalty to Russia's security services, Klebnikov was driven by blood. A descendant of czarist-era aristocrats, he quoted Pushkin with regularity and spoke fluent Russian with what some acquaintances presumed was the accent of a nineteenth-century nobleman. (*New York* magazine reported that he and two friends ran the city's marathon in T-shirts bearing the double-headed Russian eagle, and that Klebnikov led them in Russian military songs to keep spirits high. "We're fighting for Mother Russia and the czar!" went one lyric.)

He acquired his enthusiasm for things Russian at an early age. His family's Manhattan apartment was festooned with memorabilia of the old country. Descendants of Russia's displaced nobility were regular visitors, and the young Klebnikov was taught to respect his family's place in history. Stories were told around the dinner table about men such as Ivan Pouschine, a Klebnikov ancestor who was imprisoned for involvement in an 1825 uprising known as the Decembrist revolt, and great-grandfather Arcadi Nebolsin, a Russian admiral slain by mutineers during the Bolshevik revolution. An entire generation of the family had fled Russia during the 1917 uprising.

At the same time, Klebnikov became comfortable around the well-to-do. He was a guest at the homes of schoolmates from St. Bernard's, on the Upper East Side, and Phillips Exeter Academy, in New Hampshire, both exclusive schools. Later, he studied at two highly selective universities, UC Berkeley, in California, and the London School of Economics. His wife-to-be, Helen, or "Musa," as she was known, was the daughter of John Train, a wealthy New York investment adviser and bestselling author of books including *The Money Masters*.

Forbes hired Klebnikov in 1989 at the age of twenty-six, soon after he completed his research for a doctorate in Russian studies. His intimate knowledge of life in the upper class dovetailed nicely with the magazine's interests. He visited Institut Le Rosey, in Rolle, Switzerland, where he had taught tennis five years earlier, and wrote an unforgettable piece about this boarding school for the coddled rich, including the children of princes and kings. Klebnikov's inquisitive mind was evident in a later investigative report on the wealth of Iran's Rafsanjani family, whose patriarchs were among "a handful of clerics who call the shots behind the curtain and have gotten very rich in the process." It was groundbreaking work.

Along the way, he traveled regularly to Russia and wrote stories lamenting what he saw as its decline into criminality under the presidency of Boris Yeltsin. In December 1996, he made his biggest splash ever, with a story highly critical of Boris Berezovsky. The piece—headlined "Godfather of the Kremlin?"—suggested that the oligarch had become Russia's greatest baron by consorting with gangsters and being complicit in murder. The latter charge led to a Berezovsky libel suit, which was resolved when *Forbes* publicly retracted the implication that the billionaire had played a role in anyone's death.

The Berezovsky story had run without a byline, apparently out of concern for Klebnikov's safety. But it did not take much guesswork in Moscow to determine the author's identity, and death threats soon began to arrive. He continued to write about Russia, but with an armed bodyguard at his side whenever he visited the country.

Klebnikov heaped scorn on Yeltsin, soon to be succeeded by Putin. In a 1999 piece for *Forbes,* he accused the lame duck president of presiding over a "gangster state. Corrupt from top to bottom, it is ruled by a small group of political bosses and their crony capitalist friends. The gang feeds on state assets and protects itself with violence." These virtual traitors were preventing the revival of his beloved Russia, Klebnikov believed.

But Berezovsky topped his list of scoundrels. In 2000, a Klebnikov biography of the oligarch was published under the title of *Godfather of the Kremlin.* The book drew heavily on the piece four years earlier in *Forbes,* although this time there was no question mark. Klebnikov ticked off Berezovsky's alleged misdeeds on the path from small-time mathematician to wealthy kingmaker—a career, he wrote, that was "replete with bankrupt companies and violent deaths." Klebnikov thought that Berezovsky was an object lesson in why foreigners during Yeltsin's rule should have let Russia be Russia instead of trying to impose Western traditions. "If it is hard for westerners to understand how the introduction of democratic principles could have been so poisonous to Russian society, Berezovsky's career holds one of the keys," he wrote.

According to his editors, to understand Klebnikov one had to read *Eastern Approaches,* the 1951 memoir of Fitzroy Maclean. The classic account follows the swashbuckling Scot through hair-raising adventures as a British diplomat observing Stalin's 1937 purge trial of Bukharin; as a clandestine traveler to Central Asia and Afghanistan; and particularly as Winston Churchill's personal ambassador to Tito in the mountains of Croatia during World War II. I was lucky enough to meet Maclean in Georgia a few months before his death, in 1996, at the age of eighty-five. He dozed off a few times as we sat in his hotel room, discussing his hopes for Georgia's young independence. But with a bejeweled Georgian sword on the nightstand and a pair of carved Scottish canes by his side, Maclean was still at heart a man of action.

This exceptional man inspired generations of diplomats and journalists, including me. But I never thought I *was* Maclean. Klebnikov apparently did. "Most journalists think of themselves as observers. But Paul thought of himself as a participant. Like Maclean, Klebnikov wasn't only interested in recording what he saw. He really believed he could play a part in public affairs," said James Michaels, the *Forbes* editor who hired him. William Baldwin, another of Klebnikov's editors, said, "He had this messianic belief that he was going to be part of the transition from a gangster country to a civilized country."

I couldn't relate to this side of Klebnikov. I felt highly uncomfortable with the notion of injecting myself into the affairs of a foreign country. Not Klebnikov. He seemed to have acquired Lord Jim pretensions, exhibiting the vanity of a Westerner who imagined himself rescuing the natives. As to his bashing of Berezovsky, I had dealt with many such unappealing characters over the years, but I felt it was crossing a journalistic line to invest so much personal outrage in one's reportage.

But that, of course, was precisely the point for Klebnikov. He *was* personally invested in the story. He *did* take offense at the perceived misconduct of those he wrote about, Berezovsky being a prime example.

The Russian edition of *Godfather of the Kremlin* became a nonfiction bestseller, with 110,000 copies sold. Klebnikov tried to repeat that success with a book based on fifteen hours of taped conversation with a well-known Chechen warlord named Khozh-Ahmed Nukhayev. The man had been a debonair law student in Moscow and then a mobster before becoming a Chechen guerilla fighter and finally an anti-Western Islamic fundamentalist. But the book, *Conversation with a Barbarian,* was a flop, selling only six thousand copies.

Still, Klebnikov's writings about Berezovsky had impressed his editors. They offered him the editorship of his own magazine, a Russian-language version of *Forbes,* and he readily accepted. All these years,

Klebnikov had been flying from the United States and elsewhere to Moscow to do his reporting, then returning home. Now he could live in the Russian capital.

The forty-year-old Klebnikov, handsome, with piercing hazel eyes and a shock of brown hair, plunged headlong into his new assignment. He threw a champagne party for the magazine's launch, at the five-star Baltschug hotel on the Moscow River. And he set in motion an editorial project that was breathtaking by Russian standards—an American-style listing of the country's wealthiest citizens. It would throw the spotlight on Russia's profiteers and surely offend the gangster element that would be well represented on the list. Klebnikov's brainstorm seemed impossible to execute. How could anyone assemble such a list in a country where personal wealth is hidden from view, largely stashed in offshore accounts under false names? Yet Klebnikov and his team somehow succeeded, and the resulting layout, "The Golden Hundred," was an instant sensation. It appeared in the magazine's second issue, in May 2004, and catapulted *Forbes Russia* into the top tier of the country's business magazines.

One might expect Klebnikov's editorial daring to have triggered threats of physical retaliation; death threats had been quick to follow publication of "Godfather of the Kremlin?" in the magazine's U.S. edition. But I could find no record of any threats against Klebnikov while he edited *Forbes Russia*. This was somewhat puzzling. As Leonid Bershidsky, his publisher in Moscow at the time, observed, "He was doing investigative stories and was making enemies with every story."

Klebnikov now moved about Moscow without bodyguards, outwardly confident that he was in no personal danger. He was heartened by Boris Berezovsky's self-exile in London and the firm rule of Vladimir Putin, now president of Russia. A fresh breeze was blowing through the country, he thought. But the private Klebnikov seemed somewhat ambivalent about security conditions. His wife and their three children had remained in the United States; she didn't want to live in Russia and Klebnikov had agreed to take the job for just a year. When a visitor asked why his family was not with him, he replied, "I don't know if it is safe for my family."

Bershidsky, technically Klebnikov's boss at *Forbes Russia*, was employed by *Newsweek* when I first met him in Moscow in the early 1990s. I was writing for the magazine and he was a "fixer," on call to translate and solve any problems encountered by its reporters. He had since become a notable success in the business world. He told me that Klebnikov's managerial skills were lacking, but that his journalism was towering. Klebnikov, he said, could "spend a month on a project and dig out something that others wanted to but couldn't for ten years." The American editor dazzled on all fronts. "People gathered around to hear how he carried out interviews," Bershidsky said.

But as I talked with other journalists in Moscow, I discovered that Klebnikov's reputation was mixed. Again and again I was told that his main claim to fame—the book *Godfather of the Kremlin*—was based on documents and interviews provided by a single disgruntled former Berezovsky ally, Alexander Korzhakov, who had been Boris Yeltsin's chief of security. Prevailing wisdom said it was a hatchet job.

I concluded that some of the criticism was sour grapes. From the endnotes, one can see that Korzhakov provided Klebnikov with a road map—the knowledge and documents that he needed to get started. But finding fault with Klebnikov seemed to overlook how investigative journalism often begins with information supplied by an insider. Then the real work begins: The reporter must seek corroboration, authenticate documents, test the credibility of sources, and broaden the story to include all sides. Klebnikov's twenty-nine pages of endnotes are an impressive display of such footwork. Overall, the book was solid journalism, covering a vast amount of ground, with insider detail that gave the reader a "you are there" feeling.

Not that it is bulletproof. Valeri Streletsky, the publisher of the Russian-language edition, was in fact Korzhakov's former deputy, and thus an interested party. Streletsky told me that Klebnikov brought him the English-language manuscript that was being published by Harcourt, the Florida-based house, and that he simply hired a translator for the Russian edition. He didn't see anything unscrupulous about his role, and given that it was a straight translation of the English edition, I didn't either. Still, it was reckless for Klebnikov to expose himself to this appearance of partiality.

The English-language edition occasionally suffers from disingenuous writing. It hints at a Berezovsky connection to certain murders, but presents no proof. For example, Klebnikov writes that many of Berezovsky's business ventures "were marred by the assassination or accidental death of key players," but "there is no evidence that Berezovsky was responsible for any of these deaths." What was Klebnikov's point, other than to plant in the reader's mind the opposite message—that Berezovsky somehow was to blame? Klebnikov also overexerts himself in some instances to show cause and effect. For example, he intimates that Berezovsky caused the Second Chechen War by making ransom payments to Chechen kidnappers who then attacked Russia. Berezovsky's aim, according to Klebnikov? To make Putin president. Without something more in the way of evidence, the scenario is strained and unconvincing.

Some colleagues grumbled that Klebnikov was simply reporting what "everyone knew" about Berezovsky and the other oligarchs. I wrote that off as bar-stool talk. While he misfired on some occasions, Klebnikov was practicing professional, tough, American-style journalism and was among the very few writers who penetrated Russia's criminal underside.

Which raises yet another rap against him—that he was a romantic. Alexander Politkovsky, an investigative reporter and the estranged husband of Anna Politkovskaya, told me that Klebnikov "didn't really understand what was going on in Russia in reality." Oleg Panfilov, who runs a nonprofit Moscow office that teaches journalists how to protect themselves, said: "He was naïve. He worshipped Russia, and understood nothing about Russia."

Others whose advice I also respected made similar assertions—that Klebnikov's reporting on Russia was flawed from the beginning because he was less knowledgeable than he thought. If so, I wouldn't have been surprised. I had met numerous well-meaning but presumptuous second- and third-generation Americans who traced their ancestry to the former Soviet Union and came seeking to help the homeland. Their relatives in Russia and the neighboring republics often found these visitors to be condescending, and the Americans just as often were disappointed by the experience. In Armenia, some visiting kinfolk from America were told that the best thing they could do was stay home and send a check.

There was something to that advice.

I wondered how Berezovsky felt about having been the object of Klebnikov's vilification. I dropped by his Mayfair, London, office on

April 23, 2007, just hours after momentous news had arrived from Moscow—Boris Yeltsin had died at the age of seventy-six.

The billionaire, sporting a black silk shirt and striped white-and-gray slacks, was pacing and brooding. "Everything is topsy-turvy," he said. Berezovsky, who had adulated Yeltsin, went on at length about the debt Russia owed this man who "helped millions of people to be released from slavery."

He felt quite the opposite about Yeltsin's ungrateful successor, Vladimir Putin, whom the billionaire aimed to bring down. If he couldn't manage to oust him, he would at least make the autocratic Russian leader as miserable as he was.

Berezovsky had retreated to London about six years earlier, and the warfare between him and Putin had only worsened since then. Russia repeatedly sent prosecutors after him, hoping to extradite the onetime oligarch on a series of charges, including the alleged theft from a Russian manufacturer of two thousand cars worth some $13 million. But British courts refused to hand him over.

For his part, Berezovsky sank tens of millions of dollars into an anti-Putin crusade. He was the backer of *Blowing Up Russia,* the book that accused the Kremlin of complicity in the terrifying 1999 apartment bombings, and a companion documentary called *Assassination of Russia.*

In 2004, Berezovsky financed Putin's opponent when he was up for reelection, a veteran lawmaker named Ivan Rybkin (whose campaign went off the rails when he vanished for five days, then reappeared in an incoherent state that suggested he had been drugged). The same year, Berezovsky panicked Russia's ruling class by spending $30 million to support the so-called Orange Revolution in Ukraine. A Kremlin critic named Viktor Yushchenko emerged as president of the former Soviet republic after he was poisoned with dioxin, an unsolved assassination attempt that left his face disfigured. Popular opinion in Ukraine upended a rigged election and forced the rejection of a Moscow-backed candidate. Similar "street power" had unseated the president of neighboring Georgia only a year earlier, and Putin feared Russia—and he—could be next.

Berezovsky assembled a team of intellectuals and writers to help orchestrate the ouster of the Russian president. In this respect, he resembled an Old World patron of kept artists. His key allies in this endeavor were the former 1970s dissident Alex Goldfarb, the Boston-based political scholar Yuri Felshtinsky, and of course Alexander Litvinenko. These men churned out books, blog postings, and statements lambasting Putin. But Putin continued to rule, leaving Berezovsky to pout.

At its simplest, the ongoing struggle between Berezovsky and Putin was about one issue: Who would control Russia's treasures? Berezovsky wanted the nation's industrial might to be in private hands, with a large part reserved for him, naturally. Putin believed in state ownership, albeit with a generous helping set aside for his own favored oligarchs. Television was an excellent example of this. Once, the industry was controlled by media moguls such as Berezovsky, who acquired huge television holdings in the corrupt 1990s and made stations serve their political desires. Then the state wrested control, and television became the dutiful servant to Putin and the Kremlin.

As for Klebnikov, Berezovsky met with him once, for an interview in 1996. He described the *Forbes* editor as "a captive of his emotions, with all this idea of great Russia, of Russia for Russians." He did not find Klebnikov to be an impressive journalist. What particularly upset him, Berezovsky said, was the suggestion in the original "Godfather" article that he had played a role in the murder of Vlad Listyev, the talk-show host at Berezovsky's television station. He had sued, he said, "to demonstrate in the West that I am ready to protect my reputation, and I have done so."

With that, Berezovsky was off to his next meeting. A Russian journalist wanted to talk about defecting to Britain. Could the billionaire help?

Klebnikov praised Putin for beginning to correct the errors made during "Russia's flawed transition from Communism to a market economy in the 1990s," which he labeled "one of the most mishandled reforms in history." While much remained to be done, "the Russian marketplace is benefitting from the stability brought by the administration of President Vladimir Putin. Gone is the gangster free-for-all of the Yeltsin era. Putin has chosen a more measured pace of market liberalization, as well as more predictable rules." Under Putin, the admiring editor wrote, "the country is finally creating a serious consumer market. Some of the oligarchs' wealth, it seems, is starting to trickle down." The May 2004 issue of *Forbes Russia* that listed the country's richest citizens contained this exuberant testimony from Klebnikov: "Dynamism is one of the core characteristics of capitalism, and capitalist Russia is one of the most dynamic countries in the world right now."

In July of that year, his wife, Musa, came to visit for a few days. They strolled Moscow together and dined with Mark Franchetti, the investigative reporter for the London *Sunday Times*. The three had been meaning to meet socially for some time—Musa was friends with a cousin of Franchetti's—but had been unable to synchronize their schedules. Over a four-hour meal at the Pushkin Cafe, the two men debated the state of affairs in Russia. Franchetti told me that Klebnikov thought he was too negative about the country, while Franchetti felt that the American was "too much an apologist for Putin and naïve about the place."

At one point, Musa asked Franchetti, "Is it safe here, or not safe?"

Franchetti, sensing that she was worried about her husband, didn't know how to reply.

"Russia is changing," he finally said. "Now people turn to lawyers, not contract killers."

Klebnikov took Musa to the airport two days later, then returned to his grueling routine, working late hours at the *Forbes Russia* office. It was situated in a building across from the lovely Botanichesky Sad, or "Botanical Garden." Klebnikov was in the habit of commuting by metro, using a station in the park a short walk from his office.

On Friday, July 9, two days after his wife's departure, Klebnikov was working late again. He made a series of phone calls—to Musa, his brother Peter and his sister, Anna—in which he voiced high hopes for both Russia and *Forbes Russia*. Then he quit for the night. On his way out of the building, he passed an office used by *Newsweek* reporters, some of who were still working. It was about nine-thirty p.m., but still light outside.

Klebnikov walked across the street and approached the park. Suddenly, a dark Russian-made car, a Lada, halted behind him. A man inside the vehicle pointed a 9-millimeter Makarov pistol at the editor and fired four bullets. The car drove off without any words being spoken.

A guard rushed into the *Newsweek* office: "Somebody just called. He says that someone shot Paul Klebnikov in the stomach."

Reporters Mikhail Fishman and Alexander Gordeev trotted into the street, where police, ambulance attendants, and spectators formed a circle around the fallen editor. Klebnikov was on his back on the sidewalk. Gordeev saw blood coming from one of his ears, soaking his shirt. A pool of blood was visible about thirty yards away, marking the spot where Klebnikov had been hit. It appeared that he had tried to get back to the office, but collapsed. He was still conscious and able to talk.

"Do you know what happened?" Gordeev asked Klebnikov in English.

"No," Klebnikov calmly replied in Russian. "Someone was shooting."

"Do you know who?"

"No."

Klebnikov described the gunman as a Russian, with black hair and wearing black clothing. He asked the *Newsweek* reporter to call his wife and brother. Then he asked for oxygen. There was none, but fluids were administered intravenously, and Klebnikov was loaded into an ambulance. Gordeev saw that he was tensing up. His eyes took on a desperate look, and he began to shake his head, as if to say, "No." A doctor had to restrain Klebnikov from getting up. After a twenty-minute wait, the ambulance crew was told which hospital would receive them, and the vehicle sped from the scene.

Fishman, the other *Newsweek* reporter, rode along. "You can do it. It will be all right," he repeated as Klebnikov slipped in and out of consciousness. At the hospital, there were more delays. The entrance gate was locked, forcing the ambulance to wait to be admitted. Once inside, Klebnikov was loaded onto a gurney and into an elevator, but it became stuck between floors.

At 10:48 p.m., just over an hour after Klebnikov had left his office, Gordeev's phone rang. "It's all over," Fishman said. "He's dead."

Klebnikov had died either in the stalled elevator or shortly after, in the operating room. The doctors gave different stories, and no one knew whom to believe.

"None of us ever had the feeling that someone could kill him," said Klebnikov's deputy, Maxim Kashulinsky. "In retrospect, obviously everyone missed something."

Russian police sometimes resemble the Keystone Kops. But they can be quite effective if they are motivated to solve a case, and if politics doesn't get in their way. The killing of Klebnikov had their full attention.

Pyotr Gabriyan, one of the most skilled investigators in the federal prosecutor's office, was assigned to the case. His team located the Lada used in the attack the very next day, and dusted it for fingerprints. Then they applied some old-fashioned shoe leather, with a high-tech twist. Gabriyan's men reviewed cell phone activity in the vicinity of the park and discovered a number of suspicious calls to or from the area almost nightly for two weeks prior to and including the day of the murder. The callers were Chechen thugs who were identified as members of a murder-for-hire gang. Fingerprints and trace amounts of lint linked some of them to the Lada.

Four months after Klebnikov's murder, authorities announced that two Chechens had been arrested in the case. One of them, Kazbek Dukuzov, the alleged triggerman, had been captured in Belarus. Extradition proceedings moved slowly at first, arousing suspicion that corrupt Belarus officials were protecting him. When the delays suddenly ended and the Chechen was shipped back to Russia, some suspected that Putin had intervened.

"I think Putin himself called [Belarus president Alexander] Lukashenko and pushed to have him extradited," one of Klebnikov's colleagues told me. "I think that Putin has pushed to make sure that the case is pursued."

Putin openly expressed interest in the case, something that was unusual for him. In fall 2005, he met with Klebnikov's widow and one of his brothers in New York. At his annual news conference in 2007, he said, "Not long ago one of our American partners said something very true: 'Paul Klebnikov died for a democratic Russia, for the development of democracy in Russia.' I completely agree with him. I fully agree with this evaluation."

Police said they believed that the killing was ordered by Khozh-Ahmed Nukhayev, the central figure in Klebnikov's book *Conversation with a Barbarian*. The book was highly critical of the Chechens in particular and Muslims in general. It was said that Nukhayev had become so incensed that he hired the Chechen gang to assassinate its author. But he disappeared from sight after Klebnikov's slaying and was never tracked down by police.

(Valeri Streletsky, the book's publisher, is skeptical about Nukhayev being the mastermind. Not long after *Conversation with a Barbarian* was released, a package arrived at the publisher's office. It contained writings by Nukhayev and a note from his representative asking if Streletsky might want to publish them. The publisher declined, but told me that the package helped to persuade him that "Nukhayev had no role in the killing." If he was so furious about the Klebnikov book, why would he want to have any dealings with the man who had made it possible?)

Once in custody, both suspects openly boasted that they had participated in the murder of Klebnikov, according to inside information that reached Russian journalists. Such braggadocio might strike Westerners as reckless. But gangsters regarded Russian law enforcement as largely impotent and had few inhibitions about virtually daring police to take them on.

The trial was closed, not witnessed by reporters or family members. But the prosecution was confident of its case, which was based on an array of circumstantial evidence: cell phone records; fingerprints and other clues gathered from the Lada; information linking the gang to other murders; and testimony that prior to Klebnikov's killing, the gang members had bragged that they were to be paid $3 million for a "big job." The boastful confessions did not figure in the trial because the two suspects refused to sign them, ruling out their use by prosecutors.

Klebnikov's supporters began to have misgivings when word got around that the defendants and defense lawyers seemed to relax as the trial wore on. Suspicions arose that someone had tampered with the jury, always a possibility in Russia. In May 2006, the jury acquitted both defendants and the judge ordered their release. The Klebnikov camp felt defeated. But six months later, the Supreme Court intervened—in Russia, there is no concept of double jeopardy—and overturned the acquittals. A new trial was ordered. The second Chechen suspect, Musa Vakhaev, appeared at preliminary hearings, but the accused shooter, Dukuzov, vanished. In his absence, the judge halted all proceedings; the retrial was pending as of this writing.

Like his book publisher, I was not satisfied with the notion that Klebnikov died because of the way he portrayed a Chechen warlord in print. I turned to Mark Franchetti for some insight. He had lived and worked in Moscow for a decade, and was a seasoned reporter. Franchetti figured that a journalist in Russia had to do one of two things to get killed: either get really seriously into someone's personal life, or ruin someone's business deal. For instance, in 1994, a twenty-seven-year-old Russian reporter named Dmitri Kholodov was investigating allegations that the then defense minister, Pavel Grachev, and others were selling off military goods for personal gain. One day, a source called to say he had documents that could help advance Kholodov's corruption probe. When the reporter opened the briefcase supposedly containing the documents, it blew up, killing him.

Investigative reporters in Russia know that the unpublished story poses the greatest danger to the writer. After a piece is printed, the damage is done. But when the makings for a potentially explosive article are still in a journalist's notebook, everything is at risk, especially the reporter's personal safety. Some believe Klebnikov was working on a blockbuster at the time of his death, a story involving large sums of money stolen in the multi-billion-dollar reconstruction of Chechnya. Klebnikov's family, which has access to his computer hard drive and other personal effects, said there was no evidence of such a story. But it is an angle worth further consideration.

It is not possible to know, of course, but I think it likely that Klebnikov would have disapproved of this book, especially my critical view of Putin and the "new Russian state" that he fathered. Klebnikov was a tough reporter in pursuit of elements he felt were sullying the state he loved, but toward the end of his life he thought it was time to write more positively about the country itself. Klebnikov's wife, Musa, and his brother Peter declined to cooperate while I was doing my research. They specifically objected to his murder being lumped in with the deaths of Litvinenko and others who had defected from Russia or were enemies of Putin, or both. Klebnikov's story was fundamentally different—he was not one of them—and he did not deserve to be in their company.

But here is the trouble with that reasoning: Klebnikov's murder repudiated his own message about Russia—that Putin was taking it toward deserved greatness and that it was on the cusp of achieving equal footing with the West. In my opinion, his death sent the opposite message: that Russia was more prosperous but ultimately the same dangerous place it had always been. Putin was following the path dictated by his autocratic predecessors for centuries, glorifying the state over the individual. He was presiding over a system that continued to protect those who killed to further its interests.

It makes no sense to pretend that Klebnikov does not belong in the company of these victims of the Putin era. He crossed the same invisible line as the rest, and it became acceptable for someone to murder him.

In the end, he became the victim of a Russia whose nature he never fully grasped.

CHAPTER 8

Murder on an Elevator
Anna Politkovskaya and the
Voiceless of Russia

I NEVER MET THE JOURNALIST ANNA POLITKOVSKAYA. WHEN I covered the First Chechen War, she was in Moscow toiling for a small-time newspaper. By the time the second war rolled around, I had left for Afghanistan and environs. That is when Anna began reporting on the horrors of Chechnya, a career-changing experience that turned her against Vladimir Putin. She soon became the most angry and acid public critic of Putin in all of Russia.

"Putin has, by chance, gotten hold of enormous power and has used it to catastrophic effect," she once wrote. "I dislike him because he does not like people. He despises us. He sees us as a means to his ends, a means for the achievement and retention of personal power, no more than that. Accordingly, he believes he can do anything he likes with us, play with us as he sees fit, destroy us if he wishes. We are nobody, while he whom chance has enabled to clamber to the top is today czar and God. In Russia we have had leaders with this outlook before. It led to tragedy, to bloodshed on a vast scale, to civil wars."

My introduction to Anna was *Putin's Russia,* her gritty 2004 account of life under the Russian leader. It is a defense of the defenseless, and its powerful language is rich in detail and often moving. She was blessed with unerring intuition and stuck to writing about what she actually saw. Anna was self-possessed, but not self-impressed.

That was all the more remarkable in view of her celebrity abroad and the admiration showered upon her by some of the most hard-bitten Western correspondents in Moscow. *Time* magazine's talented war correspondent Yuri Zarakhovich in 2003 wrote that Anna "made her name by writing detailed, accurate and vivid reports on the plight of the civilian population in Chechnya. . . . She tells stories of people who are taken from their homes at night and never come back; about extra-judicial executions; about the hungry refugees in cold and damp camps."

A year later, James Meek, a talented reporter with the British newspaper *Guardian,* described her as "one of the bravest of Russia's many brave journalists."

"Her seriousness is not just her frown, her severe glasses and full head of gray hair," he wrote. "It's the tension, anger and impatience in her whole body, making clear that her sense of the continual injustice being perpetrated in her homeland never leaves her, that she can't shut it out in a way almost all British journalists, even the campaigning, radical kind, can."

In her coda to *Putin's Russia,* Anna made this plea: "We cannot just sit back and watch a political winter close in on Russia for several more decades. We want to go on living in freedom. We want our children to be free and our grandchildren to be born free. That is why we long for a thaw in the immediate future, but we alone can change Russia's political climate."

The West wasn't going to help, she continued: "All we hear from the outside world is 'al-Qaeda, al-Qaeda,' a wretched mantra for shuffling off responsibility for all the bloody tragedies yet to come, a primitive chant with which to lull a society desiring nothing more than to be lulled back to sleep."

Anna pushed journalistic boundaries in a way that would be frowned upon in the West: She repeatedly crossed the line between journalist and active participant in events she covered. Trying to resolve the *Nord-Ost* hostage standoff was an example of that. She thought that playing dual roles was a shrewd strategy.

It was not something I could see myself doing—negotiating with terrorists—but Anna's style did lead her to a more profound understanding of the play of events and personalities than virtually anyone else I read in Russia.

It also earned her a following among the multitude of Russia's downtrodden and powerless, who saw in Anna someone who would

The aftermath of an explosion in a nine-story apartment building on Guryanova Street in southeast Moscow on September 9, 1999. In a two-week period in August and September, explosions killed nearly three hundred people in four Russian apartment buildings, leading Prime Minister Vladimir Putin to blame Chechen terrorists and order an all-out war in Chechnya. Putin's popularity rating soared.
(Tatiana Makeyeva/AP)

Nikolai Khokhlov in South Korea in 1964, while serving as an anti-insurgency adviser to the Seoul government. Khokhlov defected from the KGB in 1954 rather than carry out the assassination of an anti-Soviet leader in Frankfurt. Three years later, the Soviets attempted to murder him with a nuclear-activated form of thallium. He went on to become a professor of psychology at California State University, San Bernardino.
(Courtesy of Tatjana Khokhlov)

Vladimir Putin during a March 2008 meeting of his security council. After his rise from nowhere to be named by Boris Yeltsin as his successor, Putin won election as president in 2000, largely based on his hard-line stand in Chechnya.
(Vladimir Rodionov/AP/RIA Novosti, Presidential Press Service)

In October 2002, terrorists took over a Moscow theater that was staging the musical *Nord-Ost*. To end the three-day siege, Russian security forces used a mysterious opiate gas that was intended to—and, together with a subsequent shootout, did—kill all the terrorists, but also took the lives of 129 of the 800 or so hostages. Here, a security officer carries a body out of the theater, with the bodies of other hostages in the foreground.
(Dmitry Lovetsky/AP)

Irina Fadeeva and her fifteen-year-old son, Yaroslav. Yaroslav died at *Nord-Ost*.
(Courtesy of Irina Fadeeva)

Elena Baranovskaya with her husband, former military intelligence officer Sergei Baranovsky, and her twenty-year-old son, Andrei Nikishin. Both the men died at *Nord-Ost*.
(Courtesy of Elena Baranovskaya)

Ilya Lysak, a bass player in the *Nord-Ost* orchestra and an old family friend of Anna Politkovskaya's. He survived the hostage-taking.
(Courtesy of Vera Politkovskaya)

New York native Paul Klebnikov, editor of *Forbes Russia*.
He was murdered in Moscow in 2004.
(Courtesy of Forbes)

Anna Politkovskaya. She became one of Putin's harshest critics in her writings in *Novaya Gazeta* and in books published in English in the West. (Colleen Piano/REX USA LTD.)

Anna Politkovskaya and her daughter, Vera. In the hours before her murder, Anna was helping the pregnant Vera to shop for a basin for her apartment. When the baby was born a few months later, Vera named her Anna. (Courtesy of Politkovskaya Family Archive)

From left to right, Alexander Litvinenko, Boris Berezovsky, Akhmed Zakayev, and Yuri Felshtinsky at Berezovsky's sixtieth birthday party in January 2006. (*Courtesy of Yuri Felshtinsky*)

Alexander Litvinenko and his seven-year-old son, Anatoly, at the Queens Leisure Centre in Blackpool, England, in 2001. (*Courtesy of Marina Litvinenko*)

Marina Litvinenko.
(Courtesy of Marina Litvinenko)

Alexander Litvinenko and Anna Politkovskaya in London, in or around 2003. Litvinenko regarded Anna as a close friend and was broken up over her assassination. According to her family, she looked at Litvinenko as a source and no more.
(Courtesy of Marina Litvinenko)

Andrei Lugovoi at a news conference on November 1, 2007—the one-year anniversary of the poisoning of Alexander Litvinenko. Great Britain had charged Lugovoi with Litvinenko's murder. Lugovoi accused Britain of covering up its own involvement in the death and ran successfully for a seat in the Russian parliament.
(Sergey Ponomarev/AP)

Dmitri Medvedev, a long-time Putin subordinate from St. Petersburg and Putin's chosen successor, as Putin walks to the stage to accept the leadership of the ruling United Russia political party on April 15, 2008. This post gave Putin an additional platform, on top of the prime ministership, with which to continue to wield power in Russia.

(Dmitry Lovetsky/AP)

listen and, more important, write something. When she arrived in the office each morning, she often was greeted by a pile of mail and a line of people out the door, all hopeful that she could help them obtain justice.

In a 2001 story, she berated the wife of a Canadian diplomat who, driving a big Ford Explorer, crashed into the car of a Russian woman. The victim suffered a concussion and broken bones, but because of diplomatic immunity, the Canadian didn't have to reimburse the Russian's medical bills. Anna unearthed international conventions that she said should force the Canadians to pay up and told Russian authorities that if they did not believe her, they should come to her office and she would show them.

Nina Lavurda's story was especially sad. She was desperate to retrieve the remains of her son, Paul, whose body had been abandoned on the battlefield after he was killed in action in Chechnya. The military was unresponsive to her pleas until Anna stepped in. Finally, the mother was presented with his skull for burial; no other body parts could be found.

"Paul Lavurda had been deserted on the battlefield and then forgotten," Anna wrote. "Nobody cared that his body was lying there, or that he had a family awaiting his return. What happened after his death is typical of the army, a disgraceful episode that stands for an ethos in which a human is nothing, in which no one watches over the troops, and there is no sense of responsibility toward the families."

Anna was born in 1958 in New York, where her father was an interpreter for diplomats at the United Nations. Four years later, the family returned to Russia. Anna grew up as a member of the privileged *nomenklatura,* the Communist Party equivalent of the West's upper middle class, with access to hard-to-obtain Western goods and education at select schools.

Her readiness to challenge authority was apparent at an early age. In class, Anna's best friends cringed each time she shot up to correct something the teacher had said. But she was the top student at School 33, and in her final year she was elected chapter head of the elite Club for International Friendship, part of the Communist Party youth group Komsomol.

She was a journalism student at Moscow State University, the Harvard of the Soviet Union, when she began dating her future husband, Alexander Politkovsky. Their relationship puzzled her friends. He was five years older, prematurely gray, and from a wholly different world: While Anna and her friends were society girls, Alexander was the son of artists and a habitué of Moscow's dissident crowd. She was a serious thinker; he was a charming rogue with the gift of gab and a taste for drink. Over beers after Anna's death, he described to me an ideal day: fly-fishing at a brook (the sound of the line hitting the water—"tuk, tuk, tuk"), a flask of whiskey in his breast pocket, a nap on the grass. That was the good-time Alexander.

To Anna, he was a beguiling exotic. One friend recalled her behaving like a schoolgirl around him, asking Alexander to hold her hand and to embrace her. On summer vacation at a Black Sea resort, she could be found each morning in her hotel room with wads of paper strewn across the floor. They were false starts on another daily letter to Alexander.

The two married after twenty-year-old Anna discovered she was pregnant. Her upper-crust parents were so incensed at her choice of a husband (who showed up for the wedding toting a half-finished bottle of vodka inside a bag) that they cut Anna off financially. At first, the newlyweds and their infant son, Ilya, survived on Alexander's slim earnings as a novice journalist and Anna's pay for scrubbing floors at a tailor shop. (She lost the job after the tailor tired of her "telling them how to work, how to treat people, how to treat her, a university [student]," said a friend, Elena Morozova.)

As graduation neared, Anna chose a literary outcast as the subject for her senior thesis. Marina Tsvetayeva was a great Soviet poet whose work ranged over the human cost of the Bolshevik revolution, her crushing loneliness, and her sexuality, including hints at lesbianism. Her life was tragic: Her poems were suppressed by Stalin's government, her White Russian husband was arrested and executed, and Tsvetayeva hanged herself at the age of forty-eight, in 1941. The poet was a controversial choice for a thesis at a Russian university. But Anna was mesmerized and would not be deterred.

At home, life was tense. Anna and Alexander argued constantly. Before long, a second child was born—a girl, Vera. Alexander had earned a toehold in television, but his wages were modest and the couple was just scraping by. Then everything changed. It was the mid-1980s, and Mikhail Gorbachev's glasnost, or openness, unshackled the Russian press. Alexander became a roving correspondent for a TV news show called *Vsglyad,* or "Outlook"—a loose version of America's *60 Minutes*. The weekly program electrified the country by daring to challenge the official Kremlin version of events, and it made him an instant celebrity.

In 1990, Anna and her family allowed a Russian filmmaker and crew to share their apartment for six weeks. The resulting documentary, entitled *A Taste of Freedom,* is mainly about Alexander and the risks he took as a TV journalist challenging the system. But it also provides revealing glimpses of everyday life with the Politkovskys. Alexander, dressed down in trademark denim jacket and red plaid cap crowning his long, wavy hair, plays to the camera. Doe-eyed Anna is coquettish and vulnerable as the housewife.

Her sister Elena told me that Anna was "a crazy mom, very involved with her children," and that is evident in the film. In one scene, daughter Vera is playing the violin, accompanied on piano by Anna, who insisted that both her children learn music from an early age. (Anna's friends laughed at their memories of arriving at the door to her apartment and hearing her loud, exasperated voice from inside, "That note isn't right. Play it right." It was Anna the perfectionist, but also Anna the realist. On camera, she says that if anything happened to her, Ilya and Vera could earn a living on their own, even if that meant "playing in some restaurant.")

As the documentary unfolds, Anna is at turns frightened out of her wits about Alexander's safety while he is on a perilous assignment and chafing that she is stuck at home with domestic chores. Sometimes the dangers follow him to their apartment. Soviets not happy with his reporting leave threats on the family answering machine, including this one from a male caller: "Think about your children. You have two of them, I think."

Questioned by the filmmaker, Marina Goldovskaya, Anna declares, not entirely convincingly, that she has learned to live with the fear. "I can't cry twenty-four hours a day," she says. Should her husband be imprisoned, she adds, friends have invited her and the children to live with them in the countryside far away from Moscow.

As his television career flourished, Alexander began drinking more heavily. Part of it was the lifestyle that came with his fame; when he and Anna were at a party or a restaurant, people rushed to shake his hand and toast him with celebratory rounds of vodka. But she detested his liking for alcohol, especially when nights on the town ended with him being quite drunk, and she felt it was poisoning their marriage.

Anna also fretted over her career ambitions. She had begun writing feature stories for a small newspaper, work that she found less than satisfying. She wanted a career in television like her husband. But he was doing everything he could to block her way, she told friends. In fact, the main problem with their marriage was that neither she nor Alexander was willing or able to play a supporting role to the other, not for any extended period, anyway. Both wanted to be Number 1.

The making of the documentary revealed a preoccupation with her appearance on camera. She was nearly blind without her spectacles, but if she wore them during the filming, no one would notice her best feature—her large dark eyes. What should I do, she wondered aloud. She ended up appearing without eyeglasses throughout the film.

In 1995, she and her husband were shaken by the murders of two friends in Moscow. The television superstar Vlad Listyev, to whom Alexander was especially close, died after being shot outside his house by unidentified assailants, in March. Five months later, the second friend, a forty-six-year-old banker named Ivan Kivelidi who drove around town in a Cadillac and a cowboy hat, went into convulsions in his office, and died. Police said the culprit was a highly lethal poison, either smeared on his telephone or poured into his tea.

Anna's halting career as a writer began to brighten three years later, when she joined the staff of *Obshchaya Gazeta,* an independent weekly of note. Her editor was Yegor Yakovlev, the legendary father of the bold newspaper reportage that had erupted under perestroika. The sixty-nine-year-old Yakovlev soon expressed his confidence in Anna by offering her a prized assignment—to accompany him on a trip to Chechnya.

It is hard to overstate Chechnya's extraordinary place in the Russian soul, firmly lodged there after centuries of writing by novelists and poets—Mikhail Lermontov, Alexander Pushkin, and Lev Tolstoy, among others—who romanticized that disorderly southern region. By the 1990s, it was also a seductive place for war correspondents from around the world, and Anna would be no exception. After her first trip there, Chechnya became "a dragon in her blood," said Elena Morozova. "She didn't want to live without it."

Anna did not immediately return to Chechnya. She found a new job at a scrappy biweekly called *Novaya Gazeta*. At first, she contributed general-interest pieces, including a call for emergency measures to control the march of AIDS in Russia, and a tirade against Russia's forty million "slaves to tobacco" and their "aggressive and contemptuous" attitude toward nonsmokers.

The hectoring tone of the tobacco commentary illustrated Anna's lifelong habit of lecturing to people. She told boys whom she heard cursing in public that they were "infringing on my rights. I don't want to hear that language." When the boys responded with the equivalent of "Go to hell," friends pulled her away before the confrontation could worsen. Elena Morozova recalled the sermonizing that three drunks had to endure after asking for money. "I know that if I give you money, you'll just buy vodka," Anna told them. "And look how [awful] you look." Elena decided that her friend had a messiah complex.

Another companion, Yevgenia Albats, remarked on Anna's stubbornness. Friends often accused Yevgenia of unwillingness to compromise, "but next to Anna, I am the most compromising person on the planet," she said.

But Anna also was a stickler for ethical behavior. After the *Nord-Ost* hostage tragedy, she bonded with the survivor group Nord-Ostsi. She was especially close to Elena Baranovskaya, who had lost her son and husband in the shoot-out and gassing that ended the theater standoff. Anna arrived at Elena's apartment one day to find the survivor group waiting with a cake and a gift of dishes, in honor of Anna's birthday. Sorry, said Anna, she could not accept the dishes. Gifts were off-limits for journalists, strictly unprofessional. One of the men nonetheless slipped the dishes into the trunk of Anna's car. A few days later, Anna telephoned Elena: "I'm coming by with the dishes."

In August 1999, more than a thousand Chechen militants crossed into the neighboring Russian republic of Dagestan to support a small Islamic uprising. Russian forces pushed back, forcing the Chechens' commander, Shamil Basayev, to retreat. Then came the bombings of the four apartment buildings in Moscow and elsewhere, and the launching of the Second Chechen War by Russia's new president,

Vladimir Putin. Anna's editor at *Novaya Gazeta* dispatched her to the war-torn region.

She made no pretense at objectivity. She seemed to see nothing heroic on either side, and focused almost exclusively on casualties of the war—innocent civilians whose lives were destroyed, hapless Russian soldiers flung into deadly combat. In one of her earliest dispatches, about a man named Vakha who had been blown up in a minefield, she wrote: "Now dead, Vakha lies on a field again, but this time fearlessly, with his wounded face looking up and his hands spread wider than they've ever been in his life. The left hand is about ten yards from his black jacket, which has been torn to pieces. The right hand is a bit closer, about five steps away. And Vakha's legs are quite a problem: They disappear, most likely turning to dust at the time of the explosion and flying away with the wind."

Her husband, Alexander, told Anna that he was not pleased with her absences and the danger she was facing. But after all the years of living in his shadow, she had no intention of stopping. Within a year, in her mid-forties, Anna hit her stride as a war correspondent, distinguished not only for her unapologetic irony and sarcasm, but also for a willingness to go to places where few others dared venture. Her career became forever intertwined with the callousness of the Chechen war and the conduct of Putin, its chief prosecutor.

At turns she sympathized with and castigated the Chechen leadership. She wrote increasingly accusatory stories about the Chechen prime minister, Ramzan Kadyrov, whose political career was launched after his pro-Moscow father, Akhmad, was killed in a bombing by Chechen opponents. While Anna thought Akhmad was brutal, she thought worse of Ramzan, whom she called "psychopathic and extremely stupid," the "deranged" leader of a torture-and-murder paramilitary force. She ridiculed his loyalty to Putin. "What kind of qualifications do you need to be a favorite of Putin?" Anna wrote. "To have ground Chechnya beneath your heel, and forced the entire republic to pay you tribute like an Asiatic bey, is evidently a plus."

Her salary wasn't much, and her newspaper's circulation wasn't large. But its readers were passionate, especially the dwindling number of liberals who admired Anna for writing regularly on painful subjects that most of the population seemed happy to ignore. And she relished the attention that came her way. Even official Russia—especially agencies dealing with foreign policy and security in Chechnya and the Caucasus as a whole—read what she wrote and took it seriously. As she became known as an expert on Chechnya, "she started liking it," her brother-in-law said.

Outside the country, Anna was a journalistic celebrity. Her articles—and, eventually, four books that were largely expansions of her reporting—attracted speaking invitations from around the world. She visited the United States, France, Norway, and Great Britain, and over three years collected almost $100,000 in prize money from organizations that supported human rights, press freedom, and achievements in reporting.

With the money—no small sum, even in booming Moscow—she at last was able to establish a comfortable life for herself and her family. Above all, she wanted Vera to have a place of her own, and so Anna gave her apartment to her daughter and bought another for herself in a lively neighborhood of cafés, within strolling distance of the historic Mayakovski Theater. Anna looked at Vera as a wisp of a girl, different from her son, the sturdy Ilya. He exhibited the discipline, steeliness, and ambition of his mother, and had become director of an advertising company. I thought Anna underestimated her daughter. It was true that Vera inherited her father's artistic gifts and devil-may-care manner, but I also sensed in her a tough inner strength and street smarts.

Anna's marriage to Alexander, under increasing strain, finally collapsed. As her fame had grown, his had gone into a steep decline. He could not attract commercial support for the kind of programs that suited his talent. In the familiar tradition of broadcast journalism everywhere, others had risen in his place. But Anna had learned from his natural talent and absorbed his appetite for risk, and then taken both to new levels.

The two never officially divorced, although Alexander made only sporadic appearances in her life. Anna complained to friends that he was distant from the children; she was especially angry at him for not sharing the costs of their son's wedding reception in 2003, which Anna arranged (including a traditional troika with three white horses). When I last saw Alexander, in late 2007, he had taken a second wife, a woman twenty-three years his junior, and was making short documentaries in his own small studio, while mentoring the occasional young journalist.

Anna was often called fearless, but she was the first to say she was not. "I'm afraid a lot during every trip [to Chechnya]," she told a Polish journalist. "But, if I wanted to live without fear and risk, I would be-come a teacher or a housewife."

The dangers that she faced because of her fiery articles were quite real. She was imprisoned for four harrowing days by a Russian military unit while in Chechnya to investigate accounts of civilians being bru-talized in a concentration camp. Anna said her captors tortured her, but she declined to describe "the details of the interrogations, because they are utterly obscene." One officer put her through a mock execution and threatened to rape her in a bathhouse. Another officer, identified as an FSB agent, intervened, and she was confined to a bunker until her re-lease.

Anna received multiple threats after writing that a Russian Interior Ministry officer named Sergei "Cadet" Lapin had tortured a prisoner who then vanished. Lapin said he was coming to Moscow to kill her, while an anonymous letter to her newspaper warned that a sniper would be sent to exact revenge. Anna's editor ordered her to stay home and police assigned four officers to guard her. When a fresh set of threats erupted after she appeared in a televised interview, Anna took temporary refuge in Vienna. Soon her children were calling to report that a woman of Anna's approximate age, height, and hair color had been murdered in front of her apartment house. They were sure the killer had mistaken the victim for their mother. As for Lapin, he was later convicted in the case Anna had exposed, and sentenced to ten years in prison.

Ramzan Kadyrov, the Chechen prime minister, whom she had ac-cused of atrocities and called an imbecile, also threatened to kill her. Many Chechens seemed to think the pro-Putin Kadyrov was serious, according to Anna. But she discounted his threat. He wouldn't risk harming her because he would be too obvious a suspect, she reasoned. "The people in Chechnya are afraid for me, and I find that very touch-ing," Anna wrote. "They fear for me more than I fear for myself, and that is how I survive." In fact, she did not believe that the greatest risk to her lay in Chechnya; more danger lay elsewhere.

In 2004, Chechen terrorists seized an elementary school in Beslan, in the southern Russian region of North Ossetia. They took some 1,200 children, parents, and teachers hostage and strapped explosives to the interior of the sweltering building. Anna, in Moscow, took mat-ters into her own hands. She telephoned Akhmed Zakayev, the European representative of rebel Chechen leader Aslan Maskhadov, and urged that the latter go quickly to the school and negotiate for the children's immediate release. Zakayev (who was a friend of Alexander Litvinenko and lived across the street from him, in London) told her that he would get in touch with the rebel commander and try to make that happen.

Along with a mob of other journalists, Anna rushed to a Moscow airport to catch a flight to Beslan, but none could be had. Then a young man approached and identified himself as an airport employee. "Are you Anna Politkovskaya?" he said. "We very much respect your newspaper. We are going to let you on this flight," referring to a departure to Rostov, from which she could drive to Beslan. According to Anna's account, he said that someone from the FSB had directed him to put her on the flight.

On board, Anna asked for a cup of tea. Within minutes of drinking it, she became extremely ill. She later recalled that aircraft crew members "beat me on the face and asked me, cried to me, 'Please don't die. Don't die.'" An unconscious Anna was hospitalized in Rostov and given emergency care. A nurse later told her she was "almost hopeless" when brought in. "My dear, they tried to poison you," the nurse said. Doctors who treated her later in Moscow confirmed that her symptoms were consistent with poisoning. But the substance that nearly killed her was never identified.

Anna was irritated at her own carelessness. How vain to think that airport personnel would recognize her so readily. She should have had second thoughts when they let her on the plane without demanding a passport or any other document. The thought that something was wrong had never crossed her mind.

She never made it to Beslan, where bedlam broke out after a three-day standoff. Shooting and explosions erupted as children began to pour out of the schoolhouse and terrorists tried to make their escape. In the end, some 330 children and adults were killed.

Anna's commitment to Chechnya made those close to her anxious about her well-being. Dima Muratov, her editor, wondered if it was time she turned to topics right in Moscow. At one point, he ordered her to stop going to Chechnya, but she went anyway.

Many family and friends thought she was in grave danger and regularly pleaded with her to stay home. Elena Baranovskaya, the *Nord-Ost* mother who now was Anna's friend, said she and others in the Nord-Ostsi survivors' group were aghast at the Chechnya articles. "Why are you writing this stuff?" Elena asked. "It's so dangerous." Anna's curt response was, "Well, don't read it."

But she let down her guard in a conversation with Alexander Litvinenko in London. She told the onetime KGB officer that she feared entering her apartment building—every time she stood in its dimly lit entryway, she thought someone might be lurking in the shadows. He gave her tips on how to safely enter the building, but said the only sure way to be safe was to leave Russia.

It was the same advice she got from her brother-in-law, Yuri Kudimov, himself an ex–KGB officer and now a wealthy banker in Moscow. "You live in a country where someone could be shot because of a thousand-dollar debt," he told Anna. "Think about that," he said.

You're right, Anna replied, but I'm not ready to give up my job. "I've got to do it because I like it," she said, "but it's also how I make my money."

Yuri thought that Anna should at least have a sure way to get out of the country—just in case. The wisest course, he argued, was to take advantage of her birthright and obtain an American passport. With Anna's consent, he prevailed on U.S.-based friends from his KGB days to collect the necessary documentation from New York archives. The U.S. embassy in Moscow issued the passport, but she showed no inclination to put it to immediate use.

Her friendship with Yuri puzzled me at first. As an undercover KGB agent, he had traveled the globe in the guise of a journalist. His wife, Elena—Anna's older sister—had accompanied him. One would think that Anna would be bothered by his service in an agency she hated, and surely displeased that her sister had married him. But the matter was not that simple.

Anna and Yuri had been friends for a quarter century, ever since he began dating her sister. There is a charming story of how he impersonated a visiting Canadian to enable Anna to save face at her high school. Elena, already a university student, came home one day to find her sister "at the point of breaking." Anna had agreed to organize a school assembly with a foreign student as guest of honor. She had found a Cuban boy to fill the role, but at the last minute he had canceled. Now Anna's prestige was on the line.

Elena called Yuri, her strapping twenty-one-year-old boyfriend. "Don't worry," he said. "I'll be the foreigner."

The following day, Anna stood before the assembly. We have a Canadian guest, she told the students. Yuri stood. He was wearing a borrowed denim jacket and T-shirt, with a pack of Philip Morris cigarettes stuffed in the front pocket—his best effort to look like a Westerner. Using what he later called "bad Russian" (he didn't think his English would pass muster), he proceeded to describe life in Canada. He talked about Canadian literature and politics, and handed out cigarettes to some of the boys. He was an absolute hit, and Anna was showered with praise. Her English teacher was the only skeptic, suggesting that next time it would be more "ideologically correct" to invite a Communist brother from Poland or Czechoslovakia.

Some time later, a fellow student visited Anna at home. There was Yuri, sitting in the kitchen with Elena. "What is the Canadian doing here?" the bewildered schoolmate asked. No one had yet caught on to the ruse. Indeed, an amusing rumor quickly reached Yuri's ear—his girlfriend Elena was defying custom by dating a Westerner.

Anna and Elena traveled different paths as young women. While Anna chose to marry the freewheeling Alexander who shocked her parents, Elena chose Yuri, by all accounts a decent if straightlaced fellow who appeared to be going places. The two young men, both army veterans, were already friends when they began courting the sisters. But when KGB agents separately approached them after graduation and offered attractive pay and benefits to enlist, Yuri signed up and Alexander said no. The couples very soon ran in separate circles, though they never lost touch with each other.

When I met Elena at a chic Japanese café in Moscow, I had to remind myself that she was Anna's sister, so pronounced was the contrast in their appearances. Anna was bookishly attractive and a conservative dresser. Elena was glamorous, statuesque in a skintight black top and pants, easy to imagine as the jet-setting wife of a secret agent.

After Anna was poisoned on her way to the schoolhouse in Beslan, it was Yuri's money that paid for a charter plane to whisk her back to Moscow. A cynic could attribute that and other deeds—such as arranging for a U.S. passport—to Yuri's understandable desire to please his wife by helping his sister-in-law. Yet I sensed a genuine bond between Anna and Yuri that had survived for years. Perhaps their relationship is best understood as one more piece of evidence that Russia is full of contradictions.

Despite her newspaper's limited audience, Anna's reporting had an impact within Russia. Her exposés of official malfeasance sometimes generated enough public outrage to force a response by the government. She caused prosecutions to be launched and participated in some of the trials that followed. Anna's readiness to be a peacemaker in moments of crisis, typified by her attempt to negotiate the release of the *Nord-Ost* hostages, forced state-controlled television to acknowledge her existence.

The Kremlin did its best to get in her way. Except for news events such as *Nord-Ost,* Anna was essentially barred from Russian television. "I am a pariah," Anna wrote.

Yet Putin did not respond publicly to her slashing attacks on him and his policies. Nor were there punitive actions directed at Anna personally. She traveled unhindered in and out of Chechnya. Her Russian passport was never seized, even as she went abroad to excoriate Putin and meet with his critics in London—Oleg Gordievsky, the 1980s KGB defector; Akhmed Zakayev, the Chechen opposition representative abroad; and Litvinenko. Fabricated criminal charges were a favored tactic to punish "enemies" of the Russian state, but none were ever lodged against Anna. Indeed, she said that she could meet and interview almost any top official, as long as the encounter was kept secret.

Putin's public silence was attributable to his media savvy. He knew that television and radio were what really mattered inside Russia; he had been elected twice largely due to the heavy propaganda hand that the state wielded over the airwaves. Relatively few Russians read newspapers, and most of those who did bought the major dailies. Anna's employer, *Novaya Gazeta,* was no threat to him. Putin seemed to have written off *Novaya Gazeta* as a grudgingly tolerated relic, like Russia's only remaining independent radio station, Echo Moskvy.

None of this is to suggest that the threats against Anna's life ever lessened. After her poisoning, she wrote: "If you want to go on working as a journalist, it's total servility to Putin. Otherwise, it can be death, the bullet, poison or trial—whatever our special services, Putin's guard dogs, see fit."

"I know this is all going to end badly," she told one friend. To another, she said, "I know I am not going to die in my bed." While handing Anna a journalistic award for courage, Mariane Pearl, the widow of slain *Wall Street Journal* reporter Daniel Pearl, could "feel that this woman knew she was going to die. Everybody in the audience could."

Anna began telling her daughter, Vera, where she kept important personal papers, such as financial records. "I'm putting this document here," Anna said. "If I'm not here, remember it is here."

She almost certainly realized that she had crossed an invisible line, the boundary in Russia beyond which it is acceptable to murder someone. Sergei Lapin (no relation to "Cadet," the police lieutenant in Chechnya who threatened Anna) was deputy chief prosecutor of Moscow until 2006. He knows about the boundary and how murder happens in the segment of Russian society Anna reported on.

No smart political leader or businessman outright orders a killing. He doesn't have to. When a threat of any kind appears on the horizon, his organization understands that it must be dealt with. The responsibility to do so falls to underlings "whose job, to say it softly, is to make sure the business develops smoothly," said Lapin.

"Everyone does his job. They understand they want to do a certain deal. Then they see that it isn't working. They say, 'We tried to negotiate, it didn't work. So that's it.' Rarely the head of the organization will say explicitly that he wants someone killed. But [his deputies know] the deal needs to get done. The head finds out ex post facto."

Vera tried to shrug off what her mother was saying. "One could hardly believe this would really happen," she said. Still, Vera and her brother and their father, Alexander, tried to think of ways to persuade Anna to take fewer risks. It seemed an impossible task.

Then, in early 2006, the daughter discovered she was pregnant. The father was a young man she was dating. Vera would not marry him, but she would have the child, she announced. That gave Anna pause. She was going to be a grandmother. Her two children recalled a pledge Anna made that she would lead a quieter life if one of them produced a grandchild. "She never simply promised," Vera said. "It meant she really would."

Later in the year, there was reason to think Vera's optimism was well placed. Anna told a friend that she was thinking of quitting journalism altogether and becoming a stay-in-Moscow grandmother. At an August 30 dinner celebrating her forty-eighth birthday, Anna expressed delight about the impending birth. The hostess sensed that her friend wanted to "return to a normal life," meaning no more trips to Chechnya.

On October 5, Radio Liberty asked Anna to comment on the thirtieth birthday of Ramzan Kadyrov, now the prime minister of Chechnya. Anna savaged him as usual, calling the pro-Putin ruler the "Stalin of our times" who tortured and murdered fellow Chechens to stay in power. He was a likely candidate for a revenge killing, she warned, adding: "I don't wish death on anyone, but as far as this particular person is concerned, I think he should take serious care of his security."

Early on the afternoon of October 7, mother and daughter separately left Anna's house to shop. Both were on the lookout for a bathroom basin large enough to bathe the baby. Each time Vera came across a basin that might work, she used her cell phone to alert her mother, and Anna did the same. Their hunt for the right basin bordered on the comic: They soon realized they were crossing each other's tracks, sometimes visiting the same shops only minutes apart.

Later in the day, Vera told her mother to go home and rest. Despite her public persona of invincibility, Anna had not fully recovered from the effects of the poisoning two years earlier en route to Beslan. More than once, the children had had to summon an ambulance when her symptoms worsened.

Around four-thirty p.m., Vera called Anna at home, but there was no answer. Then her cell phone rang. It was Ilya. He also had telephoned their mother's apartment and got no answer. Thoughts of the poisoning arose.

"You are close. Why don't you go check?" Vera suggested.

Ten minutes later, her brother called back.

"They killed Mama," he said.

A man in a baseball cap had secreted himself inside Anna's apartment building. When she stepped out of the elevator on her floor, he was waiting. He stood before her and fired four shots point-blank. Three bullets tore into her chest and the fourth penetrated her head. The force of the shots slammed her back into the elevator car, where a neighbor found her body. The murder weapon, a 9-millimeter Makarov semi-automatic pistol with its serial number scratched out, was left at the scene.

Vera didn't believe it, couldn't believe it.

Anna's friend from childhood Elena Morozova was in her car when an acquaintance called and told her to turn on the radio. "We've got this bit of tragic news," the announcer said. "Anna Politkovskaya was killed near the entrance to her house."

Elena telephoned Masha Khaykina, another of Anna's close friends from school days. "They've killed Anka," she said.

Masha screamed.

In London, Alexander Litvinenko's wife told him, "Oi, Alexander, I have terrible news for you. They shot Anya." He began pacing "like a wounded animal."

Vladimir Putin was at a party in honor of his fifty-fourth birthday. A guest conveyed the news of Anna's assassination. He issued no immediate statement.

Asked about her death three days later, in Germany, Putin famously replied that it was a pity but that her "influence on the country's political life . . . was minimal."

By one expert's measure, Anna's killing was out of the ordinary. Oleg Panfilov, with whom I worked in Tajikistan in 1992, directs a Moscow center that defends press rights in the former Soviet states. He said twenty-six reporters were killed in the former Soviet Union in 2006, the last year for which he had complete statistics. But he believed that only one—Anna—probably died for what she wrote. The other deaths likely could be attributed to personal disputes or business disagreements, he said.

Anna had a long list of enemies. Almost every time she wrote a story, she was protesting an injustice that someone had suffered. That also meant she was attacking someone—the person or persons at fault. And Anna named names. So the number of characters who might have wanted her dead is large. Ramzan Kadyrov, the Chechen leader she repeatedly berated, is thought by many to be a prime suspect. He had publicly threatened her. The murder happened two days after his birthday, giving rise to speculation that it was a present from thuggish admirers. Three Chechens were among the ten men arrested in the case, perhaps an additional reason to focus attention on him.

My hunch is that this was not a murder that required approval at the top. But it is reasonable to suspect that the FSB was complicit in Anna's death, at least at some level. Those who engineered her killing almost certainly assumed they would get away with it. They knew it would be seen as a political killing and that there would be repercussions. But they must have had reason to believe that they could weather the repercussions with relatively little effort. It is a level of confidence that one would expect to find within the FSB, or among those close to the organization. (One of the first suspects to be arrested was an FSB officer, who was accused of providing Anna's address to the triggerman. Will it be shown that he was ordered by someone higher up to provide this assistance? Perhaps, but that's not a requirement. He could have been operating under the usual understanding that certain people are fair game. The wisdom of former prosecutor Sergei Lapin may have application here.)

What about Putin? Did he order Anna's murder? I have not heard anyone present a credible case against the Russian president. I don't believe it happened at his explicit direction, or even his vague suggestion. Some have suggested a theory like the one linking Anna's killing to Kadyrov—that it was a gangland-style present to Putin. She was slain on the exact date of the president's birthday. In the end, though, such speculation is an almost pointless exercise. Putin is responsible because, as with *Nord-Ost* and Paul Klebnikov's murder, he created the climate of impunity in which someone decided that Anna could die. Putin's rule protects those who are inside the system or at least accept it. Outsiders cannot expect the same protection. That applies to business, politics, or journalism. Violence can be permissible against those deemed to be outsiders.

Anna's legacy is that she made a difference, no matter Putin's cold dismissal of her worth. She did what she did because she saw no one else doing it. She refused to be intimidated, and she made people's lives better.

But I suspect that she didn't care much about a legacy. For Anna, it added up to this: She did her best, she lived her life, and that was about it. Yes, it would have been pleasing to think that people would remember her. But would that have changed how Anna answered her calling? I think not.

Irina Fadeeva, one of the Nord-Ostsi women, who lost her teenage son, Yaroslav, in the theater tragedy, related the following to me:

A while after Anna's death, Irina dreamed that the two of them were out walking. They came to a glass house, and Anna headed toward it.

"I'll walk with you," Irina said.

"No, you can't come with me," Anna replied. "With me it's very dangerous. They could kill me."

Anna pulled her hat tight over her eyes, and disappeared inside.

CHAPTER 9

The Traitor

Alexander Litvinenko: A Defector in London

SIX DAYS AFTER THE OCTOBER 7, 2006, SLAYING OF ANNA Politkovskaya, actress Vanessa Redgrave led mourners in a flower-laying ceremony at Westminster Abbey. A tribute to Anna followed at the House of Lords. Days later, a somber panel discussion was held at the Frontline Club, a popular West London inn and saloon run by former war correspondents.

A scruffy-faced blond man in the Frontline audience rose to his feet. "My name is Alexander Litvinenko," he said in a mixture of English and Russian. "I'm a former KGB and FSB officer. Because I'm here, [I feel] I should speak up."

The killing of the crusading journalist had unsettled the Russian defector, a fixture in London's émigré community for nearly six years. He had known Anna during the last few years of her life and had admired her tough reporting on many of the same matters that occupied his interest.

Litvinenko quickly unloaded on Russia's leader: "Someone has asked who killed Anna Politkovskaya. I'll give you a direct answer—Mr. Putin, the president of the Russian Federation, killed Anna."

Toward the end of his remarks, he rephrased the statement, but its essence was unchanged. "Without the sanction of Putin, no one would touch someone of Anna's stature," he insisted. "She was their political enemy, and that's why they killed her."

As far as I could tell, it was the first time that Litvinenko had publicly blamed Vladimir Putin for Anna's death. His blunt accusations caused a stir in the room. Afterward, some in the audience invited him to speak elsewhere, and journalists who were present pressed him to elaborate. A five-minute videotape of his impromptu speech eventually found a global audience in the tens of thousands, through the magic of YouTube. Valid or not, Litvinenko's remarks helped to bolster a growing suspicion abroad: The Kremlin was killing its enemies.

The onetime Russian agent had been tossing rhetorical hand grenades in the direction of the Kremlin ever since he and his wife, Marina, and their six-year-old son, Anatoly, arrived in Great Britain on November 1, 2000. After his nerve-racking escape from Russia and failure to obtain political asylum in the United States, Litvinenko settled into the life of an exile in London. He was a health fanatic who neither smoked nor drank, and ran alone up to twelve kilometers a day through north London. His wife adjusted well, taking English lessons and finding work as a dance instructor at a health club. The jowly, balding Berezovsky, also living in exile in London, made sure they were financially comfortable.

Well before fleeing Russia, the forty-three-year-old Litvinenko had experienced a kind of personal conversion. He found himself questioning the worth of his more than a decade in Russian counterintelligence, and the values that service represented. His gradual disillusionment had led to a change of heart so intense that he sometimes resembled a religious zealot.

In London, he embraced the Chechen struggle for independence from Russia. Two years after his arrival, he and Marina moved into a row house in north London. Soon after, Akhmed Zakayev, the European-based leader of the Chechen opposition, moved in across the street, and the two men became extremely close. At times, Litvinenko seemed to see himself as an adopted Chechen. That was most apparent in his articles for the opposition online news service, called ChechenPress. Marina sometimes felt that his writing was too emotional, "like a person in a bazaar," causing him to "lose face." She advised her husband to tone it down so readers would expect that "probably there is something serious" in any article bearing a Litvinenko byline. But her advice does not seem to have influenced what he wrote.

Litvinenko's rejection of his past could be traced to his service in the First Chechen War; he saw firsthand the brutality of that conflict, including the torture of captured Chechens. His interrogation of a Chechen teenager strengthened his sense that this was no ordinary conflict. When Litvinenko asked the youth why he was not in school, the boy replied that his entire class had gone off to fight the Russian army. Litvinenko's flight to England coincided with the Second Chechen War, the cruelty of which reinforced his belief that the Russian military campaign there was immoral.

Some friends thought that his well-publicized attacks on Russia's most powerful men put Litvinenko at risk of assassination. He usually batted away such suggestions, insisting that he felt well protected in the United Kingdom. At the same time, he trusted no one, according to colleague Yuri Felshtinsky. "He thought everyone was working for the KGB," Felshtinsky said. "He thought people in Boris's office were working for the KGB, which perhaps one or more were."

Litvinenko hammered at the idea of Putin and the Russian intelligence apparatus as the unseen hands behind all sorts of outrages. He declared that the FSB trained Ayman al-Zawahiri, the deputy chief of al-Qaeda; that Putin was responsible for the Beslan school massacre; that the FSB organized the *Nord-Ost* hostage-taking (Anna alleged an FSB role as well); and that the FSB killed *Forbes Russia* editor Paul Klebnikov. He made a link to the 2004 dioxin poisoning of the Ukrainian presidential candidate Viktor Yushchenko as he campaigned against a pro-Moscow candidate. Litvinenko told *The New York Times* that the assault fit the profile of a Russian undercover operation. "The view inside our [intelligence] agency was that poison is just a weapon, like a pistol. It's not seen that way in the West, but it was just viewed as an ordinary tool," he told the newspaper.

He got exceedingly personal with Putin. The president's career in the KGB had been initially derailed because "his bosses learned that [he] was a pedophile," Litvinenko said. He claimed to have a videotape of Putin cavorting with underage boys, but never made public the purported recording or any other evidence to support what most regarded as a preposterous assertion.

Some who knew him said Litvinenko also exaggerated certain personal relationships. Anna Politkovskaya, for example, was unable to disregard his past as a KGB agent and remained highly suspicious of him, according to her family. Her only interest was whatever information he could provide on the FSB and Chechnya, they said. Litvinenko, on the other hand, regularly said he and Anna were close personal friends. Perhaps he thought his contact with her lent him credibility, allowing him to bask in reflected glory.

Skeptics abounded when Litvinenko once cast himself as concerned for Vladimir Putin's safety. He rang the London police to say that two Russian men had approached him with plans to assassinate their president. The allegation received wide attention in the British press and resulted in the men's brief incarceration, after which they were sent back to Russia. Suddenly, if only briefly, Litvinenko appeared to be the soul of moderateness.

More often, he seemed to be a man of contradictions. Most of his allegations appeared wide of the mark. Yet he had solid sources within Russian security agencies, according to his wife and Oleg Gordievsky, the former KGB colonel. They told me that he was able to reach FSB contacts by phone, and through them obtained access to inside information and documents. His judgments were accurate at times simply because he knew from personal experience how the FSB and its companion agencies worked.

His claim that Putin okayed or knew in advance of the slaying of Anna Politkovskaya is highly improbable. But his broader accusation that the Russian intelligence community was involved is far less so. In fact, as Russian prosecutors themselves later alleged, at least one FSB officer *did* assist in Anna's murder by telling the killers where she lived.

Some journalists reported his assertions as straightforward news, while others treated him as a crank and possibly unhinged. Even some admirers thought he sounded shrill.

Yet Litvinenko found an ear in British intelligence. The country's domestic and overseas intelligence services, MI5 and MI6, both debriefed him after his 2000 defection. What he told his interrogators has never been made public, but the questions likely paralleled those asked by American agents when he first sought asylum, in Georgia—for example, the identities of Russian spies in Britain and British double agents anywhere in the world. He cooperated with enthusiasm. After the rough methods of the KGB, the more polished, low-key style of the Britons appealed to him. For a while, he was disgruntled in that his hosts refused to provide him with a salary. But that was to be expected since he hadn't negotiated his defection in advance, when he might have had some leverage. In addition, he was not a truly high-value catch, not like Oleg Gordievsky, for instance, or even Nikolai Khokhlov, the first officer to defect from Stalin's assassination unit. By those standards, he failed to qualify for a regular salary; political asylum and the chance to attain British citizenship would have to suffice.

Litvinenko's best-known broadside against the FSB was *Blowing Up Russia,* the book he coauthored with Felshtinsky. It argued that the FSB had engineered the four apartment house bombings that terrorized Russia in 1999 and killed some three hundred people, and that the blasts had been part of an elaborate plan to catapult the agency's boss, Vladimir Putin, into the presidency.

Berezovsky, now in full-throated opposition to Putin, financed the book as a political weapon. He and Litvinenko were united in their desire to upend the Russian regime, with Berezovsky anxious to discredit the president and Litvinenko going after the FSB. *Blowing Up Russia* had the virtue of attacking both.

The exiled billionaire spent generously to promote his creation. He launched the book with a London party worthy of royalty and flew some four dozen journalists in from Moscow to attend a press conference. *Novaya Gazeta,* Anna's newspaper, published excerpts in a special issue. Berezovsky also bankrolled a fifty-two-minute documentary, entitled *Assassination of Russia,* which was based on the book. The French-produced film had its premiere in London but was also shown to a select audience in Moscow.

Putin's regime labored to defend itself against the book and other attacks by Litvinenko and his billionaire ally. Boris Labusov, spokesman for the foreign arm of the FSB, scorned the defector's claim that Russia's secret services had escalated their activities in North America and Europe. "There is no need to analyze Litvinenko's fabrications. You can say at once that he is fulfilling another social order by his superiors," Labusov said, seeming to refer to Berezovsky. Early one morning in 2004, someone lobbed Molotov cocktails at the north London homes of Litvinenko and Akhmed Zakayev, the exiled Chechen leader. Litvinenko blamed Russia, and Labusov responded with scorn. "Discussing our involvement is really a laugh," he said, suggesting instead that the exiles might have torched their own homes. "History knows a lot of cases when some individuals imitated attempts on their lives, trying to attract the public's attention to themselves for various purposes."

But there was no denying that Litvinenko had struck a nerve in Moscow. FSB marksmen used large portraits of their former colleague for target practice—all the better, it seemed, to motivate their accuracy. The Russian embassy left a summons at his London home to appear in Moscow and be tried on charges of beating a suspect and stealing explosives when he was an FSB agent (he had been cleared of similar allegations in 1999). Litvinenko, naturally, had no desire to return to Moscow under the threat of a prison sentence, and ignored the summons. He was convicted in absentia a month later, and a three-and-a-half-year suspended sentence was entered against him. Putin's priorities seemed misdirected—pursuing an empty conviction with the likely intent to vilify a political exile, while exerting little energy to solve the country's biggest murder cases.

Later in the year, word reached Litvinenko that the FSB apparently had hatched a plot to kill him. The tip came from Mikhail Trepashkin, who said he had been threatened with murder by the boss of Litvinenko's FSB anti-crime unit and sat with him at the famous whistle-blower press conference in Moscow in 1998. In the end, the FSB turned against both of them, but he and Litvinenko became close friends.

A former FSB colleague of theirs had proposed that Trepashkin, still in Russia, go to London and be the point man in a surveillance operation targeting Litvinenko. In Trepashkin's telling, the former colleague defined the purpose of the mission as sorting out "all matters linked to Litvinenko and Berezovsky once and for all."

Apparently, the agency expected that Trepashkin's loyalty to FSB tradition and his Russian patriotism would overcome whatever misgivings he might have at violating an important friendship. But Trepashkin quickly concluded that the agency was trying to draw him into a scheme to murder Litvinenko, and friendship prevailed.

Trepashkin told an interviewer how he responded to the ex-colleague: " 'Are you out of your mind?' I said to him. 'Are you trying to recruit me to help carry out an assassination? Forget it.' "

Episodes such as the surveillance plot did nothing to calm the paranoia and sense of drama that seemed to overwhelm Litvinenko at times. A Russian-born doctoral student named Julia Svetlichnaja, writing in a British newspaper, provided a vivid account of grandiose-to-eccentric behavior on his part. She had spent time with Litvinenko while doing research on Chechnya, and her article depicted him as a somewhat pathetic figure. Acting the superspy, he made abrupt turns in his car to lose a "tail" and insisted on standing and walking while being interviewed, supposedly to foil any attempts by unseen persons to record him. He posed in front of a British flag, belligerently brandishing a Chechen sword, and said of the Kremlin, "Every time I publish something on the ChechenPress website, I piss them off. One day they will understand who I am!" She said Litvinenko described plans to blackmail one or more Russian oligarchs with evidence he had of their corruption. He even invited Svetlichnaja to partner with him on the project, she said.

Felshtinsky, his writing partner, doubted that the latter invitation was genuine. Litvinenko, he said, would have been suspicious of a Russian woman he did not know claiming she was in London conducting research on Chechens. "He was probably thinking she worked for the KGB; all of it was his checking if she worked for the Russians or not," Felshtinsky said. That rang true. Always, it seemed, Litvinenko was on the lookout for another plot.

By 2005, Litvinenko began to feel as if he were living on the dole. He had been in England for almost five years, but was still entirely dependent on Berezovsky's goodwill and monthly stipends. He had exhausted all the evidence that he and Felshtinsky had gathered to portray the FSB and Putin as complicit in the apartment house bombings. Their investigations had resulted in a book and a film, and Litvinenko had written a second anti-FSB screed called *Lubyanka Criminal Group*. Now what would he do? He knew he was no businessman, but he excelled at intelligence work. That, he told Marina, "I can really do well." Everyone was for sale in Russia and "everything has its price," he said confidently.

Litvinenko was familiar with the detective agencies that had blossomed in London's Mayfair district, especially their hunger for the kind of information he could provide. Their clientele included Western businessmen exploring joint ventures in Russia and elsewhere in the

former Soviet Union, who were anxious to know more about their potential partners before taking the plunge. The detective agencies were
happy to supply the needed intelligence in exchange for handsome fees.

And so Litvinenko, drawing on his sources inside and outside of
Russia, began selling information to the Mayfair operatives. His initial
experiences were not encouraging. The agencies were relative tight-
wads when it came to paying their investigators. Sometimes they refused to pay anything for the information that he submitted, scoffing,
"We ourselves could have discovered this." Litvinenko was awkward in
the art of wheeling and dealing, and accepted these financial slights.

But over time, he developed good relationships with a few select
companies, especially one called Titon International Security Services.
Titon was a boutique operation known for in-the-trenches investigations that larger rivals were reluctant to undertake—just the type that
were Litvinenko's forte. One of his notable successes at Titon was a
probing report on Viktor Ivanov, a longtime Putin intimate and former
KGB officer. After Putin appointed Ivanov chairman of Aeroflot,
Litvinenko profiled Ivanov for a British firm thinking of doing business
with the state airline.

At the same time Litvinenko was feeling his way as a private investigator, his relationship with Berezovsky was becoming strained. Given
their long history together, this seemed a surprising development. The
billionaire Russian had been his mentor and a willing provider for the
Litvinenko family. Back in 2000, it was Berezovsky who had made possible Litvinenko's cloak-and-dagger flight from Russia and had overcome Marina's doubts about uprooting herself and her son from their
native country. Berezovsky's pledge to take care of them financially had
persuaded Marina to go along with the plan to flee, she told me. In
London, the exiled oligarch had installed them in an apartment in the
desirable Kensington district, paid for their son's schooling, and provided Litvinenko with a generous salary of £5,000 a month. (Litvinenko chronically griped that he had no cash. A skeptical colleague who
knew his habits when it came to managing money once remarked to
him, "Sasha, if I deposited my entire salary in the bank, I also would
have no money in my pocket.")

But Berezovsky didn't regard himself as a philanthropist. He was a
businessman who always demanded something in return for his invest-
ments. And Litvinenko, despite his obvious gifts as an investigator,

seemed unable to come up with new projects that were worthwhile, nothing like *Blowing Up Russia,* which Berezovsky had been willing to support because he thought it could wound the reviled Vladimir Putin. Berezovsky began to avoid meetings with him, no longer willing to listen to Litvinenko's highly emotional and long-winded presentations. As Berezovsky put it, his fellow exile "demanded considerable attention," while the oligarch had more pressing matters to attend to. On top of that, Litvinenko seemed obsessed with matters he regarded as absolutely vital but others thought were inconsequential at best. He seemed consumed by his conspiracy theories. At least that was how Berezovsky saw it.

Yuri Felshtinsky knew firsthand what it meant to be sought-after by Litvinenko. Phone calls came at all hours, and the voice at the other end usually was filled with urgency. But Litvinenko seldom had anything pressing to say. More often, it was "something that could wait two months, [much] less until the next day," Felshtinsky told me. "I'd say, 'You're waking everyone up. Next time, please wait before you call.' He'd say, 'I don't care. What's the problem? So I woke them up.' "

In Litvinenko's mind, his behavior was perfectly reasonable—for an *oper,* that is. This is FSB jargon for a special kind of intelligence agent, the operations man who tracks criminals in anticipation that they will commit illegal acts. Litvinenko had been trained as an *oper,* a word he used so often that Berezovsky soon picked it up. Now Litvinenko's prey was the FSB; he was in constant battle with its shadowy operatives, always attempting "to provoke, to see how they react to him," Felshtinsky said.

He sometimes struggled to decipher Litvinenko's assertions. "When he is saying he has a tape that Putin is a pedophile, there are several possibilities of what that means," Felshtinsky offered as an example. "There is the possibility he has a tape; another possibility is that he knows someone who has the tape; a third is that he is trying to provoke a reaction, such as that Putin may think he has a tape, or that someone who has the tape will understand he wants the tape, or that someone might make such a tape."

In addition to being exhausting, the process of trying to understand Litvinenko tended to discourage friendship. In fact, Felshtinsky recalled his colleague saying that intelligence agents "don't have friends." People were either sources of information or they were targets of investigations. His wife and son were the only exceptions to this rule, Litvinenko said. "After that was when I stopped calling him a friend," Felshtinsky said.

Litvinenko's estrangement from Berezovsky worsened. Marina recalled her husband saying, with emotion, that their billionaire patron no longer seemed to require his services. Finally, toward the end of 2005, Berezovsky carved out time for a chat. It ended with Litvinenko informing the oligarch that he would seek work elsewhere—he was doing little in return for the money that Berezovsky was providing, and it was time to move on. Litvinenko had hoped to hear some mention of regret from the billionaire, even a suggestion that he reconsider. His old anxiety about being unwanted seemed to be in play, the unsettled sensation that went back to his boyhood. But Berezovsky expressed no misgivings. It was a good idea and Litvinenko was free to go, the billionaire said. But he promised not to abandon the Litvinenko family; they could remain in the home that he subsidized, he would still pay a salary to the ex–KGB man—though reduced to £1,500 a month—and he would continue to cover the cost of son Anatoly's tuition.

Berezovsky's pledge to continue his patronage after severing their business relationship might seem utterly contradictory. But the oligarch still felt indebted to Litvinenko for favors carried out before the two had separately fled Russia. Most prominent of these was Litvinenko's courageous stand in 1994 to prevent Moscow police from taking Berezovsky into custody for closed-door questioning in a murder investigation. Their intentions seemed threatening, and the billionaire thought that Litvinenko's action had probably saved his life. He also was fulfilling his old promise to Marina—made as she agonized over joining her husband in exile—that she and her son would be kept financially secure. I regarded Berezovsky as an ambitious conniver, but had to respect him for adhering to a certain code of honor, at least where the Litvinenkos were concerned.

On January 23, 2006, Berezovsky observed his sixtieth birthday in lavish style. He hosted a black-tie celebration at Blenheim Palace, the famous birthplace of Winston Churchill. It was always that way with the oligarch's milestone birthdays—he had thrown a similar affair five years earlier in Nice, near his seaside villa on the Côte d'Azur.

Alexander and Marina Litvinenko were among the guests, invited as a nod to old times. So too was a snappy dresser named Andrei Lugovoi, former security chief for Berezovsky at ORT, the Russian television station that was once a valuable part of the oligarch's empire. He was also a former KGB bodyguard for senior government officials.

Litvinenko was an FSB officer when the two last had contact, in the mid-1990s. At the time, he suspected Lugovoi of attempting to limit his access to Berezovsky, and their relationship was frosty as a result. But on this night, over dinner, the two veterans of Russian intelligence found that their interests might coincide. Lugovoi, now the multimillionaire proprietor of Moscow security and soft drink companies, was thinking about expanding into the British market. Litvinenko had developed contacts with U.K. businessmen, thanks to his work at Titon and other Mayfair investigative agencies. Perhaps both men could profit from an informal partnership.

During the next several months, they tried to make the idea a reality. Progress was slow. Lugovoi provided a background report for a shared project at Titon, but the company's managers were not impressed by his work. They also were uncomfortable in his presence; there was something vaguely disturbing about his look and his manner. No one said anything to Litvinenko—he surely would have shrugged off their concerns. Instead, the managers found excuses to absent themselves if Litvinenko called to say he was dropping by with Lugovoi.

In July, Vladimir Putin signed a law that caused a ripple of nervousness among Russian exiles in London. It granted the Kremlin's intelligence agencies the right—if Putin gave his approval—to assassinate Russia's enemies outside the nation's borders, including "those slandering the individual occupying the post of president of the Russian Federation." In other words, making a defamatory statement about Putin could be punishable by death. The new law lifted a quasi-moratorium that Moscow had observed on overseas assassinations for almost a half century, since the disastrous defection of Nikolai Khokhlov and two other Soviet killers who spilled secrets to the West in the 1950s.

I didn't think that Putin necessarily had any specific slanderers in mind. Rather, he seemed to be reminding his countrymen—and other nations, especially in the West—of his new persona as the chisel-faced, muscular leader of Russia reborn. His we-won't-be-pushed-around attitude certainly played well at home. It meshed with a new sense of nationalism that he encouraged, a Russia-first policy verging on xeno-phobia.

For example, the Kremlin formed a youth movement with a para-military bent, called Nashi. Literally the group's name meant "Ours," but its sense was "Our People." The proximate trigger for its creation was the Orange Revolution of 2004 in neighboring Ukraine that over-threw the pro-Moscow president. Putin was determined that what he regarded as a Western-inspired movement would not spill into Russia and threaten his own government. Viewed that way, Nashi existed to defend Russian territory against dangerous foreign influences. Its loy-alists famously pursued Estonia's ambassador on foot when the Baltic country had the temerity to shift a Soviet war memorial from the cen-ter of the capital, Tallinn, to the city outskirts. Nashi followers demon-strated for a week in front of the Estonian embassy while the normally proactive police stood by. Concurrently, the Putin government expelled natives of the Caucasus and Central Asia from Moscow—people whom Russians call "the blacks." In the nation's capital, it became understood that the government would tolerate open racism; non-Russians, partic-ularly dark-complected ones, were subject to street attacks by toughs.

Some of the exiles in London felt personally threatened by Putin's legitimizing of assassination abroad. They remarked on how neatly the new law seemed to fit Litvinenko, who had been labeled a "traitor" by some former colleagues. Litvinenko himself observed that he, his neighbor Akhmed Zakayev, and Boris Berezovsky must be among the "terrorists" the Russian leader had in mind. His friends worried anew for his safety.

"I was there with him a few times when he got a call from Moscow," said Vladimir Bukovsky, a fellow Russian exile.

"What, do you think it's safe in London?" a caller once asked Litvi-nenko. "Remember Trotsky."

In an interview, Marina said her husband believed he could outwit any potential assassin. "He believed that he would be able to sense something first," she told the Russian newspaper *Kommersant*. "He said, 'Marina, you can't imagine how keen my nose is. I'm like a blood-hound—I sense danger, my hair stands on end, and I take care of every-thing immediately.'"

He did confess to "a feeling of danger," she said, "but nothing con-crete. He was very earnestly concerned about the law that was passed in

Russia concerning the possibility of special operations being carried out abroad. He believed they would do such a thing."

By October, Litvinenko had acquired what could be considered a layer of protection. He saw Felshtinsky and filmmaker Andrei Nekrasov at the Westminster Abbey memorial service for Anna Politkovskaya and whispered that he had finally received a British passport. "I'm British," he said elatedly. "I'm an Englishman."

When his father, Valter, a retired psychiatrist still living in Russia, expressed concern about Litvinenko's safety, the son said not to worry. His new citizenship made him untouchable—his enemies in Russia would never risk attacking a Briton. Did Litvinenko, the *oper,* truly believe that? Not if one overheard what he told a confidant, Yevgeni Limarev, a France-based former KGB officer. More than once, Litvinenko raised the possibility that he would be killed, as though "expecting an attack, an assassination attempt or a murder." Perhaps Litvinenko was genuinely conflicted about the dangers he faced. Still, he seemed to take few security precautions. Unlike Zakayev, his Chechen neighbor, he rather freely gave out his phone number and home address.

October also was a time when some of the central characters in Litvinenko's life crossed paths in London. Yuri Felshtinsky flew from his suburban Boston home in search of more ivory for his private collection. He had been promised a ride on Boris Berezovsky's jet to Israel, where carved mammoth tusks might be purchased. Best of all, he would not be subject to global export controls on the return trip because no one would check the billionaire's private plane. On an evening stroll toward Piccadilly Circus, he encountered Andrei Lugovoi, Litvinenko's putative business partner. The two hadn't seen each other since Berezovsky's birthday party ten months earlier. "Are you in town to see Boris?" Felshtinsky asked. No, said the wealthy Russian, and after a few more words they parted. Minutes later, Felshtinsky encountered Alex Goldfarb, the onetime Soviet dissident who had run George Soros's Moscow human rights office and then went to work for Berezovsky. He *had* just seen the oligarch; they had dined and gone on to see a performance of *King Lear,* but Goldfarb had left early "because all the men were naked."

Litvinenko and Lugovoi met often in October, sometimes with prospective clients, attempting to build some momentum for their budding partnership. On October 16, for instance, the multi-millionaire flew in from Moscow and brought along an old school buddy, Dmitri Kovtun. The pair dined on sushi with Litvinenko at a restaurant called Itsu on Piccadilly. But not much is known about what transpired at their meetings. Kovtun said that Litvinenko excessively talked politics. Lugovoi said that he pushed would-be clients clumsily about money, describing one meeting at which Litvinenko pestered potential partners to "transfer 100,000 pounds to us." Marina, who appears to have been uninvolved in her husband's business affairs, could shed no light on the conversations.

I was more intrigued by the almost nonchalant manner that characterized Lugovoi's dealings in London. In Moscow, he was the rich proprietor of a successful security company. A business such as that relies on operatives within Kremlin intelligence agencies to provide the information and skills that are critical to its success. Such a business cannot operate without the assent of the Kremlin. So why was Lugovoi willing and able to go into business with Litvinenko, a self-exiled FSB defector who had been convicted of a crime in Russia? And how was it that he could openly consort with Boris Berezovsky, himself a wanted man in Russia and the blood enemy of Putin? It didn't add up.

On the morning of November 1, Litvinenko called his friend and neighbor Akhmed Zakayev. "I'm about to get information. A list of people who might be responsible for killing Anna Politkovskaya," he said. The list was being offered by Mario Scaramella, a dubious figure on the margins of Italian politics who would later be arrested in a criminal investigation in Italy. Litvinenko had served as a source of sorts for the Italian's attempts to undermine Romano Prodi, the country's prime minister. Scaramella several times had paid him to fly to Italy and help build the case that Prodi was a stooge of the KGB; once he even videotaped Litvinenko saying so.

The two met that afternoon at Itsu, the sushi bar. Scaramella handed over a four-page e-mail—a purported hit list from Dignity and Honor, an association of former KGB agents with a history of issuing threats against supposed traitors. Among the names on the death list were those of Scaramella, Litvinenko, Berezovsky, and Anna. Litvinenko didn't think it stood up to scrutiny. Nevertheless, he went by Berezovsky's office to make photocopies, and gave one to the billionaire. Then he headed for a meeting with Lugovoi, who just the night before had shared a bottle of red wine with Berezovsky, his old boss.

By most accounts, Litvinenko was in good spirits. That night, he and Marina were planning to celebrate the sixth anniversary of their escape to England. They would have a quiet dinner together—Marina was planning to prepare chicken, a favorite dish.

He was also buoyed by the potential profits from a Lugovoi partnership. The two had agreed that Litvinenko would receive a 20 percent cut of any business he brought to the multi-millionaire's security company. If things went well, Litvinenko told his friend Oleg Gordievsky, he could earn a half million pounds. Among other things, that would allow him to end his financial reliance on Boris Berezovsky.

Sometime after four p.m., Litvinenko made his way down the street to the Millennium Hotel, to look for Lugovoi in the Pine Bar. It would be their last business meeting.

CHAPTER 10

Polonium

The World Is Witness to an Assassination

THE NOBLE MILLENNIUM HOTEL, BUILT AS AN ELEGANT MANSION in the eighteenth century, is situated on Grosvenor Square, in London's Mayfair district. The neighborhood around the square has several historical ties with the United States. General Dwight Eisenhower established his headquarters there during World War II, and the north side of the square is dominated by a monument to FDR. On the west side, the concrete-and-glass behemoth that is the American embassy clashes with the prevailing Georgian architecture.

This identification with America explained why, after the 9/11 terrorist attacks on the United States, the British feared an assault on the embassy. Authorities beefed up patrols and installed concrete blast barriers around the complex. But some nervous Mayfair residents thought that was not enough. A Swedish financier named Peter Castenfelt organized a neighborhood revolt, demanding that police seal access roads. As long as they were open, Castenfelt said, any attacker could drive up, detonate a bomb, and injure or kill nearby residents. I have known the soft-spoken Castenfelt for several years; well connected in capitals from Washington to Moscow, he has a habit of turning up in the middle of high-profile situations. "This is the No. 1 security issue in London that has not been resolved," he said, and led the group in buying double-page protest ads in *The Washington Post* and *The Times* of London.

About five p.m. on November 1, 2006, Alexander Litvinenko strolled along the square's south side and entered the Millennium's sedate green-and-white marble lobby. He turned into the Pine Bar, where he found Andrei Lugovoi sitting with a cigar-smoking associate, Dmitri Kovtun.

Waiter Norberto Andrade knew Lugovoi as a regular and had already brought shots of gin to the wealthy Russian businessman and his companion. Although everyone knew that Litvinenko was a teetotaler, Kovtun offered the former KGB officer a drink; by Russian custom, it would have been impolite not to do so. Litvinenko declined as expected, and sipped the green tea mixed with honey and lemon that the waiter had also set before them.

The three men were there to continue exploring the possibilities of an informal partnership, one that would use Litvinenko's talents at intelligence gathering to attract British business for Lugovoi's security company in Moscow. But the meeting was cut short after about a half-hour by the appearance of Lugovoi's wife and eight-year-old son. Lugovoi and his family had booked a room at the Millennium and planned to attend a soccer match that evening between Britain's Arsenal and Russia's CSKA Moscow.

Litvinenko bid them good-bye and caught a ride home with his Chechen friend Akhmed Zakayev. Around seven-thirty p.m., he sat down for dinner with his wife, Marina, and their son, Anatoly. It was six years to the day since they had arrived at Heathrow Airport and were granted political asylum after defecting from Russia.

As Marina later would recall, her husband was expecting to meet again with Lugovoi and Kovtun the next day. He went to bed around eleven, only to complain of nausea and twice throw up "violently," she said. She gave him milk of magnesia, which made him vomit once more.

Whatever was troubling his system, he wanted it out. So, as Marina slept, Litvinenko continued to drink the milk of magnesia and vomit through the night. He noticed that what came up was oddly gray. Early the next morning, Litvinenko rang Lugovoi to say he couldn't make their meeting; he felt terrible.

Over the next two days, Litvinenko began suffering stomach pain and intense diarrhea in addition to the vomiting. Paramedics were summoned, and they concluded that he was dehydrated. Give him liquids, they advised. The next day, Marina summoned a Russian friend who was a doctor, and he was alarmed that Litvinenko cried out in pain at the slightest touch. Paramedics were summoned once again, and this time they rushed Litvinenko to nearby Barnet General Hospital. He was so weak he could barely walk.

"Marina, this is something abnormal," he told his wife. "When I was in school at the military academy, we studied poisoning like this that was caused by a chemical weapon. This really reminds me of that." Marina said she couldn't believe it. How could it be possible that he had been poisoned? But Litvinenko was increasingly certain.

Upon his admission to the hospital, doctors immediately administered intravenous hydration. Marina stroked his head, only to become newly alarmed. His hair was coming out in her hand.

During the next week, Litvinenko's condition fluctuated. He seemed to be recovering, able to stand and swing his arms for exercise. Then he began vomiting again, this time bringing up blood. His doctors said tests indicated bacteria in his intestine, and they prescribed antibiotics.

Marina became frantic. Her husband's hair covered his pillow. He could barely speak. His skin was yellow. The doctors delivered disturbing news—Litvinenko's white blood cell count had dropped sharply. His bone marrow was depleted. They flailed about for an answer, testing him for AIDS, hepatitis, and certain strains of radiation sickness. The results were negative. His symptoms seemed typical for a cancer patient, but there was no clear explanation. When the BBC's Russian-language service reached Litvinenko on his cell phone, he stated the obvious. "Look," he told the reporter, "now after a serious poisoning I am still in very bad shape, I feel badly and I am staying at one of London's clinics."

Litvinenko kept insisting that he had been poisoned. He told the hospital staff he was a Russian defector, and said that could have something to do with his sickness. Most reacted with skepticism, even longtime patron Boris Berezovsky. But then a nurse appeared with the news that he had tested positive for thallium, a heavy metal, and poisoning was suspected. She gave him a powder, presumably Prussian blue, the same substance administered to Nikolai Khokhlov after the old spy's poisoning five decades earlier. It was still the accepted treatment to remove certain radioactive materials from people's bodies, and took its odd name from a dye for Prussian military uniforms.

British police arrived in response to the hospital's report of a possible poisoning victim. After several hours of questioning, most of it focusing on where he had been in the past few days and with whom, Litvinenko was loaded into another ambulance and moved to University College Hospital, a more secure setting. He was placed under armed guard.

"It was so strange," Marina said, "because three weeks earlier no one had taken any notice of anything, and now all of a sudden everybody was trying to save him."

News from Moscow added to the somber atmosphere in Litvinenko's room. At around six p.m. on November 18, a minor Chechen leader named Movladi Baisarov was gunned down on one of the city's busiest streets by other Chechens, in full view of policemen across the street. The official account said that his attackers were there to arrest Baisarov for crimes in the republic. Instead of surrendering, he had threatened them with a rocket-propelled grenade, authorities said. The story was totally lacking in credibility. Baisarov, a willing collaborator with the Russian authorities now in command of Chechnya, had found himself on the losing end of a power struggle between pro-Russian factions there. It seemed most probable that unidentified Russian authorities had decided he was fair game for assassination, even if the killing had to be carried out on Leninsky Prospekt, one of Moscow's busiest thoroughfares. The episode seemed to underline the peril of being perceived to be on the wrong side in Russia.

As for Litvinenko, he assured friends who came to see him that he was fine. But any improvement in his condition was fleeting. On November 20, the sixteenth day of his hospitalization, he seemed to be losing his fight to survive. Doctors moved him into intensive care.

Alex Goldfarb, the Berezovsky operative who had played a central role in getting the Litvinenko family out of Russia, tried with little success to get reporters on the story. He and Berezovsky's public relations man—Tim Bell, who famously helped to get Margaret Thatcher elected as British prime minister in 1979—finally hit on the idea of photographing Litvinenko. That would tell the whole story. So it was that a previously little-known South African photographer named Natasja Weitsz was slipped into the intensive care ward. Her picture of the stricken defector was shocking—a wasted, completely bald man clad in hospital greens, staring hollow-eyed at the camera. Bell's company distributed it.

It was as Goldfarb and Bell had hoped—newspapers and television stations around the world splashed the dramatic image before readers and viewers. Litvinenko became a blockbuster story. Reporters poured in to London and wrote vivid accounts of what he was enduring. "Ex-spy's poisoning bears hallmarks of Cold War thriller," said *The Daily Telegraph*. "Different name, same tactics. How the FSB inherited the KGB's legacy," said the *Guardian*. "Exact Cause of Ex-K.G.B. Agent's Illness Eludes Poison Experts," reported *The New York Times*.

As reporters stood outside the hospital awaiting the latest report on Litvinenko's condition, filmmaker Andrei Nekrasov visited his bedside. Nekrasov would later say that his friend "looked just like a ghost." A grimly determined Litvinenko said it was necessary that he endure the suffering. "This is what I have to do to prove I'm right," he said.

On November 22, his condition worsened. He had been able to answer police questions for three or four hours the previous day, but now it was hard for him to speak. His appearance was "like a seventy-year-old man, bald, gaunt, skin over bones," said Goldfarb. As Marina prepared to leave the hospital for the evening with their son, Anatoly, Litvinenko spoke his first complete sentence of the entire day. "Oh, Marinochka, I love you so much," he uttered, using the diminutive of her name.

At Litvinenko's bedside, his father, Valter, crossed himself and said the Lord's Prayer. "Father, I've converted. I'm a Muslim now," Litvinenko said. During a visit with Akhmed Zakayev—his neighbor and friend, who was a Muslim—Litvinenko had embraced Islam.

That night, Litvinenko twice had to be resuscitated after his heart stopped. Hospital staff summoned Marina, then after a few hours sent her home.

The following evening, the phone rang again in the Litvinenko home. It was the hospital. "Come quickly," the voice at the other end told Marina.

Though her husband was unconscious, Marina arrived in time to say good-bye.

At 9:21 p.m., Litvinenko was declared dead.

Outside University College Hospital, Alex Goldfarb read a statement that he said Litvinenko had dictated two days earlier. Addressed directly to Vladimir Putin, it said in part, "You have shown yourself to have no respect for life, liberty, or any civilized value. You have shown yourself to be unworthy of your office, to be unworthy of the trust of civilized men and women. You may succeed in silencing one man but the howl of protest from around the world will reverberate, Mr. Putin, in your ears for the rest of your life. May God forgive you for what you have done, not only to me but to beloved Russia and its people."

The stunning photograph by Natasja Weitsz and the ghastly manner of his death generated international sympathy for Litvinenko and outrage toward Russia. Many viewed his life story and the way it ended as epic tragedy, and in Hollywood there was a flurry of competition to put it all on the big screen. The contest was won by Johnny Depp, who left open the possibility that he himself would play the slain Russian defector.

What killed Litvinenko? When his doctors saw his hair falling out and his white blood cell count dropping, they had immediately suspected radiation poisoning. So they tested for what they thought to be the most likely culprits—gamma and beta radiation. Finding no evidence of either in his blood, they assumed that they were on the wrong trail. A day before Litvinenko died, however, someone at Britain's Health Protection Agency had a hunch. Samples of Litvinenko's urine were sent to the Atomic Weapons Establishment, or AWE, an agency uniquely equipped to solve the mystery.

AWE was just what its name implied—it developed and kept watch over Britain's nuclear weapons arsenal. At AWE, scientists tested the urine samples for alpha-emitting elements, the rarer, relatively large, and slow-moving particles that, unlike gamma and beta radiation, cannot pass through objects but pack a wallop when they are taken into the body.

The tests came back positive for polonium-210, an alpha emitter.

Around six p.m. on November 23, the news was passed along to Litvinenko's doctors. But it was too late. He died about three hours later.

The AWE discovery was important in more ways than one. If Litvinenko had not been in such good health when he was first stricken, he probably would have died much sooner. There would have been no urgency to continue testing for radiation poisoning, and the isotope that killed him probably would have gone undetected. Without that clue, investigators might not have found their way to the evidence that

Litvinenko had been murdered. Litvinenko himself died without learning the truth.

His doctors could be excused for not knowing that their patient's body had been ravaged by a few specks of a nuclear isotope so arcane that scientists were startled to hear of its use as a murder weapon. Once upon a time, polonium-210 was something of a household name, at least as far as known elements go. It was discovered in 1898 by Marie and Pierre Curie, and named for her native Poland. Some called it the deadliest element, gram for gram, on the periodic table. A researcher working for Marie Curie died from exposure to polonium. So did Curie's own daughter, Irène Joliot-Curie, who, like her mother, was a winner of a Nobel Prize.

During World War II and through the 1960s, polonium-210 was used as a triggering device for nuclear weapons. Mixed with beryllium, it emits a neutron and starts the fission process. But by the early 1970s, the substance had fallen out of favor among atomic bomb makers because its relatively fast deterioration rate meant it had to be replaced every few months. More recently its use had been more benign—to eliminate static in smoke detectors and dust from film and lenses, for example. The commercial market's demand for polonium-210 was so small that its entire global production was just one hundred grams a year—almost all manufactured in Russia and then exported to the United States.

Few were even aware of its existence. Polonium-210 was on no published list of potential poisons, and as far as I could tell had never been used as one. The silvery isotope was so exotic that, even five years after the imposition of heightened security measures in response to the 9/11 attacks, airports around the world were ill equipped to detect it. It was absent from the usual lists of weapons of mass destruction. Its properties were so peculiar that, unlike more familiar radioactive elements such as plutonium-239, it could be stored safely in, say, an ordinary cigarette pack or an aspirin bottle. Anyone with a mind to—and the right credentials—could slip it through almost any ostensibly secure environment.

It was unclear why the isotope had never been employed in any known assassination before Litvinenko's. Yes, there were far simpler and cheaper methods of killing. But if an assassin favored the use of radioactive poison, polonium-210 was an ideal candidate. First was its novelty, meaning it was less likely to attract suspicion than its brother thallium, which assassins, including the Soviets, had used in its nonradioactive form numerous times over the decades. Second was its nature to wander: Once it invaded an organism, polonium-210 went in many different directions. This set it apart from isotopes that gravitated toward, say, kidneys or bone marrow, thus inflicting largely localized and treatable damage. And polonium-210 threw off its mass with astonishing speed—it dispensed half its atomic particles in just 138 days, a barrage superior to almost any other relatively stable isotope. By comparison, an alternative element such as americium took 432 years to accomplish the same task. A terrorist could release polonium-210 into a crowd in an enclosed space, through food or air, and cause many fatalities in a compressed period of time, with no one learning the cause— and with reduced odds of being caught.

The few scientists familiar with polonium-210 struggled for metaphors to describe its agonizing effects. Perhaps the most chilling likened the relatively large atomic particles it released to bullets, firing away mercilessly at Litvinenko's soft tissue. Another evoked a football image, the particles knocking over cells like a rampaging fullback flattening every defender in his path. All said, polonium-210 was many times more hazardous than poisons usually associated with excruciating death, such as hydrogen cyanide.

In Litvinenko's case, once the isotope had reached his stomach, it began to shoot off particles in a ferocious attack on his intestinal lining. Internal bleeding resulted, causing him to feel pain and nausea. By the end of the first day, up to half the poison was lodging in his spleen, kidneys, liver, lymph nodes, and bone marrow. It was delivering a massive punch to his red blood cells, whose natural response was to stop multiplying, and his bone marrow stopped replenishing his body with new blood cells. Ultimately, his organs were ripped apart and his immune system rendered inoperable.

In the early hours of the day after Litvinenko's death, British police and AWE scientists appeared at the family home. They told Marina to pack her things—she had to get out, and probably wouldn't be coming back. She wondered what the fuss was about, until they told her for the first time that a nuclear poison had been used to kill her husband.

"You have to understand that we've never encountered this before, that we don't even know what it is, and we don't know what the consequences will be," said one of the emergency workers.

Then began an exhaustive effort to retrace Litvinenko's movements in the last days and hours before he fell ill. Spectrography equipment revealed a clear trail of polonium in places he was known to have visited. Boris Berezovsky's office was found to be contaminated and was sealed off. Traces of polonium were detected at the sushi restaurant where Litvinenko had dined with Lugovoi and Kovtun on October 16. It was shut down. Investigators also found polonium at the Pine Bar, where Litvinenko had sipped tea with the two Russians on November 1, only to fall ill a few hours later at home. Authorities closed the bar, and would later conclude that Litvinenko had been poisoned there— that the fatal dose of polonium had been slipped into his tea.

Britain's Health Protection Agency, anxious to avert panic, issued daily briefings on what steps were being taken to secure the public's safety. In the first weeks afterward, its telephone hotlines fielded some four thousand calls from people around the world concerned that they might have been exposed. The agency found traces of polonium-210 at more than two dozen sites in London. About a dozen people, including Litvinenko's wife and son, had been exposed to levels high enough to pose long-term health risks.

The painstaking investigation found traces of polonium at a number of locations—other than the Pine Bar—where Lugovoi and Kovtun had been. In some cases, such as Berezovsky's office and the sushi restaurant, the polonium traces were detected on the very seats that were known to have been occupied by one or both Russians. Investigators also established to their own satisfaction that the polonium had entered the United Kingdom from Russia. The clincher was evidence of the substance found on a British Airways plane that had flown from Moscow to London. It showed up on a seat that had been occupied by Lugovoi.

All signs seemed to point to either Lugovoi or Kovtun—or both— as having carried out Litvinenko's assassination, or at least participated in it.

But judging by their outward behavior, the two had been as bewildered as anyone about Litvinenko's illness. Lugovoi had telephoned his business partner in the hospital to offer his sympathy, and also called Marina.

"Marina, this is Andrei Lugovoi," he said. "Everything that happened strikes me as very strange. I'll do everything I can to figure it out."

He and Kovtun voluntarily underwent questioning by officials at the British embassy in Moscow while Litvinenko was still alive. After the ex–KGB agent died, Kovtun telephoned British authorities and said he was willing to talk further if they wished. They didn't take him up on the offer until some time later, when their investigators arrived in Moscow for interviews.

Lugovoi and Kovtun were examined by doctors in Moscow, who said that both indeed had been exposed to polonium. Lugovoi said someone must have planted the substance on his person to falsely implicate him in Litvinenko's murder. He dismissed the entire affair as a British plot to discredit Putin. Kovtun confirmed his diagnosis but said an agreement with Russian investigators prevented him from saying anything more.

Some Russians said Boris Berezovsky in London had probably masterminded the killing, and the Kremlin soon added its support to this theory. Another suspect was Semyon Mogilevich, a notorious mafia figure whose supposed motivation was to win the favor of certain powerful Russians. But he was a less than credible candidate.

Others speculated—without any supporting evidence—that Litvinenko was attempting to smuggle nuclear material and accidentally poisoned himself. This scenario sounded to me like the old Soviet habit of blaming the victim. But it was widely accepted within the Russian intelligence community.

"It's natural that you're getting sick from what you are transferring," said Josef Linder, a lecturer and self-described expert on political assassination who subscribed to the Litvinenko-as-smuggler theory. The forty-seven-year-old Muscovite had a shaved head, a tenth-degree black belt in jujitsu, and an apartment that resembled the laboratory of the gadget master Q of James Bond fame.

Swords, rifles, medals, a thirteenth-century Russian wooden mace, and a fifteenth-century Malaysian knife with an ivory handle were all on display in his foyer. Linder was especially proud of his collection of knives, one of which did double duty as a small pistol. Another, he said, was "a flying knife that can be ejected five to six meters. You push the button and the knife flies."

Linder was the author, co-author, or editor of twenty books on Russian espionage, which he had tracked back a thousand years. He beamed at the opportunity to relate some of his discoveries. In the ninth century, Russian princes were so fearful of treachery that they paid for multiple layers of intelligence gathering. Leo Tolstoy's great-great-grandfather served as a sort of spy for Peter I, sleuthing around Ottoman Turkey. Then there was the agent for Czar Nicholas II who snatched a notebook from the inside pocket of a jacket worn by Kaiser Wilhelm II as the two lunched together. By the time the meal ended, the agent had photographed the pages of the notebook and returned it to the jacket pocket without being noticed. The story sounded a bit unbelievable, but that did not bother Linder. He was a romantic who celebrated what he viewed as the most patriotic of Russian professions—spying and its associated black arts.

Linder excluded Alexander Litvinenko from his pantheon. The look on his face conveyed contempt for the very notion of Litvinenko as intelligence agent. "He joined the FSB from the Interior Ministry. He is not an intelligence officer," Linder said. He added that Litvinenko "tried to make it as though he was a personal enemy of Putin's. But nobody was interested in him here."

Mikhail Golovatov, the former commander of the KGB's elite Alpha troops, was similarly dismissive. Now the director of one of Moscow's largest security companies, Golovatov was an influential man. When he spoke, the KGB cadre heard the voice of a true comrade who had served in Afghanistan, Vilnius, Tbilisi, Baku, Kishinau, and Dushanbe—all places where the Kremlin sought to put down localized rebellions during the last years of Soviet rule. After years of ostracism during the Yeltsin era, men like Golovatov were back among the cream of Moscow society.

So what did he think of Litvinenko?

"Negative. The most negative."

Why?

Litvinenko was on Boris Berezovsky's payroll, Golovatov noted. "How can you work for the state, then join the ranks of someone working against the state? If I gave an oath to protect the state, how can I betray it? If I don't agree with state politics, I would retire and not fight against the state."

Senior Kremlin officials, while welcoming the opportunity to cast the exiled Berezovsky in a bad light, cautioned that no one could say with certainty who killed Litvinenko. Lots of people in lots of countries could be responsible, they said, and it was reckless to point the finger at Russia, as many abroad were doing.

At a news conference in Helsinki a day after Litvinenko's death, Putin went on the offensive. He falsely asserted that authorities in Britain "offer no indication that this was a violent death." He questioned whether Litvinenko in fact dictated the memo that accused him of murder. "If such a note really did appear before Mr. Litvinenko's death, then this raises the issue of why it was not made public during his life," Putin said.

Finally, the Russian president chalked up all the fuss to politics. "The people that have done this are not God and Mr. Litvinenko is, unfortunately, not Lazarus," he said. "And it is very much a pity that even such tragic events like a person's death can be used for political provocations."

I wondered why Litvinenko's assassins didn't simply shoot him or run him over. Novelist Martin Cruz Smith, for instance, thought a more "perfect" criminal would have simply pushed him off a subway platform.

If the purpose was to warn others who might have been tempted to follow in Litvinenko's defiant footsteps, then any of these methods would have sufficed. But simply rendering him dead probably was the least challenging part of the mission. The question of how to carry out the killing in the most unobtrusive manner seems to have been uppermost in the minds of the assassins. Shoving the former KGB agent in front of a moving car or planting a knife in his back could cause an ugly scene in public and make it difficult for the assassins to escape unseen. Worse yet, if they were captured, the identity of whoever organized the murder might become known.

Hence the decision to use poison. Thallium must have been immediately rejected because any half-aware doctor would respond by immediately treating Litvinenko with Prussian blue, and the plot would likely fail. Biological poisons and other radioactive substances probably were rejected because of the risks entailed in handling and administering them.

Perhaps an old-timer among the conspirators would have recalled the existence of polonium-210. Its advantages would be immediately apparent. Litvinenko's killers could carry a tiny amount of the substance to London wrapped in an ordinary piece of paper and pass undetected through airport security. Their personal health would not be at risk unless some of it got into their mouths or lungs. Once taken into Litvinenko's body via food or drink, the polonium would likely defy discovery. And even if its presence were detected after a day or so, their victim would be beyond saving because of the horrible damage to his organs. Meanwhile, the assassins would be long gone from the scene of the crime. Polonium-210 had an additional appeal: If the killers were thirsting for revenge after his harsh attacks on Putin and the Russian security agencies, they could take pleasure in knowing that Litvinenko would suffer maximum pain while dying. And that it would all occur on the anniversary of his defection to Britain might have added satisfying symbolism to the affair.

I was curious to know what other Russian exiles in London were thinking about the means and methods of Litvinenko's assassins. Boris Volodarsky, a former military intelligence officer, especially interested me. He claimed to have documented some twenty murders by poisoning that the Russian government had carried out since the 1920s—all of them employing substances that had left no trace.

It was easy to be put off by Volodarsky's manner. He had adopted the persona of a high-born Briton, sporting a neatly trimmed beard, speaking with a cultivated English accent, and wearing a beautifully tailored suit with purple tie and matching silk handkerchief. The extent of his service in Russian intelligence was somewhat murky; as best I could tell, he was operating in the West when the Soviet Union collapsed, and simply never went back to Russia. He portrayed himself as a defector and was a critic of the Russian government, but there was no sign that Kremlin leaders ranked him high among exiles who irritated them. Still, I respected his knowledge of the ways of Russian intelligence.

He suggested we meet in the Cigar Room of the Connaught Hotel near Berkeley Square, an upper-crust Mayfair establishment. He flashed a pleasant, smallish smile, the wrinkles at the edges of his eyes curving upward, and exhaled the smoke of a small cigar. When I invited Volodarsky to join me in the dining room for lunch, he brought me up short: "Let's get one thing straight. You have to pay. This is a consultation and it's not free. I'll give you ten minutes' free consultation, then you pay."

It was not possible, ethically speaking, for me to pay for the interview, although I felt a twinge of sympathy. The man did have to earn a living, and I had no idea how I would support myself if I were a former spy. Still, all I could do was buy lunch. He asked me to explain the difference between paying his accustomed fee and forking over £150 for a meal. I had no answer.

He declined lunch, but lingered for a while to talk about his business ventures. He had participated in British television programs about the Litvinenko case, and was now contributing to the making of two films. One was based on a 2005 article he wrote for *The Wall Street Journal* under the headline "The KGB Poison Factory," recounting nearly nine decades of attacks on Kremlin enemies, including Nikolai Khokhlov and Ukraine's president, Viktor Yushchenko. (After Litvinenko's death, he updated the title to read "The KGB Poison Factory, Lenin to Litvinenko.") "We are talking to several important studios," Volodarsky said.

He described thirty-five minutes he spent in an Italian prison speaking with Mario Scaramella, who famously shared sushi with Litvinenko the day he was poisoned and was first thought—mistakenly—to be a suspect. No one else had gotten to Scaramella yet, Volodarsky boasted; he had left the prison with video footage and documents that might earn him some cash from curious U.K. journalists.

His theory about the Litvinenko case ran something like this: Several small teams in several countries would have come together on November 1, 2006, to carry out the mission and then disappear. He agreed with those who doubted that Lugovoi was a key player. The wealthy Russian may have known there was to be a poisoning, but didn't actually do it himself, Volodarsky believed. The person who actually dropped the poison into Litvinenko's tea probably has yet to be identified, at least not publicly, he said. He didn't think that person would have accompanied Lugovoi or Kovtun to London because "that wouldn't be professional." On balance, he judged the Litvinenko killing to be the most momentous such exploit in three decades, "a model assassination" that seemed perfectly executed.

He recited this narrative with studied bravado, though he complained that, unlike superspy Oleg Gordievsky, he was vulnerable to a revenge attack. "I don't have security, and neither did Litvinenko," Volodarsky said. "I'm not easy to find, although if they want they can find me."

Gordievsky had a different view of the need for security. The former KGB spymaster had been a high-value defector when he sought asylum in the United Kingdom two decades ago. His home outside London had been well protected before Litvinenko's killing, and the security was stepped up afterward.

Gordievsky was most interested in the role of Andrei Lugovoi, Litvinenko's companion at the Pine Bar. He had two opposing theories: that Lugovoi was the team leader in "a typical KGB operation," or had been used as bait to befriend Litvinenko and finally lure him to the bar, where the actual assassins could do their work. In support of the latter scenario, Gordievsky cited Lugovoi's "slow approach, the cultivation of Litvinenko for ten months, inducing him, promising him deals." Once Lugovoi had cemented his relationship with Litvinenko, the trap was sprung, he surmised.

Nick Priest was not a Russian exile, but he had some intriguing ideas as to how the poisoning might have taken place. The affable Priest, one of the world's few polonium experts, was a little-known professor of environmental toxicology at London's Middlesex University. When the role of polonium-210 in Litvinenko's death became known, he was deluged with phone calls from journalists, other scientists, and security experts from around the world. Through it all, he remained a patient gentleman.

I asked the bespectacled Priest to conjure up a probable chronology, starting with the poison being transported into the United Kingdom.

Unlike others, Priest thought airport security might have been a problem. Even though polonium-210 is an alpha emitter, it throws out a tiny bit of gamma radiation, which could have been detected during airport screening, he said. Priest speculated that before it was taken to London the polonium would have been divided between four people, to lessen the risk of detection. "It's quite possible each guy came with one-fourth of the total" dose intended for Litvinenko, he said. The deadly substance probably would have been carried in vials, perhaps mixed with an acid solution to keep it from sticking to the sides or bottoms of the vials, but not so acidic as to be detectable by taste. "Then they recombined it in a hotel room," Priest said. That's when the trouble would have begun—the first release of minute traces of polonium that eventually would be found throughout London. "The moment the seal [on the vials] was broken, you started the contamination," he said.

"It's entirely possible," Priest continued, "that they didn't know what they were handling or [else] they would have taken precautions. It's possible they were only told it was poison. Otherwise they might have been frightened. Also, if you had known the properties of polonium, you would have changed your clothes [after lacing the tea], then thrown them away. You'd have used gloves. You'd have to be an idiot to leave a contamination trail behind."

That didn't necessarily explain why Lugovoi left polonium on the seat of the airliner on which he arrived in London from Moscow on October 31; perhaps he was also involved in the original mixing or pouring of the polonium solution in Moscow. Still, Priest's explanation made sense. Lugovoi and Kovtun seem not to have known that they were leaving a radioactive trail. Priest's conclusion roughly tracked with Oleg Gordievsky's second scenario—that Lugovoi had been used as bait by other, unseen hands who actually dropped the polonium-210 into Litvinenko's tea.

It seems safe to say that the assassination was not a seat-of-the-pants, rogue operation. After all, polonium-210 was not easy to procure, and it was pricey—one needed some $2 million to $3 million in cash, the commercial cost of the probable dose that experts say killed Litvinenko.

Organized crime experts considered whether Litvinenko was killed by professional Russian criminals, hired by someone whom Litvinenko had angered. But they rapidly dismissed this possibility because even the most hardened thugs would not risk Putin's wrath by murdering such a high-level target on their own. They would have participated in such a killing only if they understood that it was acceptable to the senior ranks of Russian government.

Many thought the ruthless, calculated, and convoluted method of Litvinenko's assassination clearly implicated Russia's spy agencies.

"That's Russian," said a pin-striped British private eye who formerly served as a Soviet specialist for MI6, the country's overseas espionage agency. During his spying days, he and his colleagues would marvel at the elegance of Soviet missions, finding that "an overcomplicated intelligence operation is their signature. You either admire its complexity, or decide it's all out of proportion to what you want."

Would the Kremlin dare to carry out, or bless, such an audacious scheme—murder by nuclear isotope, in a major Western capital, against a British citizen? An indignant Kremlin said no. Yet the notion of Russian state responsibility could not be easily put to rest. There was the law that Putin had approved just four months before Litvinenko's death, granting the president authority to sanction the assassination of an enemy outside the nation's borders. And there was the matter of Russia's unrivaled access to polonium-210. Ninety-seven percent of the world's commercial supply came from a single state-controlled nuclear reactor 450 miles southeast of Moscow, in a shipbuilding town called Avangard. The reactor complex was well secured, but it could not be ruled out as the source of the radiation that killed Litvinenko.

Britain sent investigators to Moscow and asked to interview Lugovoi, Kovtun, and other Russians. In response, the Kremlin said it was conducting its own investigation and asked to question one hundred people in London, including exiled oligarch Boris Berezovsky and other Russian dissidents. It was a transparent effort to turn the tables on Britain. Critics said Putin seemed to regard the murder as a public relations problem rather than a matter of criminal justice, and they appeared to be right. If, as Moscow suggested, London exiles were truly culpable, why did Russia not aggressively cooperate with Scotland Yard? It was an opportunity to prove once and for all that the West was providing safe haven to unsavory characters who did not deserve anyone's protection. But Putin's statements and actions made it appear he had little real interest in absolving Russia of outside suspicion.

Britain was in a predicament. The evidence plainly implicated both Lugovoi and Kovtun. But would the British request the pair's extradition from Russia, triggering a judicial process that could lead to courtroom accusations against senior Kremlin officials? Putin himself, the sovereign president of a much-valued country, might become entangled in the drama. Were the British prepared for this to balloon into an international incident? I had my doubts. The British conducted much business with Russia—BP, the United Kingdom's biggest company, was heavily invested there—and had a less-than-vigorous history of taking diplomatic risks. It was more of a go-along, get-along country.

Yet I was proved wrong. Six months after Litvinenko's death, the United Kingdom said it would charge Lugovoi with murder, and it officially requested his extradition. Putin refused, saying that the Russian constitution prevented sending citizens abroad for trial. He said that the Britons should present their evidence to Moscow prosecutors and allow the Russian judicial system to decide the case. Britain regarded his offer as an effort to thwart justice, which seemed a correct assumption to me.

The case went nowhere. Rather, it turned into a diplomatic fracas: Britain expelled four Russian diplomats, and Moscow responded by ordering the closure of two British cultural offices in Russia, and expelling British diplomats.

Meanwhile, Lugovoi was treated as a Russian hero. In December 2007, he won election to the Russian parliament, and he was often cheered as he traveled around the country.

The foreigner who gained the closest access to Lugovoi was Mark Franchetti, the British journalist who seemed always to end up at the center of the news. After a series of interviews with Lugovoi, Franchetti aligned himself with Oleg Gordievsky and Nick Priest's relatively benign view of the accused multi-millionaire's culpability.

"Lugovoi has often asked me if I think he killed Litvinenko," Franchetti wrote. "I confronted him with the theory, which I support, that he did murder but is not a cold-blooded killer. I told him I think he was recruited by Russia's secret service but was tricked and used without his full knowledge. He did not flinch. He again voiced his innocence, and agreed he was framed, but by MI5," meaning the domestic British intelligence service.

Franchetti wrote: " 'C'mon, Andrei, we both know that if you did take part in Litvinenko's murder, you are hardly going to tell me, are you?' I often said to him. Every time he smiled a wide, spontaneous grin. For me, that has always been revealing."

As Franchetti suggested, Lugovoi seemed genuinely not to believe he had put polonium-210 into that tea. Was he delusionary? Did he spike the tea thinking it was another substance? Did he put nothing into the tea himself, but actively or unknowingly provide cover for the person who did lace it? Was the triggerman actually Kovtun?

Lugovoi now embraced the Litvinenko-as-nuclear-terrorist theory, accusing the defector of contaminating himself, Lugovoi, and Kovtun by accidentally spilling polonium-210 he intended to sell on the black market. I could not accept that Lugovoi actually believed that; now a political celebrity, he was playing to his constituents. Who knew how far he could rise by casting himself as the brave survivor of a traitor's treachery? The sky seemed the limit.

Franchetti believed that Russia would never hand over Lugovoi to the British, and that felt right. Short of someone making a deathbed confession, there seemed to be almost no chance that the world would ever know for sure who was responsible for Litvinenko's murder.

Litvinenko had put himself in peril by turning his back on the Russian intelligence services and defecting from his native land. He had exhibited undeniable bravery before and after his exile by speaking his mind, sometimes recklessly so. He had died an agonizing death after twenty-three days of atomic war within his body. But I had difficulty viewing him as heroic or especially admirable, as a number of articles and documentaries rushed to describe him after his death. Litvinenko pursued his goals—first the reform of the FSB spy agency, then the downfall of Vladimir Putin—with much energy, but did not exhibit towering morality or intellect. In the end, he was a determined but ordinary man consumed by events far larger than him.

One thing was certain, though. Those who had scoffed at Litvinenko's paranoia had been proven wrong—the devilish forces he said he was battling turned out to be all too real.

EPILOGUE

Exit Mr. Putin

As Vladimir Putin's presidency was winding down, he sent two miniature submarines on a daring 2.5-mile dive under the Arctic ice. When they reached the seafloor, the three-person crew in one of the submersibles ejected a titanium capsule containing a Russian flag. This symbolic planting of the flag in August 2007 laid claim to the underwater region of the North Pole as Russian territory—a bold challenge to four other nations, the United States, Denmark, Norway, and Canada, that also asserted undersea rights there. But the unprecedented feat was no mere explorer's vanity. According to the United States Geological Survey, some 25 percent of the world's oil and natural gas underlies the Arctic. The Russian president was sending dual messages: Don't underestimate Russian technology, nor Russia's resolve to compete for global riches.

It was the type of gesture that Putin watchers had come to expect during his two terms in office. He regarded himself as a man of action, and, judging by opinion polls and election results, Russians as a whole did, too. As he made preparations to leave the presidency in 2008, Putin had become the closest thing to an all-powerful czar that Russia had known since the rule of Josef Stalin. He made no secret of his intention to remain at the pinnacle of power, and found a deceptively simple way to do so. Rather than run roughshod over the Russian constitution, which forbade a third term, he anointed himself as the next prime minister, enabling him to share power with his presidential successor. True, prime ministers after the collapse of the Soviet Union had served at the sufferance of the president; Boris Yeltsin and then Putin had fired them at will. But Putin decided that it would be different with him—Russia would have a government of equals and the new president would not, could not, arbitrarily fire him.

Achieving this arrangement required a critical mass of agreement among the Kremlin hierarchy, the military, and the security services that Putin was indeed essential. The ways of power in Russia have never been wholly visible, but this critical mass could bring down a government if it wished. Its leaders must have decided that it was in their mutual interest—professionally and probably financially as well—for Putin to remain a key player. Only one matter had to be resolved: With whom would Putin share power?

Eight years earlier, Yeltsin had set a precedent by declaring that Putin would be his successor, and had relied on the power of the Kremlin to make it happen. Now Putin set about doing the same. Many outsiders predicted that the next president would be Sergei Ivanov, a three-decade-long Putin intimate from his St. Petersburg days who had the added advantage of having served two decades in the foreign service of the KGB. Those who viewed Putin's Russia as the "KGB State," as Western publications and think tanks were prone to do, thought the fifty-four-year-old Ivanov was a shoo-in.

In December 2007, however, Putin announced that he would support another intimate for the job—a forty-two-year-old St. Petersburg lawyer named Dmitri Medvedev. In the post-Soviet custom, the election was rigged far in advance; Putin systematically disqualified any opponent he wanted to sideline, and state-controlled media accorded Medvedev the same worshipful coverage that Putin had enjoyed as presidential contender. Three months later, Medvedev won with about 70 percent of the vote, almost precisely Putin's popularity rating in the country.

What explained Putin's choice of Medvedev over Ivanov? By some measures, they were evenly matched. Both had served as first deputy prime ministers and neither was known for particularly strong leadership skills. But Ivanov, the KGB veteran, seemed far more likely to win the respect of the difficult-to-handle generals and spy chiefs. Medvedev, the son of university professors and the holder of a doctorate in law, had no experience in the military or Putin's beloved intelligence agencies. Since Putin isn't going to share his innermost thoughts, here is where only informed speculation is possible: Putin must have decided that Medvedev was more likely than Ivanov to tolerate, and perhaps even embrace, a subordinate relationship with the designated prime minister.

In a chat with the *Financial Times,* Medvedev seemed to give credence to this idea. "The incumbent president is an effective leader and he's ready and able to continue to work to advance the development of our country, to make sure our development continues in the way set out eight years ago," Medvedev said. "This is why this tandem, or this team of two, was formed between the presidential candidate and the Russian president as a possible future prime minister."

Yet, one wonders if Putin was taking too much for granted. It is easy to call the undistinguished Medvedev colorless, but the same—and worse—was said of Putin himself when he took power eight years earlier. History is replete with mild-mannered understudies who became hubristic leaders once on the throne. In addition to Putin, there are the examples of Anwar el-Sadat and Hosni Mubarak of Egypt; Zia ul-Haq of Pakistan; and Kaiser Wilhelm II of Germany. Would Medvedev truly be content continuing his predecessor's policies and receiving second billing? Or would he seek more? Putin would not have been blind to that peril, but he apparently saw little cause for concern.

He and Medvedev did their best to fend off doubts about their proposed power sharing. They remarked on their history of mutual trust and noted how long they had known each other. Medvedev had worked quietly as a subordinate to Putin for some eighteen years, starting in the early 1990s, when the scholarly lawyer was a legal consultant in the office of the St. Petersburg mayor. As the story goes, when Putin became prime minister in 1999, he had no one on whom he could truly depend. So he summoned Medvedev to Moscow to be his chief administrative deputy. Then, when Putin became president, he named Medvedev chairman of Gazprom.

The latter appointment was an important demonstration of confidence, since Gazprom is Russia's strategically most important company, accounting for a quarter of all government revenue, according to 2006 tax figures. It also served as the main lever of Putin's foreign policy. When he decided to seize oligarch Vladimir Gusinsky's television station, it was Gazprom, with Medvedev at the helm, who actually took over NTV. When Putin ordered that the natural gas pipeline to Ukraine be shut down, incurring the wrath of European customers who depended on the same line for their supply, it was Medvedev's Gazprom that actually carried out the order.

The same alliance went into action in 2007 when Putin moved to reassert Moscow's power on the Caspian Sea, a longtime Russian preserve where the United States had been laboring for a decade to establish a strong Western presence.

There was nothing Putin could do on the western side of the sea—Washington had already cemented Azerbaijan's and Georgia's links to the West by successfully championing the construction of a non-Russian oil pipeline to the Mediterranean that made the region somewhat independent of Moscow. But the Americans had not yet brought the eastern side of the sea into its fold, and that's where—through Medvedev—Putin acted.

Washington was loosely championing a set of two new natural gas pipelines that would link the energy-rich eastern Caspian countries of Turkmenistan and Kazakhstan with Europe. The crowning glory would be Nabucco, a two-thousand-mile line that would reach into the heart of Europe.

Putin countered by proposing that Gazprom ship the same natural gas—from Turkmenistan and Kazakhstan—straight north into Russia, and from there on to Europe. The scheme would renew Moscow's bond with the two western Caspian states, both traditional Russian dominions, and would confound the West's attempt to deepen its penetration of the former Russian empire. Medvedev and Putin personally courted the Turkmen and the Kazakhs, and by the spring of 2008 it was clear that the Russian strategy had all but won; the two Caspian states had signed over much of their natural gas to Russia, and the transit countries in Europe had agreed as well. It appeared to be a signal Russian triumph.

How far Putin—and $100-a-barrel oil—had brought his country was demonstrated even more starkly at the annual NATO gathering in April 2008. On the agenda were applications by Ukraine and Georgia to join the Western military alliance. Many Russians felt that the West had already violated an unofficial pledge to Soviet leader Mikhail Gorbachev during the late 1980s. At that time, Moscow voluntarily withdrew its army from Eastern European states, and senior Russian officials have said they were under the impression that Poland, Hungary, and the rest would not be absorbed into NATO, which, after all, was an anti-Soviet alliance. When the West did so anyway, taking in eleven former Soviet and Eastern Bloc countries, many Russians felt betrayed and humiliated. Now President Bush was strongly backing the inclusion of two more former Soviet states, an act that would push the NATO alliance smack against Russia's western and southern territories. As Medvedev put it, "no state can be pleased about having representatives of a military bloc to which it does not belong coming close to its borders."

But this time it didn't go so smoothly. Lobbied heavily by the outgoing Russian president, Germany and France both suggested that, as a sign of respect, the alliance should delay consideration of the Ukrainian and Georgian applications until the end of the year, after Putin left office. Bush offered one of his trademark speeches about the march of freedom and the cause of liberty, but Germany, France, Italy, and others vetoed his proposal—solely because Putin objected.

That could not—and did not—happen during the time of Yeltsin, whose wishes NATO routinely ignored. Putin had not only made Europe listen; he had compelled it to act.

Russia's ascendance to a new level of influence was reflected in the difficulty encountered by a second Bush proposal at the NATO meeting—the construction of a missile-defense system in Poland and the Czech Republic. It was approved unanimously by the twenty-six members of the alliance. Yet, possibly for the first time in his presidency, Bush elected to give ground on what he had identified as a primary strategic objective. He agreed to freeze the actual deployment of the missile shield until Moscow could be brought on board, something that clearly could not be achieved before his presidency ended.

Bush then turned his dual defeats into something resembling obsequiousness by flying to Putin's vacation home in Sochi. He went there without any sign of a face-saving concession from Russia on any issue, and in violation of his own definition of when a U.S. president should put his prestige on the line by deigning to visit another country. He said only that he wanted to pave the way to a more cooperative relationship between the two countries. One would be foolish to carry this too far, but it did not seem excessive to say that, as far as Bush was concerned,

Russia had finally earned equal ranking with the world's most powerful nations; its wishes had to be respected. It was quite a turnaround for both leaders—a shot of hard-fought-for respect for Putin, and a step down for the customarily uncompromising Bush.

Some observers in the West searched for signs that Medvedev would be his own man, and his soft speaking style—along with an open fondness for the 1970s band Deep Purple—fed optimism that he would be more conciliatory toward the outside world. But Putin remarked publicly that if the West thought that Medvedev would be easier than he to deal with on foreign policy issues, it was wrong. And Medvedev agreed.

Indeed, the signs were that the long Russian continuum stretching from the time of the czars to the present would go on. There was no indication that Medvedev would inherit Putin's influence over the *siloviki,* nor that, even if Putin did relegate true control over the military and spy agencies to his successor, Medvedev would change their operating style. Medvedev expressed no misgivings about unsolved murders, the indifference of the system, or the impunity enjoyed by killers. In Medvedev's public appearances, it was difficult to find any opinions distinguishing him from Putin. Asked by *Financial Times* reporters what he had learned from Putin, Medvedev replied, among other things, that "Russia needs the maximum consolidation of power, consolidation of the Russian elite and consolidation of society. Only in this case we can attain the goals we have set in front of us."

Marina Litvinenko Carries On

Late in 2007, I dined in London with Mariane Pearl, the French widow of Danny Pearl, my *Wall Street Journal* colleague who was gruesomely murdered in Pakistan five years earlier. Mariane was writing a popular series of articles for *Glamour* magazine on women leaders around the world, and told me that she was coincidentally in town to see Marina Litvinenko. Mariane—not an easy person to impress—was obviously taken with Marina, and pushed me hard not to judge her and those close to her too harshly. I had been dismayed by some of the self-promoters who had attached themselves to Marina Litvinenko after the assassination of her husband, but I said I would take a second look.

The next day, I met with Marina for lunch. Mariane's sentiments were obviously mutual. Marina had seen photographs of Mariane with the actress Angelina Jolie and had wondered how she managed to handle Danny's murder. "It was completely incredible," Marina said. "We discovered we had very much in common. Not only in what happened to us, but in our lives in general. That we gave birth at the same age. That she used to love dancing, and that I do, too. Some of the complexities in our families. Incredible. I hope it will lay the foundation for a long-term friendship. I just hope." Who could genuinely understand what Marina Litvinenko was feeling? Perhaps only another widow, such as Mariane.

After her husband's murder, tension remained between Marina and Alexander's children from his first marriage, to Natalia. The son, Sasha, was bitter because he believed his father had died for nothing, and the daughter, Sonya, felt that she and her brother were afterthoughts in their father's second family. Alexander and Marina had hosted Sonya in England three times in the six years they were there, and Marina had thought that she and the young girl had established a rapport. But that did not seem to be the case after Alexander's murder. "Marina is making money from my father's death," Sonya said. Marina said such comments from her stepdaughter made it difficult "to speak with her right now. I'm offended."

By March 2008, Marina had given up hope that Andrei Lugovoi would be extradited to Britain to face trial. So she asked her lawyer to petition the country's coroner to hold a public inquest and reveal publicly the evidence that led it to charge Lugovoi with murdering her husband fifteen months earlier. In a first-person article in *The Times* of London, Marina said that Scotland Yard and David Miliband, Britain's foreign secretary, had advised against the petition because such a hearing could prejudice any future trial. Marina said she proceeded anyway because "I cannot wait for another ten years for a slim chance that their approach would bear fruit."

Marina was right—there seemed to be no chance that the British case against Lugovoi would advance any time soon. In the same vein, Alex Goldfarb, who had helped the Litvinenkos flee Russia, filed a freedom of information request with the U.S. Department of Energy seeking a trace on the origin of the polonium-210 used in the murder. Notwithstanding the confidence of British investigators, the Kremlin claimed that there was no hard evidence that the isotope came from Russia. But Goldfarb cited sources who had told him that the U.S. government's Lawrence Livermore National Laboratory had examined a sample of the poison, at the request of British investigators. "We hope to show the polonium originated in Russia," Goldfarb said.

The Continuing Fear

Ivan Safronov, a fifty-one-year-old retired lieutenant colonel in Russia's Space Forces, which control the country's military satellites and missile defense strategy, was one of the country's leading military analysts. By most accounts, Safronov, a military affairs reporter for *Kommersant,* Russia's leading business paper, was a happy man on March 2, 2007. He had rung up his editors to say he had a scoop on a backdoor government scheme to sell sophisticated fighter jets and missiles to Syria and Iran. The Russian officials behind the deal planned to use Belarus as the middleman state, to avoid being challenged by the West for arming nations that were under United Nations sanctions, Safronov said. A little before four p.m., Safronov arrived home after shopping for oranges, went up to the fifth floor of his apartment building, and, according to the official story, jumped to his death. Police ruled it a suicide.

Most of Safronov's colleagues were skeptical of the police account. Safronov's son, Ivan, was about to enter college, and his daughter, Irina, was pregnant with his first grandchild. As for his health, he had just had a checkup and, though his doctor warned him of an ulcer, he was told he was otherwise fine. "He had no reason to do it," said one of his editors, Ilya Bulavinov.

A few people said that in fact Safronov's mood had appeared a bit dark of late. And there was always the possibility that it was neither suicide nor foul play—that Safronov for some reason had gone out onto the ledge of the fifth-floor window for one reason or another, and fell. Yet, it was precisely his accomplishments as a reporter—revealing illegal and quasi-legal business deals involving huge sums of money—that could get a journalist into deep personal trouble. When one got in the way of a business deal, one could be in peril. In addition, Safronov was at an especially dangerous point in his reporting. He had the arms sale story already in his notebook but had yet to publish it. If those who would be damaged by the story knew that it was in hand, they might have decided to attack in hopes it would never be published.

As of the publication of this book, authorities still regarded Safronov's death as a suicide.

Unlike in past years, the Safronov case was not accompanied by a spate of other sensational deaths. After Litvinenko, there seemed to be a sort of moratorium on lurid murder in Russia. But that had not eased the apprehension of some Russian journalists. In April 2008, a former Kremlin correspondent named Yelena Tregubova obtained political asylum in Great Britain. Tregubova had gained notoriety for her 2003 book, *Tales of a Kremlin Digger*. The combination of saucy insider detail and the thirty-year-old *Kommersant* reporter's blond good looks made the book a Russian bestseller. One of her stories described a 1998 dinner with Vladimir Putin while he was FSB chief. Putin commandeered an entire sushi restaurant for the evening. Such an occurrence would normally be of no consequence, given the natural order in the Kremlin, but it attracted attention as the only thing approaching an indiscretion on Putin's public record. "I couldn't decide if he was trying to recruit me—or pick me up!" Tregubova wrote.

After the book's publication, Tregubova said she received a few verbal death threats. In February 2004, a package left outside her apartment door exploded. She was fired from *Kommersant*. Finally, she decided it was too dangerous to stay in Russia and—on the same day that Boris Yeltsin died—sought asylum in Britain. She said that she seemed to be under surveillance by a woman similar in description to one who was said to be watching Anna Politkovskaya prior to that reporter's death. "They would have found a way to kill me," Tregubova said. "That is the reality in Russia today."

Remembrance

Anna Politkovskaya's friends and family worked to keep alive her memory—and the investigation of her murder. In March 2008, Russian prosecutors said they now knew the triggerman's name and were hunting him down. But her newspaper, *Novaya Gazeta*, dismissed the announcement as a ploy meant in part to persuade a judge to continue to detain other suspects in the case. In an article, the newspaper noted that the chief police investigator had said precisely the same thing six months earlier. Her editors worried that authorities were seeking to warn Anna's killers that they could be caught soon. "It's easy to guess [that] the investigation has made significant progress. And some people [have begun] to feel anxious," the newspaper said.

Before Anna's murder, a doctor informed her daughter, Vera, that she was going to give birth to a girl. Vera and Anna discussed what to call the baby, but could not reach a decision.

Five months later, the baby was born.

There was no question what her name would be.

Anna.

AFTERWORD

As I crisscrossed America on speaking engagements after the publication of *Putin's Labyrinth*, the audiences I met were attentive and even rapt. More people than I expected were familiar with ongoing events in Russia and wanted to know more about them. But almost always, at least one person would express unease with my book's less-than-optimistic prognosis for Russia. Was the nation's future truly as bleak as I seemed to believe?

At Bard College in New York City, a young international affairs student demanded, "Why do you say that Russians are uncivilized?" The student was alluding to a passage early in the book that judged Russia to be "apart from other nations that call themselves civilized." The words were meant to apply to the actions of the Russian state, I told her, not to Russians as a people. I surely did not believe, for instance, that the thousands of Russians living in Brooklyn were poised to engage in some uncivilized act.

Yet I understood her indignation. Such a broad-brush suggestion about any nation's character can easily offend, and risk seeming polemical. That is especially so when rendered by a citizen of the United States, whose own country stands guilty of shocking outrages in Iraq and elsewhere. But in the many months since I turned in the manuscript of *Putin's Labyrinth*, the actions of Prime Minister Vladimir Putin and his government have only reinforced my conclusions.

Putin began 2009 by shutting off natural gas to more than a dozen European countries, just as he had done just two years earlier. Once again, he provoked panic across the continent, as heat and electricity shut down in all or part of Austria, Bulgaria, Hungary, Poland, Serbia, and other countries. At issue? A utility dispute with Ukraine, the transit route for 80 percent of the Russian natural gas destined for European customers. Essentially, Ukraine wanted to pay less for its own 2009 natural gas supplies than Gazprom demanded, and also sought an increase in transit tariffs for the gas passing through its pipelines to Europe. (There also was the matter of the under-the-table profits to be shared by officials on both sides, but there was no way for outsiders to know how much that amounted to.) Putin turned the affair into TV entertainment for Russians. In a national broadcast, Putin, at ease in his suburban Moscow home, listened as Gazprom CEO Alexei Miller raised the alarm. Ukraine was actually stealing Russian natural gas as it flowed to Europe, Miller said. If it continued, the loss would amount to "billions" of dollars. Russia had no choice other than to cut back the flow.

"All right, I agree. Reduce it from today," Putin ordered Miller.

Again, Putin was burnishing his credentials as Russia's ultimate champion, thumbing his nose at the West and using blunt language against yet another ungrateful Russian neighbor. ("Today's situation highlights the high criminalization of [Ukraine's] authorities," Putin said.)

But Putin's seemingly impregnable position, so reliant on Russia's new prosperity fueled by its energy exports, had become threatened since *Labyrinth* was published. The global financial crisis has sent the price of oil plummeting to levels not seen since 2004. From a peak of $147 a barrel in summer 2008, prices were down dramatically by the beginning of 2009, at one point falling to $33 a barrel. That put a huge hole in Russia's national budget. Despite prior assurances that the break-even point was $39 a barrel, the Kremlin now disclosed that the state actually required $70 to $90 a barrel to avoid budget deficits. Russia had saved almost $600 billion in a rainy-day cash reserve fund, money that Putin began to draw on. But the fund rapidly shrank by 25 percent: Putin began to pay up to $10 billion a week to keep the ruble's 18 percent decline in value from turning into a free fall (the ruble's collapse years earlier having helped lead to the cratering of Yeltsin's popularity) and to bail out favored oligarchs and companies. Indeed, it turned out that Putin's economic miracle had not been fueled entirely by Russia's oil riches, but also by hundreds of billions of dollars in bank loans from the West. In 2009 alone, Russian companies had $110 billion in foreign debt coming due. Putin agreed to spend $78 billion from the reserve to help some of the oligarchs avoid losing their property.

It was a stunning fall. Only months earlier, Russia and Putin had seemed invincible. In August, Russia went to war with its southern neighbor Georgia for five days. For a decade, Georgia and the rest of the former Soviet Caucasus and Central Asia had seemed to be an increasingly Western preserve. That was especially the case because of the construction of a thousand-mile U.S.-backed oil pipeline starting in the Azerbaijan capital of Baku, crossing Georgia, and ending at the Turkish Mediterranean port of Ceyhan. Now Russia stormed into Georgia, seeming to dare the mighty U.S. military to stop it from seizing huge swaths of the republic. For good measure, Russia dropped some four dozen bombs all around the Baku-Ceyhan pipeline, showing its former colonies how vulnerable they remained to Moscow's will.

That was Russia's peak moment. Soon, Standard & Poor's cut its rating for Russian debt for the first time in a decade. As 2009 began, Putin's popularity at home remained above 80 percent. But tens of thousands of Russians had been thrown out of work or put on a shortened weekly schedule, jeopardizing the general feeling of well-being among Russians that was pivotal to Putin's national standing.

Putin's public remarks gave no indication that he was concerned. Quite the opposite. While lashing out for good reason at the global damage done by America's lax financial oversight, he vowed that Russia would be just fine. But his actions said otherwise. He and the predictably weak president, Dmitri Medvedev, clamped down on critics and bolstered their own powers. In December 2008 and January 2009, the two eliminated jury trials for crimes against the state; moved to broaden the definition of treason to potentially include, according to critics, simply talking to a foreigner; and increased the presidential term to six years from four. One might chalk up the first two initiatives to Putin acting in character. But taken as a whole, the actions seemed to reveal a regime concerned about its longevity. Putin was preparing to crack down hard if necessary.

In the same period, Russian police raided an office of Memorial, the group devoted to documenting the murderous reign of Stalin. When I had last paid a visit, its Moscow office was lined floor to ceiling with files on the Stalin period, and its St. Petersburg office contained a dozen hard drives of scanned photographs, recorded interviews, and videos from about one hundred thousand victims and witnesses to the terror. On December 4, the police rummaged through the St. Petersburg office for several hours before leaving with the hard drives. Putin was already on record decrying what he called attempts to "impose a sense of guilt on us" because of violence in Russia's past. Irina Flige, director of the Memorial office in St. Petersburg, told journalist Charles Clover that confiscation of the hard drives was part of a government attempt to make authoritarian leadership appear legitimate by sanitizing history. "It is a war over memory," Flige said.

The two-year extension of the presidential term was especially revealing in what it seemed to portend. Medvedev said he did not intend to take advantage of it in his first term. So there seemed no credible explanation other than that the extension was intended for Putin. I recalled Vyacheslav Nikonov, the Kremlin adviser, telling me that Putin and his circle intended to remain in power through at least 2028. This extension of the presidential term would allow Putin to serve a new twelve-year stretch as president. When he would move to do so seemed to depend on circumstances. If his popularity remained high, he could relax for now, serve out his term as prime minister, and then run for the presidency in 2012. But if matters seemed on the verge of deteriorating dangerously and Putin looked to be going the way of Yeltsin in terms of low public favor, Medvedev could step down, call a snap election, and allow Putin to run for and win the presidency before his popularity dropped precipitously. In that respect, the extension seemed to be an insurance policy for Putin, and by extension Putinism.

In an essay published in January in *The New York Times*, British historian Simon Sebag Montefiore, an expert on Stalin, placed the political system into the context of Russian succession going back to Ivan. "If the Russians are happy with it, should their peculiar semi-modern, semi-medieval system concern us?" Montefiore asked. His own reply was that the Russian way of governing does concern the West, "because the whims of the system are reflected in Russia's lurchingly inconsistent foreign and military policies, which are unreadable to outsiders."

Putin had forcefully brought down the curtain on the liberalizations of the Yeltsin era. His actions now pushed Russians a few years further back, into the Soviet period. He did not go as far as trying to limit Russians' much-cherished freedom of travel, a highly unlikely move that would probably have been guaranteed to provoke a tide of disobedience. But in many other ways, Russia was reverting to its past. Oil prices would eventually recover and refill Russia's coffers. But the economic slump revealed the essential hollowness of Putin's economic boom. It turned out to be the same as the oil-driven Soviet boom of the 1970s, one that ground to a halt a few years later when oil prices plummeted and led to the 1991 Soviet collapse. Putin, too, had not built a sustainable economy. He would require more than tirades to deliver a resilient new Russian state.

ACKNOWLEDGMENTS

This book was the idea of Will Murphy, the incomparable editor at Random House. A couple of weeks after the death of Alexander Litvinenko, Will called to ask whether I saw a book in the assassination. The following discussion led to our agreement on a broader theme: what a string of untimely deaths in Russia said about the country. Will is a writer's editor. He set a tight deadline, and made me swear I would meet it, but he did not say a word when I missed that date and two additional deadlines. Will edited the manuscript with his usual smart and elegant touch. Whatever success has been achieved is largely due to Will's inspiration and support.

With Will's idea in hand, I telephoned my friend Noel Greenwood. Noel, a former senior editor with the *Los Angeles Times,* is a freelance book editor and writer's coach with whom I worked on my first book. I knew that I would need his counsel and skill to pull off the feat that Will demanded. After some hesitation on whether it was possible to write a serious book on Russia in a year, Noel signed on. He gave me the confidence to pull away from a third-person journalistic voice and write a more personal book. We worked as a tag team from beginning to end. It simply would not have been possible to write this book without Noel. His imprint is on every page.

Tom Wallace is the most loyal and supportive agent in New York. He never expressed a doubt that the book could and would meet Will's expectations. Tom, himself a talented longtime editor, read the manuscript twice in its entirety, and supplied excellent commentary that much improved the book.

At Random House, I also thank Jennifer Hershey, Jack Perry, Evan Camfield, Vanessa Mickan, and London King. Lea Beresford and Courtney Turco are wonderful professionals.

My wife, Nurilda, made me swear that I would not write another book after *The Oil and the Glory*, at least not soon—not after she and our girls had to spend a summer in Kazakhstan on their own so I could finish that book in isolation at Stanford University. But, after a bottle of pinot noir and a long chat at Cru, a wine bar near our home, Nuri wholeheartedly agreed that I must write the book. Then she supported the project more than one could hope for as I was absent either physically or mentally for a year while completing the manuscript. This book is as much Nuri's as mine. I also thank our daughters, Alisha and Ilana, for tolerating my absences and remaining cheerful throughout.

Nino Ivanishvili provided a home, meals, and wise advice in Moscow. I have known Nino for sixteen years—almost since I first arrived in the former Soviet Union—and throughout she has been among the smartest journalists in the field. Fred Harrison was a great friend and a key supporter of this book, even though we met for the first time when I arrived in London to begin the research. Fred is responsible for my getting some of the most important interviews in the book. My longtime colleagues Guy Chazan, Alan Cullison, Mike Collet-White, Monica Whitlock, Jenny Norton, and Ian McWilliam opened up their Rolodexes so I could reach the people I needed. Mary Gordon provided the names and numbers of bankers in Moscow. The owners and senior investigators at certain London detective agencies were vital in my cracking Mayfair; they have asked that their names not appear in this book, so I thank them anonymously.

Anna Chernyakovskaya was my aide-de-camp in Moscow. Anna deftly and tactfully opened up the Russian capital so that I could learn about the lives of the people profiled in this book, and about the transformation that had occurred to the city since the last time I was there. The book could not have been completed without her.

Alexander Politkovsky and Marina Litvinenko were extremely generous with their time and with introductions to others.

It is easy to make false assumptions and clumsy factual mistakes. The manuscript was read in its entirety by Guy Chazan, Tom De Waal,

Carter Page, and Tom Wallace. All rescued me from errors of fact and judgment; Carter expressed serious disagreement with some of my conclusions. I take responsibility for any errors that remain.

Dolores LeVine has supported whatever I've attempted. She did so again with this book. Thanks so much. Avery LeVine was wholeheartedly enthusiastic about the project at all times. In various ways, the book was helped immensely by Heidi Bradner, Zhenya Harrison, Doug Mazzapica, Michael McFaul, Jennifer Morgan, Seymour Philips, and Rick Webb.

NOTES

Introduction

Chapter 1: Russia's Dark Side

and Vasily Pugachyov, thirty-two, were convicted by a Qatari court of murder and sentenced to life in prison. They were let go in January 2005. On February 17, 2005, the BBC quoted a Russian prison official named Yuri Kalinin that the pair was not in any Russian prison, and that in any case the Qatari conviction was "irrelevant here in Russia" (http://news.bbc.co.uk/2/hi/europe/4275147.stm).

5 **Her most recent study** Detail and quote from author interview with Olga Kryshtanovskaya, September 3, 2007.

5 **Yuri Sinelshchikov, a former deputy** Detail and quote from author interview with Yuri Sinelshchikov, April 10, 2007.

6 **"The local attitude is, 'Shit happens' "** Author interview with Rory MacFarquar, March 20, 2007.

6 **"Life isn't straightforward here"** Author interview with Al Breach, March 19, 2007.

6 **"I would advise you"** Author interview with Alexei Miller, August 28, 2007.

6–7 **"People say that Russians"** Author interview with Alexander Kamenskii, September 3, 2007.

7 **Russia's first crowned czar** Physical description of Ivan from Robert Payne and Nikita Romanoff, *Ivan the Terrible* (New York: Crowell, 1975), 215.

7 **"thrust into his fundament through his"** Edward Augustus Bond, *Russia at the Close of the Sixteenth Century* (London: Hakluyt Society, 1861 reprint of 1591 manuscript of Sir Jerome Horsey), 173. Horsey was an agent of the Russia Company and was described as having lived in Moscow more or less continually from 1575 to 1591.

7 **"cut off his nose, his tongue"** Benson Bobrick, *Fearful Majesty* (New York: Putnam, 1987), 207.

7 **Convinced that one Prince Vladimir** Payne and Romanoff, *Ivan the Terrible*, 263–64.

8 **"to make an example"** Robert K. Massie, *Peter the Great* (New York: Alfred A. Knopf, 1980), 270.

8 **"In case also that anyone"** Ibid., 726.

9 **Josef Stalin executed nearly all** Number of dead under Stalin from Robert Conquest, *The Great Terror* (London: Pimlico, repr. 1994), 286, 339.

9 **"teacher, teacher"** Simon Sebag Montefiore, *Stalin: The Court of the Red Tsar* (London: Weidenfeld & Nicolson, 2003), 350.

9 **"constantly compared his terror"** Ibid.

9 **"he should have killed"** Ibid., 206.

9 **"victorious Russian rulers"** Pavel and Anatoli Sudoplatov with Jerrold L. and Leona P. Schecter, *Special Tasks* (Boston: Little, Brown, 1994), 5.

9 **Indeed, his book is a** Assassinations as described in Sudoplatov et al. *Special Tasks,* 27, 46–49, 67–83.

9 **Dressed in a silk scarf and a** Detail and quotes from author interview with Musa Eitington Malinovskaya, August 30, 2007.

10 **Another defector, Bulgarian novelist** Description of Georgy Markov's assassination based on the documentary *Umbrella Assassin* (PBS, 2006). Markov was jabbed on September 7, 1978, and died four days later, on September 11, 1978.

11 **In summer 1993, three gunmen** *The New York Times,* August 16, 1993.

11 **In April 1995, two gunmen killed** *The New York Times,* June 7, 1995.

11 **And in November 1996** *The New York Times,* November 11, 1996.

11 **In a 1994 case, police came** *The New York Times,* December 11, 1994.

Chapter 2: How Putin Got Elected

14 **"a mixture between"** John Lloyd, *The New York Times Magazine,* August 15, 1999.

14 **The story of Vladimir Putin's ascent** The number of Yeltsin's heart attacks had been a closely held secret until Yeltsin disclosed it in a January 2004 interview with RIA Novosti, the Russian news agency, according to a BBC dispatch, January 20, 2004.

15 **In recent months, allegations had surfaced** Sharon LaFraniere, *The Washington Post,* September 8, 1999.

16 **"a man of"** Oleg Kalugin, quoted by Paul Klebnikov, *Godfather of the Kremlin* (Orlando, Fla.: Harcourt, 2000), 297.

17 **By the end of 2006** Olga Kryshtanovskaya, quoted by Reuters, December 15, 2006.

18 **"I think the best plan would"** Mikhail Fridman, quoted by John Lloyd, *The New York Times Magazine,* October 8, 2000.

19 **Yeltsin warned that** Boris Yeltsin, quoted by CNN, April 9, 1999.

19 **"transformed the Russian political"** Klebnikov, *Godfather of the Kremlin,* 302.

20 "Ryazan was planned" David Satter, *Darkness at Dawn* (New Haven: Yale University Press, 2003), n265.

20 "those who needed another" Ibid., 69.

21 Opposition lawmaker Vladimir Golovlyov Vladimir Golovlyov was killed August 21, 2002; Sergei Yushenkov and Yuri Shchekochikhin were killed on April 17, 2003, and July 3, 2003, respectively. Mikhail Trepashkin was jailed on October 22, 2003.

23 "There are no people" Vladimir Putin, quoted in *The New York Times,* February 2, 2002.

24 Russia possessed 26 percent of BP Statistical Review of World Energy 2007.

24 As prime minister, Putin Andrew Jack, *Inside Putin's Russia* (London: Granta Books, 2004), 14.

24 "This profession employs" Vladimir Putin, quoted in *The Washington Post,* December 22, 2006.

Chapter 3: Getting to Know The Putin

27 Europe was an important energy BP Statistical Review of World Energy 2006. It is understood by energy experts that Europe's reliance on Russian natural gas did not diminish in 2007 and 2008.

28 According to the SOVA Center Statistics from the SOVA Center are at http://xeno.sova-center.ru/6BA2468.

29 He thought Washington simply didn't understand Quotes, paraphrases, and detail from author's interview with "Viktor," August 29, 2007.

31 "I heard it from the Kremlin" Author interview with Vyacheslav Nikonov, April 29, 2007.

31 "overstepped its national borders" Vladimir Putin, quoted in official transcript of his February 10, 2007, speech before the 43rd Munich Conference on Security Policy.

31 When the United States said February 21, 2007, in *The Washington Post.*

33 "Gentlemen, Russia has" Sergei Yastrzhembsky, quoted in *International Herald Tribune,* February 22, 2007.

34 "Putin may be back" Author interview with Vyacheslav Nikonov.

35 "everything is the state" Author interview with Boris Volodarsky, February 28, 2007.

Chapter 4: Nikolai

36   "copper-colored skin was"   Nikolai Khokhlov, *In the Name of Conscience* (New York: David McKay, 1959), 353.

37   "artistic whistler"   Ibid., 13.

38   In short order, Nikolai signed   Sudoplatov et al., *Special Tasks*, 35.

38   "Kube is killed"   Khokhlov, *In the Name of Conscience*, 71, 73, 75.

38   "kill a man whose"   Ibid., 54.

40   "blond, blue-eyed good looks"   Sudoplatov et al., *Special Tasks*, 247–48.

40   "a young Sudoplatov"   Nikolai Khokhlov spoke in person and by phone and communicated via e-mail numerous times during 2007. This particular quote came from a telephone interview with the author on June 9, 2007.

40   "I have big plans for you"   Khokhlov, *In the Name of Conscience*, 95.

40   "if he admitted"   Author interview with Nikolai Khokhlov.

41   "the finest and most"   Khokhlov, *In the Name of Conscience*, 184–85.

41   "didn't care"   Author interview with Nikolai Khokhlov.

41   "short-witted"   Khokhlov, *In the Name of Conscience*, 216.

41   "apparently a very good man"   Ibid., 201–02.

42   "Is it possible that this"   Ibid., 240.

42   "I've come to you from"   Ibid., 246.

42   "rigorous questioning"   Author interview with Thomas Polgar, intelligence adviser to CIA station chief at the time, July 21, 2007.

42   he was a high-value catch   Based on author interview with David E. Murphy, who was in charge of Soviet affairs for the CIA in Munich at the time of Nikolai's defection, July 21, 2007.

43   "blow for blow"   Khokhlov, *In the Name of Conscience*, 318.

43   "keep Yana in the embassy"   Khokhlov, *In the Name of Conscience*.

43   "I was desperate"   Author interview with Nikolai Khokhlov.

43   "a slight, scholarly-appearing blond"   Reporter quoted in *The New York Times*, April 23, 1954.

43   "Nobody went to your family"   Khokhlov, *In the Name of Conscience*, 345.

44   "say anything"   Author interview with Thomas Polgar, July 20, 2007.

44   "he was never told"   Author interview with David E. Murphy.

45   "nauseatingly friendly"   This quote and details of the telephone calls and Yana's sentence are from an unpublished addendum to *In the Name of Conscience*, provided to the author by Nikolai Khokhlov.

46   **"things began to whirl"**   Khokhlov, *In the Name of Conscience,* 350.

46   **"To be honest, it's hopeless"**   Ibid., 357.

46   **He later told crusading**   Anna Politkovskaya, *Novaya Gazeta,* July 1, 2004.

46   **"due to poisoning, probably"**   *The New York Times,* October 15, 1957.

47   **"square accounts"**   Khokhlov, *In the Name of Conscience,* 354.

47   **"disgusted"**   Author interview with Nikolai Khokhlov.

47   **"done everything right"**   Author interview with Nikolai Khokhlov.

Chapter 5: *Nord-Ost*

50   **Five years later**   Unless otherwise noted, detail and quotes throughout this chapter are from separate author interviews with Ilya Lysak, Irina Fadeeva, Elena Baranovskaya, and their families. The interviews were conducted on May 4, 2007, and May 5, 2007 (Lysak); May 3, 2007 (Fadeeva); and April 14, 2007 (Baranovskaya). In addition, the author interviewed Fadeeva and Baranovskaya at a dinner of the Nord-Ostsi (the "People of *Nord-Ost*") on August 30, 2007.

52   **Among the lucky ones was Alim**   Detail and quotes from author interviews with Alim and Zauddin Tlupov, August 26, 1997.

55   **Anna entered the lobby area**   Quotes and detail from Anna Politkovskaya's account of her visit, *Novaya Gazeta,* October 28, 2002. I relied on a translation approved by Politkovskaya and published on the website of the International Women's Media Foundation (http://www.iwmf.org/features/anna/).

57   **Anna telephoned a trusted friend**   Quotes and detail of exchange with Dima Muratov and Alexander Voloshin from author interview with Muratov, September 4, 2007.

57   **"You'll help him"**   Elena Baranovskaya quoted by Anna Politkovskaya, *Novaya Gazeta,* October 23, 2003.

59   **The assault had been organized with**   Mark Franchetti, *The Sunday Times* (London), November 3, 2002.

59   **Still, after the fentanyl was released**   Detail on the continued pumping of fentanyl into the theater is from a former senior Kremlin official who observed the decision-making on the use of the gas firsthand. He spoke to the author on condition of anonymity so as to preserve his relations within the Kremlin.

62   **A former Kremlin official who had**   Ibid.

63   **"The gas was rather harmless"**   Author interview with Vyacheslav Nikonov.

63   **Yuri Sinelshchikov, a former deputy**   Quotes and detail from author interview with Yuri Sinelshchikov.

63   **Anna Politkovskaya had her suspicions**   Politkovskaya's interview with Khanpasha Terkibayev, *Novaya Gazeta,* April 28, 2003.

64   **After the interview, Terkibayev**   Natalya Serova, *Politkom.ru,* April 29, 2003.

65   **"taken me by a finger"**   Irina Fadeeva quoted by Anna Politkovskaya, *Novaya Gazeta,* November 25, 2002.

66   **"a severe wound in our heart"**   Vladimir Putin quoted by RFE-RL on October 23, 2003. Putin was in Kyrgyzstan when he issued the statement on the anniversary.

Chapter 6: The Exiles

68   **This somewhat vain political**   Boris Shikhmuradov was arrested in Turkmenistan either on December 25 or December 26, 2002. His arrest was announced the latter day.

72   **"doesn't go out to cleanse"**   Background on Russian gangs and quote from author interview with Mark Galeotti, February 25, 2007.

73   **"have hotter blood so are"**   Author interview with Natalia Litvinenko, September 1, 2007. She and her two children with Alexander Litvinenko—their son, also named Alexander Litvinenko, and daughter, Sonya—also met for lengthy interviews with the author's assistant, Anna Chernyakovskaya, May 26, 2007.

73   **"felt sidelined"**   Alex Goldfarb and Marina Litvinenko, *Death of a Dissident* (New York: Free Press, 2007), 21–22.

74   **The two met when Litvinenko**   Ibid., 29–31.

74   **"[T]hey developed a bond shared"**   Ibid., 37.

74   **"You will be the one to"**   Ibid., 124.

75   **"grave threat to our country"**   Ibid.

75   **Yet Litvinenko decided that Berezovsky**   Detail of the men's and Berezovsky's initial actions from whistle-blowers' news conference, November 17, 1998; and Goldfarb and Litvinenko, *Death of a Dissident,* 122–24, 130–34.

76   **Litvinenko and the other whistle-blowers**   Information on the thinking of the whistle-blowers from author interview with Yuri Felshtinsky, June 14, 2007.

76   **"thoughtless statements"**   Goldfarb and Litvinenko, *Death of a Dissident,* 145.

76 **"a strange-looking man who"** Quotes and detail from author interview with Felshtinsky.

77 **"used for settling scores"** Alexander Litvinenko's statement quoted on "How to Poison a Spy," *Panorama,* BBC television broadcast, January 22, 2007.

77 **"extraordinary"** *The Independent* (London), November 18, 1998.

77 **"Moscow has talked of"** *The New York Times,* November 21, 1998.

77 **"internal scandals public"** Vladimir Putin quoted by Yelena Tregubova in Goldfarb and Litvinenko, *Death of a Dissident,* 160–61.

77 **"was glad to have me"** Quotes and detail from author interview with Felshtinsky. Felshtinsky's account in general coincides with that presented in *Death of a Dissident.*

79 **"Berezovsky was winning"** Author interview with Felshtinsky.

79 **Felshtinsky's recollection is that** Quotes and detail from author interview with Felshtinsky.

80 **According to *Death of a Dissident*** Goldfarb and Litvinenko, *Death of a Dissident,* 219–20.

80 **Not too long after, Natalia Litvinenko** Author interview with Natalia Litvinenko.

80 **"You know we have"** Detail and quotes from author interview with Felshtinsky. The account does not conflict with *Death of a Dissident,* which relates Alex Goldfarb's role in Litvinenko's flight.

81 **"Tell me Boris, I don't . . ."** Goldfarb and Litvinenko, *Death of a Dissident,* 210–11. In an April 24, 2006, interview with the author, Berezovsky said that the book could be regarded as a completely factual account of events in which he was a participant. I regarded the book as one from the perspective of the Berezovsky camp.

82 **"If we don't go to the American embassy"** Quotes and detail on Litvinenko's escape from author interview with Felshtinsky. The account generally coincides with the Goldfarb account in *Death of a Dissident.*

84 **Felshtinsky and Goldfarb began instantly** Detail and quotes from author interview with Felshtinsky. Information on Marina Litvinenko's feelings of betrayal from author interview with Marina Litvinenko, April 24, 2006.

84 **"They're here already . . ."** Goldfarb and Litvinenko, *Death of a Dissident,* 11.

84 **"I won't go alive"** Ibid., 12.

85 **"You left Tbilisi"** Detail and quotes from author interview with Felshtinsky.

85 "We can't be subject"   Author interview with Felshtinsky.

85 Goldfarb left to his   Goldfarb and Litvinenko, *Death of a Dissident*, 15–18.

85 Berezovsky put up Litvinenko   Detail on allowance from author interview with Marina Litvinenko.

86 "quite a positive figure"   Quotes and background from author interviews with Oleg Gordievsky, February 7, 2007, and February 27, 2007.

87 Like Nikolai Khokhlov, Gordievsky   Background on the Gordievsky family's flight to London from "Family Joins K.G.B. Spy in London," Reuters, September 7, 1991.

87 "She wanted the money"   Detail and quotes from author interview with Gordievsky.

Chapter 7: The Crusading American

88 A descendant of czarist-era aristocrats   Detail about Klebnikov's accent from author interview with Maxim Kashulinsky, May 4, 2007.

89 "We're fighting for Mother Russia"   Song quoted in *New York* magazine, October 25, 2004.

89 His family's Manhattan apartment   Atmosphere of Klebnikov's upbringing from Otto Pohl, "The Assassination of the Dream," *New York* magazine, October 25, 2004; Nicholas Stein, "The American Who Knew Too Much," *Men's Vogue*, August 21, 2006. Klebnikov's wife, Musa, recommended the two articles to the author as authoritative accounts of her husband's life.

89 He visited Institut Le Rosey   Paul Klebnikov, *Forbes*, July 5, 1999.

89 "a handful of clerics"   Paul Klebnikov, *Forbes*, July 21, 2003.

90 "a gangster state"   Paul Klebnikov, *Forbes*, November 1, 1999.

90 "replete with bankrupt companies"   Klebnikov, *Godfather of the Kremlin*, 4.

90 "If it is hard for westerners"   Klebnikov, *Godfather of the Kremlin*, 6.

91 "Most journalists think of themselves"   James Michaels quoted in *Men's Vogue*, August 21, 2006.

91 "He had this messianic belief"   William Baldwin quoted in *New York* magazine, October 25, 2004.

91 The Russian edition of *Godfather*   Sales figures of the two books obtained in an author interview with Valeri Streletsky, Klebnikov's Russian publisher, May 3, 2007.

92 "He was doing investigative stories" Author interview with Leonid Bershidsky, May 3, 2007.

92 "I don't know if" Quoted in *New York* magazine, October 25, 2004.

93 "spend a month on a" Author interview with Bershidsky.

93 Streletsky told me that Klebnikov Author interview with Streletsky.

93 "were marred by the assassination" Klebnikov, *Godfather of the Kremlin,* 4.

94 Klebnikov also overexerts himself Ibid., 298–302.

94 "didn't really understand what" Author interview with Alexander Politkovsky, April 18, 2007.

94 "He was naïve. He worshipped Russia" Author interview with Oleg Panfilov, March 25, 2007.

95 "Everything is topsy-turvy" Author interview with Berezovsky.

95 For his part, Berezovsky sank tens Figures on Berezovsky's spending to oust Putin from Goldfarb and Litvinenko, *Death of a Dissident,* 316.

96 "to demonstrate in the West" Author interview with Berezovsky.

96 "Russia's flawed transition from Communism" Paul Klebnikov, *Forbes,* March 17, 2003.

97 "Dynamism is one of the core" Paul Klebnikov, *Forbes Russia,* May 2004; repr. *Forbes,* July 22, 2004.

97 "too much an apologist for" Author interview with Mark Franchetti, January 21, 2008.

97 He made a series of phone Detail on calls from *Men's Vogue,* August 21, 2006.

97 A man inside the vehicle pointed Some accounts speak of two weapons being fired. Absent an ironclad account of who precisely shot, I am using the single-shooter account.

97 A guard rushed into the *Newsweek* Account of aftermath to Klebnikov's killing from author interviews with Alexander Gordeev, April 19, 2007, and Mikhail Fishman, August 29, 2007, in addition to Gordeev's written account, e-mailed to author by Gordeev.

98 "None of us ever had" Author interview with Kashulinsky.

99 "I think Putin himself called" Ibid.

99 "Not long ago one" Vladimir Putin, annual news conference, official Kremlin transcript, February 1, 2007.

100 "Nukhayev had no role" Author interview with Streletsky.

100 **Once in custody, both suspects** Author interview with a Russian journalist who asked not to be identified because he feared losing access to his police sources.

100 **"big job"** Quoted in *Forbes,* May 5, 2006.

100 **Franchetti figured that a journalist** Author interview with Franchetti.

Chapter 8: Murder on an Elevator

103 **"Putin has, by chance"** Anna Politkovskaya, *Putin's Russia* (New York: Henry Holt, 2004), 242–44.

104 **"made her name by writing"** Yuri Zarakhovich, *Time,* April 13, 2003.

104 **"one of the bravest of Russia's"** James Meek, *Guardian,* October 15, 2004.

104 **"We cannot just sit back"** Politkovskaya, *Putin's Russia,* 255.

105 **In a 2001 story, she berated** Anna Politkovskaya, *Novaya Gazeta.*

105 **"Paul Lavurda had been deserted"** Quote and details from Politkovskaya, *Putin's Russia,* 4–13.

105 **In class, Anna's best friends** Author interview with Masha Khaykina, April 15, 2007.

106 **Their relationship puzzled her** Author interviews with Khaykina, and with Elena Morozova, May 2, 2007.

106 **Over beers after Anna's death** Author interview with Alexander Politkovsky.

106 **One friend recalled her behaving** Author interview with Morozova.

106 **The two married after** Information that Anna was pregnant from author interview with Politkovsky.

106 **Her upper-crust parents were so** Wedding-day detail and that parents cut off Anna and Alexander financially from author interview with Morozova.

106 **"telling them how to work"** Author interview with Morozova.

106 **But Anna was mesmerized** Information about Anna's admiration for Marina Tsvetayeva, from author interview with Politkovsky.

106 **Alexander had earned a toehold** Detail on how the couple was scraping by and on Politkovsky's instant celebrity from author interviews with Morozova and Politkovsky.

107 **The resulting documentary, entitled** Marina Goldovskaya, the filmmaker, was a professor of Politkovsky's at Moscow State Uni-

versity. The documentary was financed by Turner Network Television. Goldovskaya is currently a professor at the University of California, at Los Angeles.

107   **"a crazy mom, very"**   Author interview with Elena Kudimova, March 26, 2007.

107   **"That note isn't right"**   Author interview with Morozova.

107   **As his television career flourished**   Detail on Alexander's drinking and Anna's attitude toward it from author interview with Morozova.

108   **She wanted a career in television like**   Detail on Anna's career desires and feeling that Alexander blocked her way from author interview with Morozova.

108   **She was nearly blind without**   Author interview with Morozova, to whom Anna made the remark about her glasses.

109   **"a dragon in her blood"**   Author interview with Morozova.

109   **"slaves to tobacco"**   Anna Politkovskaya, *Novaya Gazeta,* June 14, 1999.

109   **"infringing on my rights"**   Author interview with Morozova.

109   **"but next to Anna, I am"**   Author interview with Yevgenia Albats, April 15, 2007.

109   **"I'm coming by with the dishes"**   Author interview with Elena Baranovskaya, April 14, 2007.

110   **"Now dead, Vakha lies"**   Anna Politkovskaya, *A Small Corner of Hell* (Chicago: University of Chicago Press, 2003), 35.

110   **"psychopathic and extremely stupid"**   Anna Politkovskaya, *A Russian Diary* (New York: Random House, 2007), 134, 167–68.

111   **"she started liking it"**   Author interview with Yuri Kudimov, husband of Politkovskaya's sister, Elena, April 29, 2007.

112   **"I'm afraid a lot"**   Anna Politkovskaya interview with *Rzeczpospolita* (Polish daily newspaper), April 27, 2002.

112   **"the details of the interrogations"**   Anna Politkovskaya, *Guardian,* February 27, 2001.

112   **Lapin said he was coming**   Author interview with Dmitri Muratov, April 19, 2007.

112   **Anna's editor ordered her to stay**   Anna Politkovskaya interview with Committee to Protect Journalists, November 13, 2001.

112   **Soon her children**   Ibid.

112   **"The people in Chechnya are afraid"**   Anna Politkovskaya, *Guardian,* February 27, 2001.

112   **In fact, she did not believe**   Detail on Anna Politkovskaya's belief that she was safe in Chechnya from author interview with her son, Ilya Politkovsky, April 27, 2007.

113   **She telephoned Akhmed Zakayev**   Detail on Anna's reaction from Sergey Sokolov and Dmitry Muratov, *Novaya Gazeta,* September 4, 2004.

113   **"Are you Anna Politkovskaya?"**   Author interview with Elena Baranovskaya, to whom Anna recounted the incident.

113   **According to Anna's account**   Anna Politkovskaya, *Novaya Gazeta,* September 9, 2004.

113   **"beat me on the face and"**   Anna Politkovskaya quoted by *Newsnight,* BBC, September 13, 2004.

113   **"almost hopeless"**   Anna Politkovskaya, *Novaya Gazeta,* September 9, 2004.

113   **Anna was irritated at her**   Author interview with Baranovskaya.

114   **She told the onetime KGB officer**   Author interview with Marina Litvinenko, Alexander's wife.

114   **"Think about that"**   Author interview with Kudimov.

115   **"at the point of breaking"**   Quotes and foreign visitor anecdote from author interview with Morozova. In an interview with the author, Kudimov confirmed the details.

116   **"I am a pariah"**   Anna Politkovskaya, *The Washington Post,* October 15, 2006.

117   **"If you want to go on"**   Anna Politkovskaya, *Guardian,* September 9, 2004.

117   **"I know this is all going"**   Author interview with Baranovskaya, to whom Anna made the remark.

117   **"I know I am not going"**   Author interview with Yevgenia Albats, to whom Anna made the remark.

117   **"feel that this woman knew"**   Author interview with Mariane Pearl.

117   **"I'm putting this document here"**   Author interview with Vera Politkovskaya, May 2, 2007.

117   **"whose job, to say it softly"**   Author interview with Sergei Lapin, April 14, 2007.

117   **"One could hardly believe"**   Author interview with Vera Politkovskaya.

118   **"She never simply promised"**   Author interview with Vera Politkovskaya.

118   **"return to a normal life"**   Author interview with Khaykina.

118   **"Stalin of our times"**   Anna Politkovskaya interview with RFE-RL on October 5, 2006.

118   **"You are close"**   Detail of October 7, 2006, and quote from author interview with Vera Politkovskaya.

119 **A man in a baseball cap** Details of murder from *The Independent* (London), October 8, 2006. All credible accounts coincide on these details.

119 **Vera didn't believe** Author interview with Vera Politkovskaya.

119 **Anna's friend from childhood** Detail and quote from author interview with Morozova.

119 **Elena telephoned Masha Khaykina** Detail and quote from author interviews with Morozova and Khaykina.

119 **"Oi, Alexander, I have"** Author interview with Marina Litvinenko.

119 **Vladimir Putin was at** Author interview with Yuri Kudimov, who knew of the birthday party from his KGB friends.

119 **"influence on the country's"** Vladimir Putin, quoted by the BBC News online, October 10, 2006.

119 **Oleg Panfilov, with whom I worked** Author interview with Panfilov.

121 **A while after Anna's death** Author interview with Fadeeva.

Chapter 9: The Traitor

122 **"My name is Alexander Litvinenko"** Alexander Litvinenko, appearance at the Frontline Club, YouTube videotape, October 19, 2006.

123 **"like a person in a bazaar"** Author interview with Marina Litvinenko.

124 **His interrogation of a Chechen teenager** Goldfarb and Litvinenko, *Death of a Dissident,* 89–90.

124 **"He thought everyone was working"** Author interview with Felshtinsky.

124 **"The view inside our"** Litvinenko quoted in *The New York Times,* December 16, 2004.

124 **"his bosses learned that"** Alexander Litvinenko, *ChechenPress,* July 5, 2006.

124 **Some who knew him said Litvinenko** This was a consistent assertion of those close to Anna. One of them was Ilya Politkovsky, Anna's son, who expressed this opinion in an interview with the author.

125 **He rang the London police** British authorities briefly arrested Andrei Ponkin and Alexei Alyokhin after Litvinenko alleged that they had attempted to recruit him to help murder Putin, according to Interfax news service, October 21, 2003. Ponkin, who was one of

the FSB whistle-blowers in the famous November 1998 news conference, said he met with Litvinenko and Boris Berezovsky to discuss a business affair, when they were introduced to British intelligence officials who attempted to get them to defect.

125   **Yet he had solid sources**   Separate author interviews with Marina Litvinenko and Oleg Gordievsky.

125   **Yet Litvinenko found an ear in**   Background on Litvinenko's cooperation with British intelligence from a well-connected source who discussed it on condition of anonymity.

126   **"There is no need to analyze"**   Boris Labusov quoted by Interfax, September 4, 2003.

126–27   **"Discussing our involvement is really"**   Boris Labusov quoted by *Nezavisimaya Gazeta,* October 18, 2004.

127   **"History knows a lot of cases"**   Boris Labusov quoted by Interfax, October 16, 2004.

127   **FSB marksmen used large photographs**   The story of Litvinenko's image being used in target practice by Russian special forces broke in Poland's *Dziennik Online,* January 30, 2007.

127   **The Russian embassy left a**   Author interview with Marina Litvinenko.

127   **"all matters linked to Litvinenko"**   Mikhail Trepashkin quotes and detail by Mark Franchetti, *The Times* (London), December 9, 2007.

128   **"Every time I publish something on"**   Quote and detail from Julia Svetlichnaja, *The Observer,* December 3, 2006.

128   **"He was probably thinking"**   Author interview with Felshtinsky.

128   **"I can really do well"**   Quote and detail from author interview with Marina Litvinenko.

129   **"We ourselves could have"**   Ibid.

129   **One of his notable**   Author interview with a source familiar with the firm who asked not to be identified.

129   **"Sasha, if I deposited my"**   Author interview with Felshtinsky.

130   **"demanded considerable attention"**   Author interview with Berezovsky.

130   **"something that could wait"**   Author interview with Felshtinsky.

131   **On January 23, 2006, Berezovsky**   Description of birthday party from author interview with Felshtinsky; detail on Lugovoi's relationship with Litvinenko from author interview with Marina Litvinenko.

132   **Litvinenko was an FSB officer**   In a series of long interviews with Mark Franchetti of *The Sunday Times* (London), Lugovoi

claimed that Litvinenko had called *him* prior to Berezovsky's sixtieth birthday seeking a business relationship. Franchetti's story on the interviews was published in the paper on November 25, 2007.

132 **Lugovoi provided a background report** Author interview with a source familiar with the attitude at Titon; the source wished not to be identified.

132 **"those slandering the"** Law quoted in "Russia law on killing 'extremists' abroad," BBC online, November 27, 2006.

133 **"traitor"** Litvinenko's former supervisor at the FSB, Alexander Gusak, quoted in "Litvinenko 'a traitor'—ex-boss," BBC online, February 7, 2007.

133 **"I was there with him a"** Vladimir Bukovsky, speaking in documentary by Jos de Putter, VPRO, 2007.

133 **"He believed that he would"** Marina Litvinenko quoted by *Kommersant,* December 21, 2006.

134 **"I'm British," he said elatedly** Author interview with Felshtinsky; Andrei Nekrasov speaking in VPRO documentary of 2007.

134 **When his father, Valter** Valter Litvinenko, quoted in *Poison Plot: The Killing of a Spy,* CNN, December 4, 2006.

134 **"expecting an attack, an assassination"** Yevgeni Limarev, interview with Red TV (Moscow), December 23, 2006.

134 **"Are you in town to see"** Author interview with Felshtinsky.

135 **"transfer 100,000 pounds"** Quote and detail from Spiegel Online, December 11, 2006.

135 **"I'm about to get information"** Akhmed Zakayev, speaking in VPRO documentary of 2007.

135 **Litvinenko had served as a source** Maxim Litvinenko, Alexander Litvinenko's brother, quoted by Reuters, January 5, 2007.

135 **Scaramella handed over** The e-mail was provided to Scaramella by Yevgeny Limarev, a Russian émigré who lives in France.

135–36 **who just the night before** Author interview with Berezovsky.

136 **The two had agreed that** Litvinenko's cut is according to Andrei Lugovoi, quoted by Mark Franchetti in *The Sunday Times.*

Chapter 10: Polonium

137 **"This is the No. 1 security issue"** Peter Castenfelt quoted in *USA Today,* July 28, 2006. The ads appeared in the newspapers on the previous day.

138 **He turned into the Pine Bar** Detail on Norberto Andrade and the serving of Litvinenko's tea from *Evening Standard,* November 6, 2007. Detail on the drinks and cigar smoking from Spiegel Online,

December 11, 2006. Detail on Lugovoi's family's plans from *The Washington Post,* December 13, 2006.

138 **He went to bed** Detail on Litvinenko's condition from Marina Litvinenko interview with Natalia Gevorkian, *Kommersant,* December 21, 2006. In terms of the poisoning itself, the interview was, in my opinion, the most complete of dozens in which Marina participated. In its main points, it coincided with the other interviews she gave. Since the thrust of her comments was virtually identical in all her interviews, I relied on those published accounts and skipped over the subject of the poisoning entirely when we twice met, so as to avoid repetition. This allowed me to cover topics that other interviewers had not.

139 **"Look," he told the reporter** Alexander Litvinenko interviewed by BBC Russian Service, November 11, 2006.

140 **"It was so strange"** Marina Litvinenko interview with *Kommersant.*

141 **"Ex-spy's poisoning bears hallmarks"** *The Daily Telegraph,* November 21, 2006.

141 **"Different name, same tactics"** *Guardian,* November 21, 2006.

141 **"Exact Cause of Ex-K.G.B. Agent's"** *The New York Times,* November 22, 2006.

141 **"looked just like a ghost"** Andrei Nekrasov, quoted in VPRO documentary of 2007.

141 **"like a seventy-year-old"** Goldfarb and Litvinenko, *Death of a Dissident,* 329.

141 **"Oh, Marinochka, I love you"** Marina Litvinenko interview with *Kommersant.*

141 **"Father, I've converted. I'm a Muslim"** Valter Litvinenko quoted in VPRO documentary of 2007.

141 **"Come quickly"** Marina Litvinenko interview with *Kommersant.*

141 **"You have shown yourself to"** Alexander Goldfarb reading Alexander Litvinenko's statement, November 23, 2006.

145 **"You have to understand that"** Marina Litvinenko interview with *Kommersant.*

146 **"Marina, this is Andrei Lugovoi"** Ibid.

147 **"He joined the FSB from"** Author interview with Josef Linder, April 18, 2007.

147 **"Negative. The most negative."** Author interview with Mikhail Golovatov, April 17, 2007.

148 **"offer no indication that this"** Vladimir Putin, official transcript of news conference following a Russia–European Union summit meeting, November 24, 2006.

148 **Novelist Martin Cruz Smith** Cruz Smith quoted in *The Wall Street Journal Europe,* December 29, 2006.

149 **"Let's get one thing"** Author interview with Boris Volodarsky, February 28, 2007.

151 **"a typical KGB operation"** Author interview with Oleg Gordievsky.

151 **"It's quite possible each guy"** Author interview with Professor Nick Priest. I interviewed Priest numerous times in person and by phone. This interview took place February 15, 2007.

152 **"That's Russian"** Author interview with a former MI6 agent who asked not to be identified by name because of a condition placed upon him when retiring from the agency, February 9, 2007.

154 **"Lugovoi has often asked me"** Mark Franchetti, *The Sunday Times* (London), November 25, 2007.

Epilogue

157 **As Vladimir Putin's presidency** Detail on the dive from National Geographic News online, August 3, 2007.

159 **"The incumbent president is an"** Dmitri Medvedev quoted in *Financial Times,* March 24, 2008.

159 **As the story goes** Some said that in effect Putin himself was chairman of Gazprom, pulling the strings behind the scenes. That may have been true—outsiders could not know for certain what went on in the Kremlin.

161 **"no state can be pleased"** Dmitri Medvedev quoted in *Financial Times,* March 24, 2008.

162 **But Putin remarked publicly** Quoted in the *Daily Telegraph,* March 3, 2008.

162 **And Medvedev agreed** Quoted in *Financial Times,* March 24, 2008.

162 **"Russia needs the maximum"** Dmitri Medvedev quoted in *Financial Times,* March 24, 2008.

163 **"It was completely incredible"** Quotes from author interview with Marina Litvinenko.

163 **"Marina is making money from"** Quote from Sonya Litvinenko interview with Anna Chernyakovskaya, author's assistant.

163 **"to speak with her right"** Author interview with Marina Litvinenko.

163 **By March 2008, Marina** Detail and quote from Marina Litvinenko from *The Times* (London), March 27, 2008.

163   **In the same vein, Alex Goldfarb**   Detail and quote from Alex Goldfarb from Reuters, February 28, 2008.

164   **"He had no reason to"**   Ilya Bulavinov, *Kommersant,* April 10, 2007.

165   **"I couldn't decide if he"**   Yelena Tregubova quoted by BBC News online, November 21, 2003.

165   **"They would have found a way"**   Yelena Tregubova quoted by the *Daily Mail* (London), April 4, 2008.

165   **But her newspaper, *Novaya Gazeta***   Detail and quote from *Novaya Gazeta,* April 2, 2008.

166   **Before Anna's murder, a doctor**   Detail on how Vera decided to name her daughter from author's interview with Vera Politkovskaya.

Afterword

168   **"All right, I agree"**   Alexei Miller and Putin quoted in *Financial Times,* January 11, 2009.

168   **"Today's situation highlights"**   Putin quoted by *Los Angeles Times,* January 9, 2009.

168   **Russia had saved almost**   Economic data from "The Putin Defense," *Financial Times,* December 29, 2008; and "Oligarchs Seek $78 Billion as Credit Woes Help Putin," Bloomberg, December 22, 2008.

170   **"impose a sense of guilt"**   Quoted in "Stalin-era Files Raided in 'War Over Memory'" in *Financial Times,* December 27–28, 2008. Putin made the remark in a 2007 meeting with history teachers.

170   **"It is a war"**   Ibid.

170   **"If the Russians are happy"**   Simon Sebag Montefiore, "In Russia, Power Has No Heirs," *The New York Times,* January 12, 2009.

BIBLIOGRAPHY AND
NOTE ON SOURCES

This book is largely the result of interviews conducted in Moscow and London during 2007, buttressed by reporting during the eleven years I was based in the former Soviet Union, from 1992 to 2003. I relied heavily on archival material—books, contemporarily written articles and films—for the historical passages and also to inform the account of present events. The deaths described in the book are among the most-chronicled events of our time, and I am grateful for the excellent work of colleagues. The sources for the quotations I have used are indicated in the notes, and work on which I relied informatively is listed below.

Books

Albats, Yevgenia. *The State Within a State: The KGB and Its Hold on Russia Past, Present and Future*. New York: Farrar Straus & Giroux, 1994.

Alibek, Ken. *Biohazard: The Chilling Story of the Largest Covert Biological Weapons Program in the World—Told from the Inside by the Man Who Ran It*. New York: Random House, 1999.

Andrew, Christopher, and Oleg Gordievsky. *KGB: The Inside Story*. New York: HarperCollins, 1990.

Andrew, Christopher, and Vasili Mitrokhin. *The Sword and the Shield: The Mitrokhin Archive and the Secret History of the KGB*. New York: Basic Books, 1999.

———. *The Mitrokhin Archive II: The KGB and the World*. London: Allen Lane, 2005.

Baker, Peter, and Susan Glasser. *Kremlin Rising: Russia and the End of the Revolution.* New York: Scribner, 2005.

Beazley, Raymond, Nevill Forbes, and G. A. Birkett. *Russia from the Varangians to the Bolsheviks.* London: Clarendon Press, 1918.

Belfield, Richard. *The Assassination Business: A History of State-Sponsored Murder.* New York: Carroll & Graf, 2005.

Bobrick, Benson. *Fearful Majesty: The Life and Reign of Ivan the Terrible.* New York: Putnam, 1987.

Bond, Edward Augustus. *Russia at the Close of the Sixteenth Century.* London: Hakluyt Society, 1861 repr. of 1591 manuscript.

Cherkashin, Victor, with Gregory Feifer. *Spy Handler: Memoir of a KGB Officer: The True Story of the Man Who Recruited Robert Hanssen and Aldrich Ames.* New York: Basic Books, 2005.

Conquest, Robert. *The Great Terror: A Reassessment.* London: Pimlico, 1994 repr.

Deriabin, Peter. *Watchdogs of Terror: Russian Bodyguards from the Tsars to the Commissars.* Frederick, Md.: Foreign Intelligence Book Series, 1984 repr.

Deriabin, Peter, and T. H. Bagley. *The KGB: Masters of the Soviet Union.* New York: Hippocrene, 1990.

Deriabin, Peter, and Frank Gibney. *The Secret World: The Terrifying Report of a High Officer of Soviet Intelligence Whose Conscience Finally Rebelled.* New York: Doubleday, 1959.

Felshtinsky, Yuri, and Alexander Litvinenko. *Blowing Up Russia.* London: Gibson Square, 2007.

Freeland, Chrystia. *Sale of the Century.* New York: Crown, 2000.

Goldfarb, Alex, and Marina Litvinenko. *Death of a Dissident: The Poisoning of Alexander Litvinenko and the Return of the KGB.* New York: Free Press, 2007.

Handelman, Stephen. *Comrade Criminal.* New Haven, Conn.: Yale, 1995.

Hochshild, Adam. *The Unquiet Ghost.* Boston: Houghton Mifflin, 1994.

Hoffman, David E. *The Oligarchs: Wealth and Power in the New Russia.* New York: Public Affairs, 2002.

Jack, Andrew. *Inside Putin's Russia.* London: Granta Books, 2004.

Kalugin, Oleg. *The First Directorate.* New York: St. Martin's, 1994.

Khokhlov, Nikolai. *In the Name of Conscience: The Testament of a Soviet Secret Agent.* New York: David McKay, 1959.

Klebnikov, Paul. *Godfather of the Kremlin: The Decline of Russia in the Age of Gangster Capitalism.* Orlando, Fla.: Harvest Books, 2000.

Knight, Amy. *How the Cold War Began.* New York: McClelland & Stewart, 2005.
———. *Spies Without Cloaks.* Princeton, N.J.: Princeton University Press, 1996.

Kouzminov, Alexander. *Biological Espionage: Special Operations of the Soviet and Russian Foreign Intelligence Services in the West.* London: Greenhill, 2005.

Krivitsky, W. G. *In Stalin's Secret Service.* New York: Enigma, 2000.

Lauchlan, Iain. *Russian Hide-and-Seek: The Tsarist Secret Police in St. Petersburg, 1906–1914.* Helsinki: Finnish Literature Society, 2002.

Ledeneva, Alena V. *How Russia Really Works: The Informal Practices That Shaped Post-Soviet Politics and Business.* Ithaca, N.Y.: Cornell, 2006.

Lee III, Rensselaer W. *Smuggling Armageddon: The Nuclear Black Market in the Former Soviet Union and Europe.* New York: Palgrave Macmillan, 1998.

Linder, I. B., and C. A. Churkin. *Istoria Spetsialnikh Sluzhb Rosii X–XX Vekov* (The History of the Special Services of Russia from the Tenth Through Twentieth Centuries). Moscow, 2005.

Lloyd, John. *Rebirth of a Nation: An Anatomy of Russia.* London: Michael Joseph, 1998.

Lucas, Edward. *The New Cold War: Putin's Russia and the Threat to the West.* New York: Palgrave Macmillan, 2008.

Massie, Robert K. *Peter the Great.* New York: Knopf, 1980.

Matlock Jr., Jack F. *Autopsy on an Empire: The American Ambassador's Account of the Collapse of the Soviet Union.* New York: Random House, 1995.

Meier, Andrew. *Black Earth.* London: HarperCollins, 2004.

Montefiore, Simon Sebag. *Stalin: The Court of the Red Tsar.* London: Weidenfeld & Nicholson, 2003.

Payne, Robert, and Nikita Romanoff. *Ivan the Terrible.* New York: Crowell, 1975.

Pipes, Richard. *Russia Under the Old Regime.* New York: Scribner's, 1974.

Politkovskaya, Anna. *Putin's Russia: Life in a Failing Democracy.* New York: Henry Holt, 2004.

———. *A Russian Diary: A Journalist's Final Account of Life, Corruption, and Death in Putin's Russia.* New York: Random House, 2007.

———. *A Small Corner of Hell: Dispatches from Chechnya.* Chicago: University of Chicago Press, 2003.

Putin, Vladimir, Nataliya Gevorkyan, Natalya Timakova, and Andrei Kolesnikov. *First Person: An Astonishingly Frank Self-Portrait by Russia's President.* New York: Public Affairs, 2000.

Ruud, Charles A., and Sergei A. Stepanov. *Fontanka 16: The Tsars' Secret Police.* Montreal: McGill–Queens University Press, 1999.

Satter, David. *Darkness at Dawn: The Rise of the Russian Criminal State.* New Haven, Conn.: Yale University Press, 2003.

Skrynnikov, Ruslan G. *Ivan the Terrible.* Gulf Breeze, Fla.: Academic International Press, 1981, trans. by Hugh E. Graham.

Smith, Hedrick. *The New Russians.* New York: Random House, 1990.

Sudoplatov, Pavel, and Anatoli Sudoplatov, with Jerrold L. and Leona P. Schecter. *Special Tasks.* Boston: Little, Brown, 1994.

Talbott, Strobe. *The Russia Hand.* New York: Random House, 2002.

Weiner, Tim. *Legacy of Ashes.* New York: Doubleday, 2007.

Videos, Films, Documentaries

"In Memoriam Aleksander Litvinenko." Directed by Jos de Putter. VPRO, 2007.

"The Last Days of a Secret Agent." *Dateline NBC,* February 25, 2007.

"Poison Plot: The Killing of a Spy." *Anderson Cooper 360°,* CNN, December 4, 2006.

"A Taste of Freedom." Directed by Marina Goldovskaya. Turner Network Television, 1990.

INDEX

STEVE LEVINE is the author of *The Oil and the Glory: The Pursuit of Empire and Fortune on the Caspian Sea*. He is the chief foreign affairs writer for *BusinessWeek* and is based in Washington, D.C. He was a foreign correspondent for eighteen years, posted in the Soviet Union, Pakistan, and the Philippines, reporting for *The Wall Street Journal, The New York Times, Newsweek, Financial Times,* and other publications.